# CHINA AND THE WEST

# CHINA
## AND
# THE WEST

## Hope and Fear
## in the **Age of Asia**

# FOKKE OBBEMA

I.B. TAURIS
LONDON · NEW YORK

Published in 2015 by
I.B.Tauris & Co. Ltd
London • New York
www.ibtauris.com

**N** **ederlands**
**letterenfonds**
**dutch foundation**
**for literature**

The publisher gratefully acknowledges the support of the Dutch Foundation
for Literature

ISBN: 978 1 78453 384 7
eISBN: 978 0 85773 922 3

A full CIP record for this book is available from the British Library
A full CIP record is available from the Library of Congress

Library of Congress Catalog Card Number: available

Typeset by Fakenham Prepress Solutions, Fakenham, Norfolk NR21 8NN
Printed and bound by ScandBook AB, Sweden 2015

*For Carine, Zana and Djuna*

# Contents

## Part III
Politics and Values

# Introduction

During my first visit to China in 2008 I became fascinated with the dynamic of its big cities Shanghai and Beijing. They gave me the feeling of being 'where it's at'. As I conducted interviews with intellectuals and business people, I was accompanied by a Chinese man my own age with whom I got on surprisingly well. While we experienced the odd culture clash, this only heightened my fascination. That fascination can be summed up by the question that underpins this book: what are we to do about China? Inevitably followed by the counter-question: what is China to do about us?

Having decided to visit locations where the Chinese and Europeans meet, I travelled around Germany, France, the United Kingdom, Hungary, Italy and the Netherlands. And then back to China again. I ended up speaking with entrepreneurs, students, politicians, labourers, diplomats, social workers, prostitutes, shopkeepers, writers and government ministers. And above all with experts, some of whom had been studying China for decades. As a relative novice, I felt privileged to hear their views on the subject.

I relied on their contributions to get to grips with a topic so big it overwhelmed me at times and also posed the huge risk of unwarranted generalisation. In fact, the German-Chinese author Vera Yu warned me: 'Everybody is always trying to capture what *all* Chinese people are like. But that's absolutely impossible. Surely you can't make claims about *all* Europeans either?' I have tried to take that warning to heart, but without letting it interfere with my objective: a book about Chinese–European relations. To my surprise I failed to find such a book in the countries I visited.

What images have we been projecting onto China throughout the ages? And how did they view us, the 'barbarians' who headed for their shores in droves in the nineteenth century? The superiority complex I encountered on both sides is something that continues to define both parties to this day.

As a journalist I could not escape the consequences of this public perception, or distortion rather, attributable in large part to the media. I am guilty of it too, as evidenced by my search for Chinese buyers of French vineyards. The media's tendency to stir up fear is a book topic in its own right, and the same is true for one of the most exciting media developments in the world right now: Chinese internet. I will address it in Part I.

Are we heading for a clash when China, like the West, becomes a knowledge economy? And will China's appetite for resources prove to be the world's undoing, Europe's especially? These questions will be explored in Part II, which focuses on globalisation. I for one believe globalisation will have a positive impact: its financial benefits as well as the large numbers of students and academics travelling back and forth will, if anything, contribute to a better mutual understanding.

As the nation to emerge victorious from globalisation China has become a lot more important for us Europeans. But mostly as a trading partner; for all the brouhaha about China 'taking over' Europe, this has not yet been reflected in investment levels.

'The Chinese Are Not Coming' could well be a bigger threat to Europe than 'The Chinese Are Coming'.

Part II also considers China's role in Africa. We often look askance at the undiscerning and occasionally ruthless Chinese business practices on the African continent. Again, our media present us with a distorted picture. Some more modesty would not be out of place, especially given our historic roles in colonisation.

Do the Chinese occupy their own wing in the house of mankind, entirely separate from the rest? Or does the observation made by the Italian missionary Matteo Ricci in the seventeenth century still hold true: 'They are human beings, just like us.' I explore both perspectives in Part III. The former tends to foreground 'The Eternal China', which is virtually immune to external influences and will in due course treat us to its own distinctive values. Martin Jacques, the British author of *When China Rules the World*, is a rather vocal representative of this perspective. The second approach stresses social trends such as consumerism and individualism which are just as conspicuous in China as they are here. The similarities here outweigh the differences, as can be seen in the work of the German writer and sinologist Tilman Spengler.

I compare these two diametrically opposed perspectives, in conjunction with the other, much better-known antitheses: those between our political systems and our disparate views of human rights. To begin with, the emphasis will be on China's political system: is it as effective as many in the West believe it to be? And what are we to make of the new leader Xi Jinping and his emphasis on a 'Chinese Dream'? What do his efforts to increase Chinese soft power around the world tell us about his worldview?

But I also view Europe and the US through China's power-political prism. The dissension among European nations, which decreases Europe's chances to play a significant role on the world stage, is not just a disappointment to us. As for the US, despite cracks in its image, it is still perceived by the Chinese as the real superpower. Distrust about American motives is widespread, both among the leaders and the population, and mixed with feelings of inferiority and admiration. As a result China is unwilling to be the 'responsible stakeholder' the US would like the country to be. How to respond? Some American voices are calling for a firmer stance on China, especially in the light of its territorial ambitions and its industrial espionage. In my view it would be unwise to take a tougher stance, as it would only fuel China's already powerful nationalism. A Cold War 2.0 is not the fight the West should want to pick with China.

When it comes to China's future I'm convinced that it will become more powerful; with the necessary effort the country can develop into a knowledge economy, something Europe and the US will have to prepare for. But the West tends to underestimate the country's internal problems and overestimate the capacity of its leaders to solve them. As a result we tend to view China as more threatening than it really is. China will certainly not eclipse the rest of the world in the years to come. And the West should have more faith in its own strength. As for the mutual relations, the daily undercurrent of contacts at micro level between China and the West can hopefully lay the groundwork for trust.

I hope this book will deepen the understanding of one of the most important developments of our time: the rise, or renaissance, of China. Writing this book has taught me a great deal. Hopefully reading it will have the same effect on you.

Fokke Obbema
January 2015

# Part I

# History and the Media

*Past and Present Perspectives*

# Chapter 1

# Pounding on the Table

*A Chinese Professor in Brussels*

'Europe is full of pride and prejudice. You never give an inch in negotiations. If you really were our friends, you could become China's most important partner within the next five years; our number one. We could form a united front against the United States. But only if you stop discriminating against us and acknowledge us as a market economy.'

A speech like machine-gun fire, practically shouted out. This is the first time I see it happening: a Chinese man shedding his traditional, modest role in a large Chinese–European gathering. The man on the rostrum is Xia Youfu, professor and director of a think tank for Chinese–European economic cooperation. Short and stocky, and bursting with energy and passion, he has been invited to Brussels by Friends of Europe, a group of idealists who believe in the European Union and are confidently seeking to establish a dialogue with China. The setting, Le Cercle Gaulois, is a beautiful nineteenth-century ballroom on Rue de la Loi, at the heart of Belgium's government district. It is late 2011 and some 500 Chinese and European delegates have flocked to this symposium on Chinese–European relations. One of the speakers is Xia.

He refuses to adopt the submissive attitude prescribed by former Chinese leader Deng Xiaoping for dealing with foreigners, even for a moment. Speaking heatedly, albeit with a broad smile, Xia tries hard to open our eyes to the true enemy. 'Who is behind your crisis? The United States of course! They are trying to pin the blame for the debt crisis on you. And who will come out on top? The United States. They are undermining the peaceful relations between Asia and Europe. European investments in China have hardly increased since the beginning of the crisis, and neither have our exports to Europe.'

As Xia pounds his notes covered in Chinese characters with his fist, the well-turned English phrases roll off his tongue. Louder and louder, until even Leon Brittan, who is seated on the podium beside him, opens his eyes. Having been made a peer, the distinguished septuagenarian was introduced as Baron Brittan of Spennithorne. His heyday as UK home secretary and European commissioner for competition behind him, he is now sitting out his career on the boards of various international companies. He delivered a short, sharp speech after which he shut his eyes in full view of the hundreds of listeners. Who knows, maybe this is fuelling Xia's agitation. It is hard not to see the dozing Briton and the excitable Chinese speaker as symbols of Europe and China.

'Your economic growth is low, yet your social systems are extremely expensive. This will have to change,' Xia tells his European audience. The European Central Bank should 'concentrate on creating full employment and not just on fighting inflation. This too will have to change.' His assertive, high-pitched voice puts an end to the respectful silence in the ballroom. Suddenly the place is buzzing. Two young Chinese diplomats next to me do not know which way to look, embarrassed at their countryman's impudence.

At the same time, I cannot help but appreciate the attack. For a while the meeting was threatening to get bogged down in good intentions, conflict avoidance and lethargy – the very things that often plague symposia like this. The organisers clearly tried to inject a note of tension into the day's proceedings with the title: 'Europe and China: Rivals or Strategic Partners?' But from the word go the European and Chinese diplomats who funded the event have been trying to take the sting out of it. Of course we are not rivals, is the common consensus. The Chinese ambassador to the European Union and co-sponsor is praised to the sky and back before he takes the floor himself. Top diplomat Song Zhe conveys Prime Minister Wen Jiabao's very best wishes and expresses his delight at so much European interest in China. It is wonderful to see such excellent cooperation in so many fields. Yawn.

The Brussels-based official speaking on behalf of EU President Herman van Rompuy does not do a much better job. 'Rivals or partners'? He claims he does not even understand the dilemma. In his sugar-coated way of thinking the first is not an option. He reiterates the EU mantra: China is important; China is an opportunity; China and Europe are equal partners. I am beginning to wonder why all this amassed intellect from China and Europe is prepared to waste its time with this. Unfortunately the idealists from Friends of Europe who organised the symposium do the same. Their leading man claims we have advanced beyond mere courtesies and are seeing 'real progress' – a phrase that, on a day like this, seems as clichéd as the assertion that China is 'an opportunity'. I fail to see the leap forwards.

But luckily there is Lord Brittan. Establishment through and through, but always good for some trenchant observations. It is all very well, this official 'strategic partnership' between Europe and China, 'but it is no more than a hollow political sound bite unless the obstacles to a mutual relationship are removed', he argues. The sums invested on both sides are still very small, 'despite the fact that even the most backward company in Europe now knows what is going on in China. The days of feigning ignorance are over.'

Next he outlines what he sees as the problem areas: intellectual property in China, public contracts in China, subsidies to companies by China. Incidentally all areas where Europe is very sure of its own position, I cannot fail but notice. In passing he praises the European Commission for having so far resisted the temptation of protectionism. Hitting back by protecting your own market is ill-advised, Brittan believes. 'Not because we're such good boys, but because it would reduce our chances on the Chinese market. An open economy is best for everyone. We will have to convince our Chinese friends of that.'

Sounding amused and not quite as vitriolic as Xia, the Englishman expresses himself more eloquently than his Chinese neighbour. But is his message really substantially different from that of his opponent? Both avoid self-criticism and take aim at the other instead. As a European I am inclined to agree with Brittan; his criticism seems perfectly valid from a European perspective.

My first impulse upon hearing Xia disparage our social systems is to tell him to mind his own business; this is all very easy to say for someone from a country without safety nets. Only later do I realise that this kind of 'meddling in our internal affairs' is something we ought to take seriously if we want to view the Chinese as equal partners. Chinese government officials regard our talk of human rights violations as 'meddling' in their affairs. Is their indignation comparable to what I felt when Xia dismissed our social security system?

## The elephant and the frog mother

I got an inkling of just how difficult that openness is when a large Chinese delegation visited the editorial office of my newspaper. Led by an under-secretary, this delegation travelled around Europe making courtesy visits to various media in 2010. But all was not as innocent as it seemed. The under-secretary took advantage of his visit to *de Volkskrant* to express his displeasure with news reports from our correspondent in Shanghai. He pulled an article from his pocket which said that the latest meeting of the National People's Congress had produced nothing new. According to the under-secretary, however, some very important reforms had been introduced. He also cracked a joke about a frog mother warning her children about their neighbour, an elephant. It was an attempt to remind us of the balance of power, and while we tried to laugh it off afterwards, it also struck us as quite exceptional. 'The Chinese would never have dared to do this in the old days', a veteran foreign commentator said. 'I can't believe they expect this kind of behaviour to be effective', the editor-in-chief remarked. Having an official from a one-party state trying to curb our freedom of expression – every journalistic bone in our bodies railed against the idea. As it was, the Chinese under-secretary's intervention was counterproductive, arousing resistance and briefly fanning the flames of anti-Chinese sentiment among us. Eventually the incident was swept away by fresh waves of news.

Yet it is important that we face up to our own 'pride and prejudice'. Not just European journalists, but all Europeans.

Europe is brimming with pride – Xia has a point – as evidenced by our perception of Europe's leading role in world history, the political system that despite its many flaws we consider the 'least of all evils', the cultural legacy we imagine to be the envy of the world and Western technological supremacy. I for one cannot deny feeling superior at times.

Xia's Chinese arrogance holds up a mirror to me. And his views have an unexpected champion in the British academic and journalist Martin Jacques, also present in Brussels. His book *When China Rules the World* made it onto US President Obama's bedside table in 2009. 'European pride and prejudice? Yes, that rings a bell', he says with an ironic smile. He predicts no less than 'the end of the Western world' now that China is casting off 150 years of lethargy to claim its rightful place in the world. He once again underlines the West's fundamentally flawed view of China. We measure success by how much a society is Westernised. 'The West likes to think of itself as cosmopolitan, but is actually extremely provincial. It is incapable of respecting differences.'

According to Jacques, Europeans look down on China because it is not a democracy, violates human rights and is increasingly polluting the environment. 'This is what China is reduced to. It betrays a great deal of ignorance, effectively hiding one of the greatest revolutions ever: in the past thirty years China has done more to eliminate global poverty than any other country. We have to treat this with respect.'

Kerry Brown, a British professor of Chinese politics at the University of Sydney, is another seasoned China expert. He too is sympathetic to Xia's strident outburst. In the West we always want the Chinese to speak out more clearly and not be so vague, he reminds us. As an example he cites former President Hu Jintao, whose biography he wrote. 'A man of many qualities, but communication was not one of them', Brown remarks drily. But neither are we happy when someone like Xia defies our expectations. 'Then we turn round and say: whoa, tone it down a bit!'

# Chapter 2

# Superiority and Humiliation

*How China Sees Us*

Did the irate professor in Brussels give us a glimpse of how China really thinks about us, or can we bank on the more common image of the friendly and smiling Chinese? My efforts to get to the bottom of the Chinese attitude towards the West have brought me to an inconspicuous white terraced house in the London borough of Chelsea on a sunny morning in autumn. It is the home of George Walden, in his early seventies and with well over forty years of fascination with China under his belt. A former diplomat in the country at the time of the Cultural Revolution, he later became a Conservative politician and is now a writer and essayist.

He is the author of the personal and compelling account *China: A Wolf in the World?*. The book proved to be a rich source of erudition, not least because of Walden's fluency in Chinese, Russian and French. He never presumes to know it all, but espouses, rather modestly, that 'each of us has his or her own personal China'. His answer to the question of how the Chinese see us has been shaped by four decades of personal experience, as well as by his interest in the country's history.

Walden gives me a shy smile when we introduce ourselves and then ushers me into the kitchen, where he makes coffee. The intimacy of the setting gives me the courage to crack a joke about a large, arty portrait of the young Mao on his wall. In Walden's book he is depicted as an even worse mass murderer than Hitler. Surely the latter won't be given a place on the wall too, I ask with mock concern. Walden, a man with blue eyes, a strong jawline and a mouth that soon talks nineteen to the dozen, bursts out laughing: 'I guess I'm guilty of double standards.'

In the living room filled with ancient and modern Asian art we embark on a conversation that races through the centuries and locations but always comes back to the Cultural Revolution. Mao proclaimed it in 1966 to rid himself of 'rightist elements' in his Communist Party. The 'proletarian' campaign resulted in years of chaos. Hundreds of thousands, perhaps even millions of people perished, either murdered or starved to death. Much of what represented the old, such as temples, monasteries and churches, was destroyed. Families were torn apart and separated by forced labour in the countryside. Ever since, the phrase 'never again' has been as pertinent to right-minded Chinese citizens over the age of fifty as to Europeans who lived through World War II.

According to Mao, the 'rightist elements' received support from foreign spies. As a young diplomat in his mid-twenties Walden had first-hand experience of the repercussions of this. He was stationed first in Hong Kong, still British at the time, and then in Beijing during the Cultural Revolution. 'A terse hostility was the best I could hope for in the street, in shops and in restaurants.' Whenever the tall Walden joined the Chinese readers of a wall newspaper, there was a good chance he would be mistaken for a 'spy' or an 'imperialist'. 'I remember people shaking fists at my face. Their aim wasn't so much to lynch me as to humiliate me. This in turn provoked a strong urge to deprive them of that pleasure. I liked to respond with a quote from Mao, who had said that foreign guests of the Chinese government ought to be treated with respect.' He quips: 'Face is no Chinese monopoly.' The Chinese may have wanted to avoid loss of face at all costs, but Walden did not fancy it much either.

His stories about xenophobia seem strange these days. How can the people who now tend to extend a warm welcome to foreign visitors have been capable of doing the exact opposite? It is the same question, I note, we ask with regard to the Germans, even seventy years on. The analogy makes sense to Walden: 'Contemporary China is as much a product of the catastrophe of

the Cultural Revolution as modern Europe is of Hitler's defeat.'
He believes that putting the past behind you, a Chinese variation
on the German *Vergangenheitsbewältigung*, i.e. the process of
coming to terms with one's past, is indispensable for progress
and reform.

Despite many subsequent visits, his memories of the Cultural
Revolution continue to haunt him. He describes his anxiety when,
thirty years later, four youngsters approached him on the street
in China. A flashback took him back to the dangers of yesteryear.
But the youths bore him no ill will. On the contrary: they thought
he was interesting and were keen to practise their English on him.
'I was struck by the friendly expressions on their faces', he writes.
The meeting reassured him.

But one such positive encounter will not tempt Walden, with
all of his life experience, to draw overly optimistic conclusions.
While foreigners may be better tolerated now, they are seldom
made to feel truly welcome. Not weighed down by memories
of the Cultural Revolution, I do not recognise this feeling. My
experiences in China are more positive, I point out. He goes one
step further: 'I experience a degree of arrogance, mixed with
resentment. Covered with only a thin veil of civility.' It is a charac-
terisation that meets with widespread support when I put it to
other China experts later.

## 'Red-haired barbarians'

This 'resentment' is tied up with an earlier period which has left
its mark on Chinese–European relations: the nineteenth century.
It remains extremely vivid in China's collective conscience as
'the century of humiliation, perpetrated by Westerners'. The
government is doing everything it can to keep it that way, Walden
tells me. After 1989, when the protests on Tiananmen Square
were crushed, patriotism reappeared on the school curriculum.
The bloodbath prompted leaders to conclude that education had
taken a wrong turn somewhere. So ever since, China's young
people are taught love of their country and its history. It has
the wondrously paradoxical effect that the age of the empire no

longer stands for the suppression of the people, as Mao used to claim. These days it is depicted as a glorious era, which Western 'barbarians' ended by occupying China and exploiting it for their own gain.

The humiliation by the West was a particularly big blow because China had been convinced of its global superiority for centuries. As Walden puts it: 'Their attitude was: why associate with the rest of mankind?' This sense of superiority was underpinned by immense wealth, advanced technology and an impressive culture replete with inventions, 'long before the West got around to it'.

Emblematic of this penchant for isolation was China's abandonment, at the start of the fifteenth century, of the maritime voyages of discovery that had brought the renowned Admiral Zheng He to the east coast of Africa and the Arab world. Some 150 years before the Spanish Armada, He was in charge of a much bigger and far more advanced fleet than the Spaniards. But the Emperor did not use his lead for aggressive conquests. The Chinese authorities like to cite this peace-loving stance to allay fears over aggression today.

Since recognition of his supremacy was an important element of these voyages, alongside commerce, Zheng He gave lavish gifts to the rulers of the countries he visited. Next he invited them to the imperial court to come and 'kowtow'. The ritual demands that a person prostrate himself nine times before the Emperor, forehead pressed to the floor. This was a reflection of the balance of power, at least in Chinese eyes. China was the Central Kingdom and the Emperor the Heavenly Son. The Chinese saw their country as the last word in civilisation and the British as 'red-haired barbarians'.

This Chinese arrogance met its European match. The British envoy Lord George Macartney categorically refused to kowtow before the Emperor: he was prepared to genuflect, as he would for the British sovereign, but no more. He was allowed to do so, although Chinese chroniclers report that Macartney did indeed prostrate himself. At the decisive moment, they write, he had been particularly impressed by the Emperor. Either way, Macartney failed to establish the intended diplomatic relations.

What if every nation demanded to have an embassy in Beijing? It would be utterly impractical, was the Emperor's reasoning. It marked the start of a supremely grim century in Chinese–European relations.

It was the opium trade from the early nineteenth century onwards that particularly fanned the flames of Chinese indignation about Western behaviour. As Walden describes the relations: 'In accordance with their sense of superiority, the Chinese had shown no interest whatsoever in ordinary British merchandise, whereas we were crazy about Chinese products such as silk, tea and porcelain.' To offset the resulting trade deficit, his compatriots came up with something that incenses the Chinese to this day. The British stimulated opium cultivation in India. The sale was banned in China for health reasons, but this interdiction did not stop them from bringing the substance into the country via Chinese smugglers. As prices were moderate to begin with, a section of the population soon became addicted. A price hike followed.

In the Chinese version of events the role of domestic opium traders is generally overlooked. The same is true for the reason the underclass got hooked in the first place – opium offered them an escape from a life of misery. In contrast, there is plenty of attention given to a national hero, Lin Zexu, a special envoy to the Emperor. In 1839 he was dispatched to Guangzhou, where most of the opium was smuggled into the country. He was incorruptible and managed to have no less than 1.2 million kilos confiscated and destroyed within six weeks. In addition, he wrote an incisive letter to Queen Victoria about the British double standard. 'We have heard that in your own country opium is prohibited with the utmost strictness and severity: this is a strong proof that you know full well how hurtful it is to mankind. Since then you do not permit it to injure your own country, you ought not to have the injurious drug transferred to another country, and above all others, how much less to the Inner Land! Of the products which China exports to your foreign countries, there is not one which is not beneficial to mankind in some shape or other. [...] Has China (we should like to ask) ever yet sent forth a noxious article from its soil?' George Walden, certainly no royalist, provides the answer: 'Definitely not the tea, the silk or the porcelain the Queen ordered from China. It is a shame that this letter was probably never seen by our moralising Queen.'

While Lin occupied the moral high ground, he was given a military thrashing by the British. His crackdown on traders was the trigger for the First Opium War, which was to last four years. It ended with a unilateral 'treaty' which was extremely detrimental to China. The Second Opium War in 1860 even resulted in the destruction of the Emperor's Summer Palace, which included many precious art treasures. It took 3,500 British and French troops three days to do. Western tourists visiting Yiheyuan, another Summer Palace, today are made all too aware of the outrage.

By the end of the nineteenth century China had been brought to its knees. While it was no official colonisation – the Emperor remained on the throne – this is what it effectively boiled down to. The Boxer Rebellion of 1899–1901 was an unsuccessful attempt to combat the unequal treaties and ended with an 'Eight-Nation Alliance' of mostly European nations. It was made up of an army of 55,000 troops, which defeated the Emperor's army. The alliance captured Beijing and demanded further major reparations. These financial demands were particularly offensive because the conflicts had not been started by the Chinese themselves, and they also delivered another heavy blow to the country's economic independence. Once an eminent world power and an ancient civilisation representing 30 per cent of the global economy in 1820, it had now become a backward region divided by European powers.

Western historians challenge this Chinese tendency to pin the blame for the 'century of humiliation' all on the West. The decline was certainly not solely Europe's doing, they argue. China itself had been deeply internally divided at the start of the nineteenth century and over the years it failed to join the Industrial Revolution that was making European countries so powerful. The corruption of officials was also a major problem at the time. Be that as it may, what matters here is the Chinese perspective on the nineteenth century, since it influences their current view of the West.

Today's rulers not only keep the memory alive through education. The state has official commemorations of its humiliations, such as the defeat to the Eight-Nation Alliance, reminding people how the poor Chinese were exploited at the hands of the brutal Westerner. Universities have professors specialising in the subject. Whether or not they are aware of it, the nineteenth century continues to shape the Chinese attitude towards Europeans. 'They carry that experience of imperialist aggression within them, in their conscious or subconscious mind, even if they never mention it', argues the German sinologist Axel Schneider, professor at the University of Göttingen.

In his capacity as a diplomat, George Walden represented the country that perpetrated the worst atrocities during the 'century of humiliation'. He believes that if you want to understand China's oversensitivity to criticism, you cannot ignore the nineteenth century. 'We like to see Deng Xiaoping [the leader known as the architect of the open-door policy, which saw the country open up its economy in the late 1970s] as a modern reformer, but he was also an old-school party man. He regarded the West's emphasis on human rights as an attempt to undermine Chinese sovereignty, like it did in the nineteenth century.' In fact, many Chinese people remain suspicious about the West. 'It may strike us as paranoid, but because of the plundering during the imperialist era plenty of Chinese people remain convinced that the West will stop at nothing to deprive China of its rightful status as a superpower.'

This Chinese sensitivity came to the fore towards the end of 2009 when China sentenced a British drugs trafficker to death. With the sale of heroin to Chinese youngsters opening old wounds, the 'bitter memory of the past' was cited to justify the death penalty. The then British prime minister Gordon Brown called for the death sentence to be quashed, without showing much understanding of the historical context. Unlike Walden, who says: 'China was criticised with regard to a subject associated with its darkest memories.' Of course his country had to stand up for its citizen, but it ought to have been mindful of the role it played in the past. The drugs trafficker was eventually executed.

Like many other historians, Walden is convinced that the humiliations from the past continue to play a role, as does China's fundamental disinterest in the West. 'I think you cannot under-estimate the essence of five thousand years of history. And these days the Chinese have more reason than ever to be arrogant. If we ask them to cease production of something because otherwise 500,000 people here will lose their jobs, we cannot expect a great deal of sympathy.'

# Chapter 3

# 'Yellow Peril'

## Our Fears about China

'In the 1950s and 1960s, Germany had no interest in China, none whatsoever. You had a small club of sinologists who studied the country, but that was it. These days all employers watch China, because they realise the country is keeping their employees in work. But intellectual interest is lagging. We must learn to understand China. And that means knowing what the country looked like before communism.'

Helmut Schmidt, Chancellor of Germany in the 1970s, is not short on strong views. I am watching him in action at a meeting in Berlin on 'Magnet China', a theme which would have been inconceivable fifty years ago. The packed conference hall hangs on every word the ninety-three-year-old in the wheelchair utters. His presence fills the large stage. As soon as he opens his mouth his physical impairments cease to matter and the years seem to drop away. Schmidt is in turns provocative, entertaining and wise, viewing China not through a contemporary lens, but from the perspective of the past few millennia. It prompts him to say: 'I respect China.'

This is quite a provocation in a country which is highly sensitive to human rights violations – for obvious historical reasons. With its poor reputation in this area China scores badly in German public opinion, however well both countries get on economically.

Schmidt defends China against critical questions from the audience. China's Africa policy may be described as 'neocolonial' in Germany, but again he applies his historical perspective. 'In four thousand years of history, China has shown little or no urge towards colonisation. Unlike us in the West. They had the power to conquer, but declined to do so. It betrays a different kind of mentality. Those who preach fear of China had better reread their own colonial history', he tells his audience. From 1898 until 1914, Germany too possessed a slice of the China pie.

This friendly attitude towards the Chinese government is certainly not above criticism, as the Tibetans and Uyghurs will tell you with indignation. But Schmidt has a point when he holds up a mirror to his European audience. We are more likely to notice the aggression in the Chinese approach than our own colonial attitude. Instead of taking your own superiority for granted, Schmidt emphasised, try to understand the other culture. But for Western China-watchers this has long been a major obstacle.

## Chinoiserie

Since the thirteenth century, when the Italian explorer Marco Polo claimed to have spent time in China, Europeans have stumbled into the twin pitfalls of damnation and glorification. The physical distance leads to romanticising; the scale of the country and the strangeness of its culture make it hard for us to obtain a satisfactory, let alone a complete picture. Few can resist the tendency to exaggerate. As we shall see, China was and still is often used to comment on developments at home. Before long, what is really going on becomes all but invisible.

Among the enthusiasts we find the German philosopher and mathematician Gottfried Leibniz. This polymath took his cue from the jubilant findings of Catholic missionaries who were greatly impressed by the highly evolved Chinese culture. Europe is in no way superior to Chinese civilisation, Leibniz concluded on the basis of their books and stories. In his *Novissima Sinica* from 1699, which translates as 'the latest news from China', he tried to ascertain objectively whose development was most advanced – and who could learn from whom and in what areas. In scientific matters, he identified a considerable lead for the West. But the Chinese surpass us ('though it is almost shameful to admit this') in 'practical philosophy', the organisation of society. 'Among the Chinese, laws are beautifully directed towards the greatest tranquillity and order.' He praised the Chinese for their reverence towards one another: 'Scarcely anyone offends another by the smallest word in conversation. And they rarely show evidence of hatred, wrath or excitement.'

Leibniz's love of the social order and the alleged conduct of the Chinese cannot be seen separately from the situation in his fatherland, where the Thirty Years War dominated the first thirty years of his life. In his view, China was an example to Germany, which was slipping into 'ever greater corruption'. If it was up to him, the Catholic missionaries who were sent to China would have counterparts: Chinese missionaries sent to Europe. He dreamed aloud about a global culture uniting the best of China and Europe.

A couple of decades later, in France, the Enlightenment philosopher and writer Voltaire was equally open to Chinese culture. Among a section of the French elite this was all the rage. This was the era of chinoiserie, when Chinese porcelain, silk and carpets were imported and depictions of Chinese houses and gardens adorned the walls. It was against this backdrop that Voltaire wrote several works about China between 1740 and 1764, including the famous stage play *L'Orphelin de la Chine* (The Orphan of China). In it he praised the wisdom of the emperors and the highly evolved morality of their subjects.

Voltaire never visited the country either and took his inspiration from the accounts of the Jesuit missionaries. They stimulated his imagination to such an extent that he even had a bust of Confucius in his study. He also wrote several poems in honour of Emperor Qianlong, whom he regarded as a 'philosopher-king' in the tradition of Plato, an enlightened autocrat who was both ruler and thinker. 'Their empire is the best that the world has ever seen', Voltaire wrote in 1764.

Like that of Leibniz, Voltaire's love of China cannot be seen in isolation from the political context of eighteenth-century Europe. The rationalist Voltaire fought a lifelong battle with officials of the Catholic Church, which accounted for 20 per cent of landown-ership in France at the time. To him, the teachings of Confucius proved that a society could be morally upright without religion.

The fact that the old Confucian civilisation had never been afflicted by the religious wars which were so prevalent in Europe particularly appealed to him.

Because of his political agenda, Voltaire paid little or no attention to the downsides, overlooking the Emperor's despotic qualities. He had nothing but praise for the way the mandarins, the high-ranking officials at the imperial court, were selected. Their selection was based on expertise rather than birthright – a meritocratic principle he liked to hold up to his compatriots. He was not bothered by the fact that the exams, which could last up to nine days, revolved primarily around the Chinese classics and totally ignored practical skills. These days, historians cite this failing as one of the reasons for the impasse in which the Chinese civilisation found itself in the eighteenth century.

The penchant for selective observation could also prompt the opposite conclusion. Voltaire's contemporary Charles de Montesquieu saw China as an example of how *not* to organise a state. The separation between legislative, executive and judicial power that he propagated was (and is) a distant reality in China. 'A despotic regime, driven by fear', he concluded in his celebrated book *De l'Esprit des lois* (The Spirit of the Laws).

## Yellow Peril

The French Revolution at the end of the eighteenth century had such a great impact that interest in China waned. During the century that followed, a far more negative perception of the country and its people gained the upper hand. Economic developments played a determining role in this: while Europe enjoyed explosive growth thanks to the Industrial Revolution, China remained stuck in the agricultural age. As corruption, natural disasters and famines weakened the empire, the European colonial powers increasingly looked to the territory for gain. The resulting economic decline continued until the second half of the twentieth century. China's reputation slumped; the weak Emperor and his people were looked down on. Negative accounts by Western merchants engendered racism.

The establishment of the first few Chinatowns in the United States played a role as well. After 1870, when the US economy took a turn for the worse, those first large Chinese communities in the West became a particular bone of contention. American politicians claimed that these cheap labourers stole jobs from white Americans. This led to discriminating legislation, the Chinese Exclusion Act of 1882, which imposed a drastic curb on immigration. The act, for which the American Senate offered its apologies in 2011, was not abolished until 1943.

The term 'Yellow Peril' became fashionable towards the end of the nineteenth century, in Europe and elsewhere. It is often ascribed to the German Emperor Wilhelm II, who had a vision in 1895 about a fat Buddha riding a dragon threatening Christian Europe. He sketched his vision and handed it to the painter Hermann Knackfuss, who made it into the painting *Völker Europas, wahrt eure heiligsten Güter* (Peoples of Europe, guard your dearest goods). The canvas warned of the advance of the Chinese hordes. The Emperor presented it to the Russian Tsar, who was very pleased with it, and distributed copies across half of Europe. Fear of China became commonplace.

It was not until the twentieth century that perceptions of China began to change for the positive, at least among European adherents of communism. The French author and politician André Malraux lived in French Indochina for several years in the 1920s. In the novels he wrote during that period he set out to put an end to the two prevailing views of China: that of a stagnant country, trapped in its own traditions, and that of a barbaric nation, a potential threat to European civilisation. In the eyes of Malraux, who did not break with communism until Stalin signed a non-aggression pact with Hitler in 1939, communism made China 'part of history' again. He viewed the country's development with Europe in the back of his mind, wondering if the Chinese way of thinking, with its emphasis on community life, could be the answer for European youths who were, according to him, at risk of succumbing to individualism? As an aficionado of Chinese culture and as a communist, Malraux was inclined to answer that question in the affirmative.

His contemporary and fellow author Jean-Paul Sartre remained in thrall to communism for much longer. Given his ideological beliefs, his view of China was even more biased than that of his eighteenth-century compatriots. Sartre made only one brief visit, in 1955, together with Simone de Beauvoir, during which he was introduced to Mao. It preceded Mao's biggest campaigns: the Great Leap Forward (1958–62), with an estimated death toll of 45 million, and the Cultural Revolution (1966–76), which claimed the lives of an unknown number of people; estimates range from hundreds of thousands to several million. It did not stop Sartre, who, like Mao, was enthusiastic about the concept of 'permanent revolution', from staking his reputation on the Maoist movement in France in the 1970s. This, incidentally, should be seen as a statement against the French political establishment rather than direct support for Mao's practices. Other, lesser-known European intellectuals did condone those, such as the French writing couple Philippe Sollers and Julia Kristeva, the Dutch filmmaker Joris Ivens and the Italian author Alberto Moravia.

He may have been well into his sixties, but Sartre's support for Maoism connected him firmly to the zeitgeist, which was hostile to all things American. In France, especially, the largely left-leaning public opinion was resolutely against the US with its Vietnam War, arms race and multinationals. This anti-Americanism resulted in a fairly accommodating attitude towards communist China. Mao was forgiven for receiving the hated American President Nixon in 1972.

This tolerance is remarkable because there were plenty of signs of systematic human rights violations. The books and essays by the Belgian sinologist Simon Leys, starting with *Les Habits neufs du président Mao* from 1971, paint a shocking picture of day-to-day reality under the Cultural Revolution. But in those years Leys was only read in small circles and fiercely criticised by French Maoists, who tended to draw a veil over human rights violations. To them China was an exemplary nation and the suffering of Chinese individuals either irrelevant or a necessary sacrifice en route to the 'New Man'.

Likewise, US President Nixon and his national security advisor Henry Kissinger did not broach the subject of human rights violations during their historic meeting with Mao. Their rapprochement was aimed primarily at isolating the Soviet Union; human rights played little or no role at the time. Forty years on, this is difficult to comprehend. Nowadays we are outraged by the months-long detention of artist Ai Weiwei, but back then both Left and Right were only moderately critical or even wildly enthusiastic about the Cultural Revolution, during which executions and torture were routine. Ignorance of the facts goes some way to explain this, but everybody in the West could have known about the excesses as early as 1971.

Looking back on more than three centuries of Western opinion building, we must conclude that our present-day advantages are striking. China has come a great deal closer and has opened up considerably. The days when only a small group of Jesuits or sinologists dealt with China are over. Western business people, as well as politicians, scientists, students and tourists visit the country in unprecedented numbers and can travel freely. Various forms of cooperation are getting off the ground. After the economic ties intensified, a wide range of academic disciplines started engaging with the country. George Walden is extremely pleased: 'After centuries of projecting fears and dreams, we are finally developing a realistic picture of China.'

An added benefit is that most Europeans are now free from the ideological blind spots that coloured the public debate back in the 1960s and 1970s. Faith in communism has all but disappeared in the West; the communist movement is now practically non-existent. In China, while the exercise of power comes straight out of the communist handbook, including the persecution of dissidents, the ideological zeal has waned compared to the Mao era. Especially in relation to the rest of the world, pragmatism prevails. This penchant for pragmatism on both sides should facilitate rapprochement, and with that the development of a relationship of trust. At least in principle.

But it would be arrogant to think that in the twenty-first century we can entirely avoid the affliction of China-watchers in earlier times: a perspective on China that is strongly coloured by our historical circumstances. What we can do is account for the flaws in our perception. The main obstacle emerging right now, as I see it, is the West's fear of China – 'Yellow Peril' in a new guise. Its context is not religious or demographic this time, but economic: China's spectacular development, in sharp contrast with Europe's and the US's performance since the start of the credit crisis in 2008. While China experienced continued growth – albeit at a lower level of around 7.5 per cent since 2012 – Western governments which were forced to rescue their banks have seen an increase in debt levels and are still experiencing economic stagnation. The implications of China's economic rise are considerable. We must prepare for a future in which China becomes a knowledge economy, and therefore a much more direct competitor to the West and a country with two unmistakable advantages: more manpower and more money. For Europe especially, the accompanying shift in the balance of power will almost certainly be coupled with a smaller role on the world stage. Europeans will have to prepare for what the German China expert Eberhard Sandschneider has termed 'Europe's successful descent'.

In his book of the same name, Sandschneider argues that the renunciation of world power does not need to be a catastrophe. 'We must prepare properly for our descent, which is inevitable and historically speaking not at all shocking.' First of all this will require intellectual curiosity about what drives the new super-power. In this respect Sandschneider agrees wholeheartedly with Helmut Schmidt. 'We must see China as it is, not as we want to see it. So far we have shown scant interest in this learning process, as we are sniffy about their internal discussions.'

This is true for both policy makers and private individuals. When Chinese delegations travel to Europe they do so with the aim of gaining expertise, while German delegations head to China 'to explain how the world works', a German member of parliament sneers. Whether consciously or not, ordinary Europeans have a tendency to express their sense of moral superiority, a Chinese journalist based in London tells me. 'Their main interest is the one-child policy. Although there are very good reasons for this, eight out of ten Europeans I encounter broach the subject to voice their disapproval.'

This sense of superiority cannot be dissociated from our past. Long after the loss of their colonies, European countries still laboured under the illusion that they, in tandem with the United States, ruled the world. The message of the past decade is that after two hundred years this Western monopoly is coming to an end. This realisation has not quite sunk in yet, which is not surprising given the pace of change. But their diminishing role is now beginning to dawn on Europeans. Since the credit crisis their economies have slumped, growth is moderate at best and most EU countries face excessive government debt and youth unemployment. Mutual distrust has been painfully exposed by the euro crisis. The global economy is growing without any substantial contribution from Europe. All this raises doubts about our future. The resulting fear converges on China, which is not only seen as one of the biggest threats but also looked down on. The risk is that the intellectual curiosity that both Schmidt and Sandschneider so heartily recommend will lose out to emotion and condescension. When that happens we might continue to misperceive China and the Chinese, as in previous centuries.

# Chapter 4

# 'We Are Still a Developing Nation'

## The Chinese View

The taxi winds its way through narrow Beijing streets full of cars, bicycles and pedestrians. Ambulances and visitors' cars block the road in front of a large hospital. It may be a sunny spring morning, but the stress is all too visible on people's faces. Luckily the taxi driver manages to slip through and a short time later he parks beside a large gate in a long wall. Two young soldiers throw me a suspicious look, but after showing them my passport I am ushered into a lush garden with mature trees and a vast lawn.

The premises are part of the former Austrian-Hungarian embassy, the target of an attack by furious Chinese people during the Boxer Rebellion of 1900. Now it is an oasis of calm, away from the hustle and bustle of the street. This is where the employees of the CIIS, the China Institute for International Studies, ponder their country's changing position in the world. In the enormous, quiet building, I am welcomed by Cui Hongjian, director of the think tank's Western Europe division, a department of the Ministry of Foreign Affairs.

This is my first interview with a government advisor. Warnings from experienced correspondents flash through my head. 'Those guys will just reiterate the official position', one of them assured me. Nevertheless I am curious. Will there be any sign of resentment, arrogance or indifference towards Europeans, the feelings instilled in the Chinese throughout the ages?

## Europe as a model

Cui, who is in his early forties with a round, slightly pale face, gained the necessary experience at the Chinese embassies in Jamaica and India. He shows me into an absurdly large meeting room, where dozens of chairs are set up in the usual open square formation. We occupy two, a little awkwardly, with a white teapot and cups between us. A joke about how we disappear in this ridiculously large space is probably impolite. My frivolity is further stifled by the tall wooden window panels that keep out the bright morning sun. It lends our meeting a solemn air. Accordingly, our conversation gets off to a difficult start, as Cui is struggling with a cold. After a while he becomes easier to understand and over the course of two hours and many cups of tea his comments become more spontaneous too, especially when I switch my recorder off. Eventually, after photographs, our goodbyes are cordial.

His message is that Europe should not be afraid. But why not, I ask; you are rapidly transforming into a knowledge economy, like us, but with more people and more money. 'Technologically, we lag too far behind the West', Cui replies modestly. 'We won't come close in the next five to ten years. We are a late developer and have a long way to go before we can compete on an equal footing.' Once China has caught up, the West has cause for concern, he believes. 'Your fear of job losses in the medium term is understandable, because your products will be more expensive than ours and this may jeopardise your export to international markets.' But that is still a long way off, he stresses. Besides, in his view the Europeans are smart enough to anticipate this. 'Life is always in flux', he says philosophically. 'So you have to change with it. And you will.'

Competition is healthy, he says with a smile. 'Besides, it is not just about competition. There is room for cooperation too. We have worked together in the past few years and this has benefited both parties to date', he notes. 'Your companies have gained access to our market in exchange for technology, much more so than Japanese and American businesses. This has worked to both our advantages. China has changed considerably in recent decades, not least thanks to Europe.'

Besides, we need not be afraid because his country still has so many internal problems to deal with: the gap between rich and poor, environmental pollution, droughts, the ageing population. 'We are still a developing nation. You need to see this to understand the challenges we are facing. We need twenty million new jobs annually, just to absorb migration from the countryside to the city.' As for dealing with the ageing population, he believes China can learn a lot from Europe. 'It is putting pressure on your welfare state, I know, but our government may still want to look at European models. We need a lot more social security here. We need a more balanced distribution of wealth.'

Europe need not be afraid, Europe as a partner, Europe as a model even – these words are meant to reassure, spoken by a diplomat with a European remit. Open-minded as he is, Cui is clearly not one of the hawks looking down on Europe. I cannot detect even a trace of resentment or arrogance. He makes no reference to socialism, which is enshrined in the Constitution and still the official ideology. To be honest, he strikes me as sympathetic and well-informed; his knowledge of our part of the world cannot be faulted. The West should be able to do business with such a pragmatic and capable diplomat. Or am I too naïve and, as my ever-critical journalist peers would put it, turning into a 'useful idiot' in the service of the Chinese government?

Of course Cui's argument toes the party line. 'Don't be afraid, trust us', urged then Prime Minister Wen Jiabao during his tour of Europe in 2011. He too was one of the 'Chinese you can do business with', Western diplomats reckoned. His track record included advocating a dialogue with the students in 1989, when the drama around Tiananmen Square was unfolding. It was good for his credibility in the West. But trust? It will have to come from both sides. The question is whether the Chinese, with their problematic past experiences with Europeans, can be deemed capable of trusting us.

## 'A reservoir of goodwill'

A remarkable survey conducted among three thousand Chinese city dwellers and some two hundred 'members of the elite', such as government officials, entrepreneurs and journalists, has yielded encouraging results. The government has long been anxious to avoid public polls, because they carry a whiff of democracy about them. A case in point was the Chinese version of the talent show *Idols*, which invited viewers to vote for their favourite performer. It threatened to be such a success in 2005 that the government promptly imposed a ban on voting by text message. But interviewing several thousand city dwellers, right across the country, went ahead. Under the auspices of the University of Nottingham in the UK and with substantial funding from the European Union, researchers and students set off with questionnaires in 2010 to gauge their compatriots' opinions.

How familiar are Chinese city dwellers with Europe? One in five has occasional contact with Europeans, while fewer than one in twenty has visited the continent. The image they have is shaped first and foremost by what they see on television, followed at some distance by newspapers and the internet as sources of information. The party does not shape their opinions directly, even if one in four in this survey is a member. It does indirectly, since it is the reporting on state television that influences their perspective on Europe. That is largely positive, as half of the respondents believe that Europeans are peace-loving and trustworthy. A sizeable minority of 30 per cent believes otherwise. The urbanites appear to be more enthusiastic about Europeans than about the Americans and the Japanese. And while an overwhelming majority of those questioned profess to be proud of their country – fertile ground for nationalism – that does not stop 85 per cent from welcoming the spread of European culture in China. Music and films are particularly popular. The European role in the world is viewed as positive in areas such as scientific progress, peace and environmental protection.

'Despite the difficulties of the past, the European Union can access a huge reservoir of goodwill in China', research leader Zhengxu Wang of the University of Nottingham concludes. Europe is also given good marks by the 'elite groups', which include government officials. They too are free from hostility. Interestingly, Europeans are deemed preferable to Americans and especially to the Japanese. The controversies they highlight are the usual ones: human rights, Tibet and intellectual property rights. The elite groups are also remarkably positive about Western forms of government, but without saying whether it might be an option for their own country. Needless to say, you cannot be too open in this kind of research. Again, more cooperation tops the elite's wish list. The greatest shortcoming they identify in themselves reflects that of the rest of the population: insufficient knowledge of Europe.

Contempt for our work ethic, but envy of our lifestyle. This, without questionnaires, is my general impression of how the Chinese view the West, whether they live in China or here. Contempt and envy are two sides of the same coin. While the Chinese are proud of their work ethic ('nobody in the world works as hard as we do!'), they are not entirely happy with it either. The younger generations especially admit they would not mind a bit more leisure time, and seize the opportunity whenever they can. In Hungary I met a Chinese opera singer in her early thirties and a Chinese chef and restaurateur in his forties, both of whom lived a European lifestyle. They had become used to working weeks of thirty hours. The chef ruled out a return to China, 'because I would have to work too hard'.

## Civilised and lazy

Over lunch in London's Chinatown, Angela Hao, a journalist in her early thirties, tells me that since moving to Europe she is finally getting round to walking and swimming. 'In China it is extremely hard to live your own life. You're always under pressure: first you have to work your socks off in school, then at university. Next, your family wants you to marry and buy an apartment. The social pressure is enormous, and people are constantly on tiptoe. That's why you see them sleeping everywhere, on buses and on trains, whenever they get the chance.' In London that pressure has now been lifted from her shoulders, much to her relief: 'Perhaps Europeans are a bit lazier than we are, but the lifestyle here is great.' She has no plans to go back, not for the time being anyway: 'At least you can have a balanced life here.'

Those same reservations about going home after enjoying the fruits of the West are expressed by a group of young students I talk to later that afternoon. They are studying at the London School of Economics, an elite institution in the heart of London. Small clusters of them congregate outside the library – it looks like another Chinatown. Chinese students make up a large proportion of the highly select student body, some 1,100 out of 9,000. Many dream of making lots of money in the financial sector, starting off in the City or in Hong Kong before considering the Chinese mainland. 'We are patriotic, we love our country. But by the time we finish, we will have spent six years paying for expensive degrees. I see it as making a return on an investment', says twenty-year-old Di, who wants to make a living as a management consultant. Despite the economic crisis, he is full of praise for Europe. 'Europe has its problems, but they are not all that serious. It certainly doesn't undermine my idea of a developed continent. We respect European culture and we can learn from it. Every culture has its benefits.'

Nineteen-year-old Sherry, an accountancy student, expresses the greatest reservations about a possible return: 'In principle I'm happy to do my bit for my country. It's where my roots are. But I wonder if I can adjust to the Chinese style of doing business', she says diplomatically. Business is all about *guanxi*, an opaque system of relationships and favours, quite unlike the more rational Western approach. She has come to prefer the latter, along with the Western vision on education. 'Here at LSE you can choose your own modules; it's a lot more flexible than in China', she reckons. She too is largely positive about the West. Neither she nor any of her fellow students mention the European atrocities during the 'century of humiliation'.

Appreciation, envy and scorn – Pál Nyíri, Professor of Anthropology at the Free University in Amsterdam, confirms that the Chinese have mixed emotions about Westerners. 'They feel both inferior and superior' is his conclusion after twenty years of studying Chinese migrants in various countries including Italy and his native Hungary. While the Chinese may be catching up economically, they still look up to the West, especially to the United States with their global brands, technology and innovative strength.

The Chinese feel superior because of their work ethic. 'Westerners are lazy, demand time off every three months and won't work six days a week, they argue.' Yet they feel inferior 'because they think Westerners are civilised and their own manners rather boorish. And they look up to democracies, even ordinary people.' Nyíri believes the feeling of humiliation is alive and well. 'The sentiment you encounter is this: "The world ransacked us during the nineteenth century and now they begrudge China its growing strength."'

In Nyíri's view, attitudes towards the West are less favourable than the survey mentioned above suggests. 'People may appreciate Westerners, yet still be convinced that Western countries are seeking to corner China. These days the animosity is directed more at the United States than at the European colonial powers.'

## National pride

Chinese nationalism is certainly something that American and European companies will have to take into account. Multinationals such as McDonald's, Nike and Apple faced a barrage of criticism on the internet following suspicions of misconduct; the bar is set much higher for them than for their Chinese counterparts. French company Carrefour even faced a boycott following the false rumour that its main shareholder LVMH was sponsoring the Dalai Lama, *persona non grata* to the Chinese government.

As befits a good diplomat, Cui Hongjian puts the growing nationalism into perspective: 'You can compare it to someone who is performing better. That person will become more confident. That's happening to China at the moment.' Self-confidence has its benefits, including less fear. 'I remember having a heated debate in 1999 when our embassy in Belgrade was accidentally bombed by NATO. "What can China do to better protect itself?" people wondered fearfully. More defence was the answer. As if China itself could come under attack. But when NATO started bombing Libya in 2011, the response here was calm. We all realised that it was unlikely we would be next in line.'

Self-confidence is one thing, but what if it turns into arrogance? Cui admits he has some concerns. 'The way some wealthy people flaunt their luxury goods abroad undermines our image. Other than that our main challenge is to avoid extreme nationalism.' But that is true for all governments, he stresses. 'Nationalism is a label you can stick on anyone you dislike. It's also an issue in Europe. And where is national pride most prominent? In the United States of course.' For China it means first and foremost that its anti-Japanese sentiments must be kept in check. 'There is nothing wrong with national pride, provided it does not tip the balance. The government knows this. We owe our progress of the past thirty years to the fact that we started opening up to the rest of the world in 1979.'

# Chapter 5

# Fuelling Our Fear of China

Over the past ten years we have been bombarded with information about China and its spectacular growth. The main message in the Western media is: they're coming. China is set to become the world's biggest economy. It has huge reserves at its disposal with which it will become a threat to the West. 'China is buying up Europe', claimed a leading European think tank in 2011. Great fodder for newspaper headlines.

Having spread this message so widely, the media have created significant misconceptions. A majority of Americans are under the impression that the Chinese economy is already bigger than their own. In reality, the size of the US economy was 17.4 billion dollars according to the IMF, substantially bigger than China at 10.4 billion. Jointly, the twenty-eight EU member states are even the biggest economy in the world, in front of the US, with a GDP above 18.4 billion dollars, despite the eurozone crisis. This statistic is probably at odds with what the average European thinks. The projections have clearly galloped ahead of reality.

Equally inflated is the perception of the role of Chinese investors in Europe. It is minor compared to that of investors from many other countries, the United States especially, and yet there is talk of Europe being bought up. The media present every potential acquisition as the beginning of China's victory march, pandering to the hype and to the fear of both the 'Yellow Peril' and the West's downfall. The tone of these reports is seldom neutral. 'The Chinese are taking over the Port of Rotterdam' ran the headline of an article in the Dutch quality newspaper *NRC Handelsblad*. On closer inspection the nightmarish vision was exaggerated. The Chinese have certainly stepped up their activities, but the Russians are also investing heavily in the Port of Rotterdam, which remains the biggest in Europe. The Americans and Arabs already had a presence and will not be edged out, nor will the Europeans. In short, there is quite a coming and going and those nuances are certainly there in the article, but a subheading reinforces the tone of the story: 'China gains control over Port of Rotterdam'. Well, if we hand over our national pride, what hope is there, the average reader will be thinking. The Swedes must have thought along similar lines when their Volvo fell into Chinese hands, and so did the French when PSA (Citroën and Peugeot) became part-owned by the Chinese. 'There we go' was the undercurrent of the newspaper analyses of these deals. The interest from Chinese buyers was taken as a symptom of failure, which is not surprising as the media like to play up to both fear and a certain defeatism about the future, as I experienced while writing an article on Chinese investments in the Bordeaux region.

## 'Oh no, not again!'

Since 2008 a number of French wine châteaux have passed into Chinese ownership. As in Volvo's case, the nationalist murmurings are all too easy to imagine: proud French wine makers complaining about the decline of their national heritage. Record those complaints and 'there's a story', as journalists put it. Without complaints there might not be a story because 'what would the headline be?' Aware of this mechanism, I hint at possible French opposition to justify my trip to Bordeaux to the newspaper. 'The Chinese in Bordeaux! The production of the world-famous wine, the industry that makes France what it is, may be falling into Chinese hands. It's bound to upset the French.' Yes, the newspaper likes the sound of that.

When I tell my friends in Amsterdam about Chinese investments in French wine, they all, without exception, react with shock. 'Oh no, not again!' they say, further proof that perceptions are at odds with reality. I did not have much choice in France, since the wine sector was one of the few that had been penetrated by Chinese investors. These days they have a broader presence.

In the high-speed train to Bordeaux doubts arise. Am I doing the right thing by writing this story? In the past few days, several people I spoke to in Paris gave me puzzled looks when I raised the subject. No, they had no idea that the Chinese had arrived in the area around Bordeaux. It appears to be accepted with a shrug. The chief editor of *Le Monde*, who has just published his book about the growing arrogance among the Chinese, confirms that the French cannot get worked up about this.

Of course I could see the cool, rational or uninformed response of those I spoke to for what it was. 'Oh well, they're Parisians whose urban lives are a far cry from those of winegrowers in the country, those who are experiencing the meaning of a Chinese takeover at first hand.' At least that is what I told myself. But on the train to Bordeaux I speak to a local journalist, César Compadre, on the phone. Ever since the first château was sold to a businessman in 2008, he has been closely following the Chinese takeovers for the regional paper *Sud-Ouest*. We are talking about half a dozen out of more than eleven thousand châteaux, he stresses, or a few hundred hectares in a wine region measuring more than 117,000 hectares. A tiny wine stain on an enormous white tablecloth. Besides, the acquired châteaux include not a single famous *grand cru*: no Lafite-Rothschild, no Margaux, no Pomerol. If they did, it might have elicited protest. But there is a historic reason for this lack of anger too, he explains. 'We have had foreign buyers for decades: British, American, Dutch, Japanese. Now they are joined by a few Chinese buyers. Nobody is losing any sleep over it, I can assure you.'

He notes, not without irony, that it is a particularly hot topic outside the Bordeaux region. Foreign journalists, led by the British and Americans, have visited with the same expectations I had: proud Frenchmen reacting with anger. But in actual fact all official bodies, most notably the association of wine producers, welcome it. They know better than anyone just what dire straits the Bordeaux region is in. So when a white knight passes by, you cannot be too picky. When I wonder out loud whether there is any point in visiting now, Compadre's answer carries a hint of reproach: 'You could always come and tell the truth, namely that the whole thing doesn't amount to much.'

Hmm, he is right of course. But a newspaper article thrives on tension, preferably a conflict of interest. That is how biased I am after twenty years of newspaper journalism. It is time I am cured, so I decide to suppress my professional reservations.

Early the following morning I am enjoying the scenery around Château de Viaud, one of the properties to have fallen into Chinese hands. I had some difficulty locating the small village of Lalande-de-Pomerol, more than forty kilometres east of Bordeaux. Assistance came from a somewhat rough-looking man in overalls, who was glad for the interruption as he worked a vineyard with a small but noisy tractor. Of course I had to ask him what he thought of the Chinese investors. How would he like working for them? 'As long as they pay, I don't really mind', he yelled above the noise of his tractor.

At Château de Viaud the leaves on the vines are yellow, red and green. The autumn sun dispels a few lingering ribbons of mist. The vineyards stand out sharply against the blue sky. Four centuries ago, the scene may well have been the same, because that is how old Château de Viaud is. The only difference is that it is no longer owned by a Frenchman.

Since I am a little early for my appointment at the château, I decide to go for a wander around the hamlet. Fortune smiles on me because before long I bump into the mayor-winegrower, Monsieur Christian Courty. After hearing the reason for my visit, he escorts me to the wine cellar where he receives his customers. His hands on the wine barrel in front of him betray a lifetime of hard work. From under his beret he regards the world with a slightly sceptical and mocking eye. He says exactly what a newspaper journalist in search of tension wants to hear.

Courty, who is nearing pension age, is not too fond of the Chinese. He had dealings with them this summer when two merchants knocked on his door, offering to buy up his entire harvest. The whole lot, all sixty thousand bottles! 'I didn't have to think twice. What would I say to my regular customers, the ones I've acquired over the course of dozens of years and some of whom have become friends? Tell them their wine will be drunk in China this year?'

He dispenses with diplomacy when he talks about the buyers of the neighbouring Château de Viaud. He grumbles about the price of close to half a million euros per hectare paid by 'those guys', when 220,000 euros per hectare is a lot of money in this region. It is unfortunate for young French people who want to get into wine making, he believes, 'because they won't get a foot in the door'. Besides, the Chinese never properly introduced themselves. 'They were here in my courtyard once, when they were lost, but that was the last I saw of them. They won't do much for the community.'

He is resigned more than angry. The vineyards around Bordeaux may have been declared world heritage sites by UNESCO, but there is nothing to stop foreigners from taking controlling stakes. In his view the French authorities rather than the Chinese buyers are to blame for that. 'If we don't want this to happen to our heritage in France, we'll have to take action. But that's not happening. The French have run out of money, so foreigners are buying our châteaux. It's as simple as that.'

As mayor, Courty objects to the arrival of *all* foreigners; he is making things hard for me, since I am particularly curious about the tensions aroused by the Chinese, not just any foreigners. Luckily he comes up with another argument: French wine-making know-how is also going to China. This could work against Bordeaux wine makers in the form of Chinese wine on the market. 'It would not be the first time. The French also helped out in Chile and Argentina. It's our speciality', he remarks cynically. He sees China as a serious competitor. 'They've got excellent terrain over there. Besides, they've hired Michel Rolland, the most expensive consultant imaginable. He'll send you an invoice just for shaking your hand.'

Strong words, spoken by an ordinary Frenchman and playing up to underlying fears: the Chinese are stealing 'our' expertise to beat us at our own game. Like the gunmaker shot with his own gun. The same applies to the high-speed train I travelled on. In Europe such trains are currently French- or German-made, but elsewhere in the world Chinese companies compete with

Europeans for orders, having picked up their technology. Could we soon find Chinese wine of Bordeaux quality on our supermarket shelves?

In little more than half an hour Mayor Courty gives me almost enough ammunition to write a scare story. I am all the more tempted when, later that day, I speak to some farm labourers during their lunch break. When I press them, they voice disapproval too. They grumble that it is an outrage that French heritage is falling into Chinese hands, but what can you do? What strikes me is their resignation; no sign of anger whatsoever. Having spent several years as a correspondent in this country, I recognise this acquiescence. From a French point of view, things have long been going awry in Europe, and in France especially. Within the space of a couple of hours, I have gathered enough quotes to write the story I proposed and my newspaper is expecting – regardless of what my colleague Compadre claimed.

But is such an approach really justified? Would I not be distorting reality by giving free rein to the grumbling that casts a bad light on the Chinese investments? The delight with which official bodies have welcomed the capital injection offers something of a counterbalance, but not nearly enough. It feels like a diplomatic gesture, insincere compared to the raw views of the mayor-vintner and the farm labourers. And yet I decide to put their gloom and doom into perspective. There are too many reasons for a positive interpretation of the Chinese presence in the Bordeaux region.

## A 'grand merci' is more appropriate

The Chinese are here in the capacity of investors, but even more so as wine drinkers – from the cheapest plonk to the priciest *grand cru*. The elite are prepared to spend astronomical sums of money on top wines, whether or not diluted with coke or Sprite, as rumour has it. A bottle of Château Lafite from 1869, bought at an auction in Hong Kong for 165,000 euros, or a somewhat younger Pétrus from 1982, sold for 52,000 euros – truly dizzying sums. But the Chinese also like to drink the cheap Bordeaux wines, which make up the remaining 95 per cent of the market, and thus help prevent the decline of this quintessentially French industry. China leads the top five nations importing Bordeaux from the bottom end of the scale (less than 3 dollars per litre) by a generous margin, ahead of Germany, England, Belgium and the Netherlands.

In the past four years, the explosive growth in Chinese demand for Bordeaux has given this wine region some much-needed respite. A graph published by the wine association shows a curve rising spectacularly to nearly a million hectolitres. The wine makers are struggling because of disappointing domestic demand, as the French lunch has not only been curtailed, but is no longer served with copious amounts of wine either. Add to this the competition from other parts of the world and one in four wine makers is operating at a loss. Their average income is below subsistence level. Now that the Chinese have started drinking wine, quite a few French vintners can at least keep their businesses afloat. A 'grand merci' may be more appropriate than distrust.

As investors the Chinese cannot be faulted either. They are taking risks in an industry in which the margins, except for the top brands, are very low. Not only that. They are buying from owners who have reached the end of the road, like the Ducos family at Laulan Ducos, north of Bordeaux. The château had been in the family since the eighteenth century, but son Frédéric could no longer keep his head above water. 'It was frustrating. We were too small and couldn't spend enough on marketing', he tells me. He does not fancy an interview with a foreign journalist – after three centuries of production the loss is too painful – but he was overjoyed when a Chinese chain of stores selling luxury products was prepared to take over his chateau. Bottles of Laulan Ducos are no longer sold in France, only in luxury stores in China. 'No, I don't mind', he says.

At the Château de Viaud it was a businessman from the Médoc who threw in the towel after several years. The buyer is COFCO, a large state-owned corporation, which also owns a Chinese vineyard of ten thousand hectares. So what do they want with the twenty-one hectares of Château de Viaud? I ask Sophie Lafargue, who has been responsible for wine production at the château for the past eight years. She is at work in a dark barn not far from the chateau, where hundreds of barrels of wine are waiting to be seen to. Thirty-nine, with regular features and a ponytail and dressed in jeans and a red jacket, she is vibrant and cool. And reserved too. This is clearly not the first time she has been quizzed about her new bosses. She pulls a chair up to a small table for her guest, while she leans against a couple of wine barrels.

She tells me she was drawn to the small scale of this château – a team of six takes care of the entire production, apart from the grape harvest. No cheap Chinese labourers will be flown in for the next harvest; the suggestion elicits a faint smile. Nor does she expect the enterprise to be upscaled. When it became clear that the Chinese were coming to Lalande-de-Pomerol those around her were particularly surprised: 'China is not known as a wine country. But I think their involvement is a very good thing. Their demand for wine keeps the whole market going.'

She will not be drawn on the motives of the new owner. 'You have to ask them.' But she does not believe that the Chinese are primarily after French know-how, as the mayor-winegrower of Viaud suggested. 'I haven't had that much to do with them yet, but my impression is that they know quite a lot about wine making already. At most there will be an exchange of ideas about details.' She reckons COFCO's motive is simple: Bordeaux sells really well in China. So again, virtually all bottles will go to the new mother country. In a brief email statement COFCO explains that the acquisition is part of their worldwide strategy. 'France is the centre of viticulture, so a French chateau is vital.' It is a bit vague.

When I put the suggestion of buying expertise to a more objective informant, César Compadre, he is amused more than anything. 'We have been spreading our expertise around the globe for decades. A bit more or less won't make a difference.'

Finally, in the lounge bar of the association of wine producers in the heart of Bordeaux, I speak with Jean-Baptiste Soula. The viticulturalist, in his early forties and with many years in the wine business under his belt, dismisses the suggestion that the Chinese are after French expertise. 'Making wine is not exactly high-tech; it's not that difficult.'

When my story makes it into the paper, I notice that the editors have fallen for the grumbling of Mayor Courty. He is quoted in the headline: 'Winemaker's know-how goes to China.' You scarcely notice that it is strongly denied by various experts. So without meaning to, I have fuelled the fear myself.

# Chapter 6

# The Lure of Sensationalism

## The Media and China

The place: the St Ursula Gymnasium, a girls' high school in Lenggries, a conservative provincial town in Bavaria. Chinese-German writer Luo Lingyuan is visiting from Berlin and answering questions. Initially, the 200 schoolgirls want to know all about human rights violations. Say 'China' and this is what springs to their minds.

But when Luo starts talking about the beauty of the language and recites poetry, the scales fall from the girls' eyes. 'They didn't know China was so much more. The entire country had been reduced to the human rights issue.'

Luo, a lively, smartly dressed woman approaching fifty, has lived in Berlin for over twenty years. She fell in love with a German while studying journalism in Shanghai, but once in Germany the relationship foundered. The fall of the Berlin Wall was one of the reasons. He was keen to explore East Germany, but she felt a great antipathy to a region that evoked the totalitarian aspects of her native country: 'I wanted to leave that world behind.'

In other words, she is no stranger to critical thinking about her home country. Her books confirm this. But that does not stop her from criticising the Western media, which keep harping on about China's harsh side. The result is scenes like the one at the Bavarian school. 'That's how big an impact the media have. They're only too happy to hint at a "Yellow Peril". Yet there's no need to fear the Chinese at all. They want more or less the same things as Europeans: good health, a decent salary and travel. There's a very real danger that Europeans will get the wrong impression of the Chinese.' After which she points to the trap that many Western China analysts have fallen into: 'When you're guided by fear you no longer see what's really going on.'

## Western prejudice

Luo's colleague Vera Yu, another Berlin-based writer, is of a younger generation. But she is equally annoyed by the one-sided representation and in fact opposed to all generalisations. Yu, the daughter of a Chinese professor and a German air stewardess, comes into contact with Chinese people as a student mentor. The students spend a couple of months in Berlin under an exchange programme, and what strikes Yu above all else is their diversity. 'Everybody is always trying to capture what *all* Chinese people are like. But surely you can't make claims about *all* Europeans either? They are too diverse. There are fifty-five known minorities in China alone.'

Thinking the world cannot handle such nuances, the media want to provide clarity and direction. I tell Yu I will not be able to avoid generalisations in my book either. She sighs. In her experience Western journalists are primarily interested in reinforcing feelings of fear. 'There are exceptions, like foreign correspondents in China who actually go out and investigate. So when they report wrongdoings, it's fine, because there's plenty wrong. But the editorial offices of newspapers have a tendency to exploit people's fears. This happens not just at *Bild*, but also at *Der Spiegel*, which has headlines like "The Threat of the Dragon" or something along those lines on its cover.' True, to accompany a story about industrial espionage, the Hamburg-based weekly does not shy away from printing on its cover a photo of a young Chinese woman's eyes peering at the reader through blinds, captioned 'The Yellow Spy'.

Another cover story, about the 'Birth of a Global Power', features a fearsome dragon tearing the world apart. Yu can see the impact of these images on her students, who are not exactly positive about press freedom in the West. The way they see it, their country is being reduced to 'human rights, Tibet and

Ai Weiwei'. They find it hard to understand, not least because human rights receive hardly any attention in their own media. This then magnifies the shock when they are confronted with Western media reports on their country. Yu tells me that one of her students lamented: 'If this is what press freedom brings, why bother fighting for it?'

It is an attitude that China expert Daniela Stockmann, a German political scientist at Leiden University, recognises in her students. 'My impression is that most of them are critical of internet censorship, but not of their government. What's more, over here they discover that Western countries aren't perfect either and have their own serious problems. It sometimes makes them even more enthusiastic about China's style of government.'

## 'China is seen as a monster'

This support came to light in 2008 when thousands of Chinese students took to the streets of Europe to demonstrate against Western reporting on Tibet. On the eve of the Olympic Games, the army had come down hard on rebellious Tibetans and the Western media were raising a hue and cry about it. But the students regarded the Tibetan demonstrators as criminal troublemakers who were attacking hard-working Chinese citizens. To them the army's intervention was entirely justified. In fact, their criticism of the Western media, born of injured pride, took on a sharp tone. At the time a popular clip on the Sina portal quoted Mao approvingly: 'Imperialism will never abandon its intention to destroy us.' What followed was a video montage showing a sequence of news flashes from the likes of CNN and the BBC. The images were meant to prove that the West is only interested in negative coverage. The clip became a huge success, to the surprise of its maker, twenty-eight-year-old Tang Jie. Shortly afterwards, he received a visit from Evan Osnos, then a correspondent with the *New Yorker*. Defying expectations, Tang was no frustrated loser, but a well-read student majoring in Western philosophy at top university Fudan.

He had long been wise to the brainwashing tactics of the Chinese media, he explained, but that the Western media were equally biased came as a huge disappointment to him. It hurt his patriotic feelings to find that his country was still viewed with suspicion despite experiencing its greatest ever prosperity. The clip's success suggests that he had touched a sensitive chord. China's economic success has only fanned the flames of national pride. If the West steps up its criticism, as it did at the time of the Tibet crisis, the loathing will increase exponentially. Tang Jie even went as far as hinting at a conspiracy theory in his video: 'Obviously, there is a scheme behind the scenes to encircle China. A new Cold War!'

Similar criticism of Western media can be heard at an official level. In their speeches, the Chinese ambassadors to Europe like to refer to what they see as the failings of the media, often going into specific detail: 'A German television channel broadcast images of the Nepalese army to show what the Chinese army was doing in Tibet!' complained a prominent ambassador. The reproach that the Western media are driving at a second Cold War has also made it into the official discourse. 'China is depicted as a monster. The media ought to portray our country as it really is, or else the Europeans could slip into a Cold War mentality', warned Liu Xiaoming, the Chinese ambassador to Great Britain, at a symposium on Europe and China in 2012. Although courteous and polite in all other respects, the diplomat made an exception for the media.

Not long before, the most prominent Chinese diplomat in Brussels, EU ambassador Song Zhe, had denounced the 'irresponsibility' of 'some media' in an opinion piece. They had had the temerity to suggest that China was trying to make support to the European countries hit by the euro crisis conditional on political gains, such as more voting rights in the IMF. 'This behaviour [of the Western media] is misleading and detrimental to our relations.'

In his opening speech to the China–Europe Forum in 2009, the same Song Zhe rejected the criticism of his country even more vehemently. The meeting brought together Chinese and European professionals who, in discussing their respective countries, also addressed the role of the media. The EU ambassador immediately upped the ante: 'On many issues concerning China some Western media have nurtured a "systemic bias", persisting with patronizing comments and ill-founded criticisms. In extreme cases, they even abandon the fundamental principles of objectivity and fairness and violate the professional ethics. They patch up a piece of news using untested or even fabricated information.'

'What we don't accept', he addressed the journalists in attendance, 'is wilful imposition of views and standards or pressuring. China never yields to any pressure. Over the past 30 years, China has made tremendous achievements in economic, social, political, cultural and other fields. These achievements are the result of the reform and opening-up policy and the hard work of all Chinese people. They are by no means the result of *media pressure* from the West.'

Pierre Calame, the Forum's idealistic organiser, witnessed the proceedings with concern. 'Song ruined the exchange of ideas by accusing Western journalists of professional shortcomings. Needless to say, it got us nowhere.' But he also tells me that the French journalists who were present confirmed the bias in their editorial offices. 'It's a subject journalists don't like to talk about, but they said that their editors have a preference for topics they think the public will like: human rights violations, environmental pollution, industrial unrest, mining accidents, corruption and Tibet. More positive issues such as China's progress, the variety and depth of the internal debate and the adjustments to the development model rarely make the news.'

Western journalists are unlikely to lose sleep over this kind of media criticism. Practically all world leaders complain that 'good news does not make the news'. The ambassadors sticking up for their country are viewed with scepticism. As representatives of an authoritarian regime that censors its own media on every level, they lack the credibility to lecture the Western media.

## 'Giving the truth a helping hand'

Western journalists are also in a position to dismiss Chinese criticism as a caricature. Like many of their countries' politicians, newspapers and television have actually paid a great deal of attention to China's growth spurt in recent years while human rights have receded into the background. This, at any rate, is the picture I get from a study by Li Zhang, a media sociologist working in the UK. Over the period 1989–2005 she analysed the coverage in three leading publications, the *International Herald Tribune* and *Financial Times* newspapers and weekly news magazine *The Economist*. In the years immediately following the student uprising of 1989 the picture of a problematic country teetering on the edge of political chaos dominated. But after 2002, China's economic dynamism and its growing role on the world stage start gaining the upper hand.

So it is certainly not true that the West is hammering on about human rights to the exclusion of all else, as the Chinese claim. But it is interesting to see that this is the perception. In my experience there is a grain of truth in the other accusation, namely that Western journalists have a tendency to turn China into 'a monster'. Positive stories about the country's growth might convey the message that China provides the West with new opportunities. But more often than not the implicit message is: 'Watch out, they're coming!' My experience in the Bordeaux region illustrates this. The lure of sensationalism, however subtle, is almost irresistible to journalists.

Besides, Western journalists are known to display a degree of arrogance when they find themselves confronted with this criticism. 'The Chinese haven't quite figured out what press freedom means, so why would we take their criticism seriously?' This unspoken assumption in turn prompts the Chinese reaction: 'You see, Western journalists think they're superior. They're happy to lecture others, but are not prepared to listen themselves.' Efforts to bridge these differences in perception have met with limited success, as the proceedings at the China–Europe Forum illustrate.

Another illustration comes courtesy of the German journalist Frank Sieren in his book *Angst vor China* (Fear of China). With nearly twenty years of journalistic experience in China under his belt, he made an after-dinner speech at a meeting aimed at bringing German and Chinese journalists closer together. He criticised his Western colleagues, who have 'a penchant for giving the truth a helping hand in order to establish a clearer distinction between good and evil'. He also took aim at China for what he described as the 'abduction' of artist Ai Weiwei. 'Abducting and detaining people just because they have a different opinion can never be a model for the world.'

This speech earned Frank Sieren furious reactions from both a German and a Chinese colleague. Back in 1989 the Chinese journalist had been one of the demonstrators on Tiananmen Square. He believes 'abduction' is too strong a word for what happened to Ai Weiwei. The artist was actually allowed to briefly visit his wife during his imprisonment. 'Abduction' is reminiscent of the dark days of the Cultural Revolution, 'and luckily those are far behind us'. Sieren apologised for using the word: 'I should have used a different term to get my point of view across without offending my Chinese colleague.' This is the degree of empathy we need for a proper debate.

The speech also upset a German journalist, who deemed Sieren's criticism of Western colleagues inappropriate, fearing it might play into the hands of the Chinese regime. If Western journalists were to portray the country as more open and liberal than it really is, they would lend themselves to propaganda, he argued. It would be inappropriate to view an 'unfinished Chinese system' as equal to that of the West. The German's reasoning is based on the assumption that the West is superior. While I believe there is a lot to be said for this as far as press freedom goes, to dismiss any kind of self-criticism as inappropriate is going too far. You would preclude corrections to your own blind spots. And those are plentiful.

## Criticism is politically correct

Take the freedom of expression of Chinese journalists and scholars. Under President Xi it is declining, as censorship is tightening. But various people I have spoken to, Chinese and European alike, have told me how much it increased in the first decade of this century. Yet this 'increasing freedom' will have escaped the attention of the average Western citizen, who would have labelled China as first and foremost a champion of censorship in those years.

Both are true. Yes, there is an impressive system of censorship, and yes, people had more freedom. But I searched the Western press in vain for stories highlighting the positive developments. There is certainly no shortage of negative reports that highlight the shortcomings. It appears that Western journalists are suffering from peer pressure. A positive story about growing academic and journalistic freedom in China is perceived as a sure-fire way to ruin your reputation as a critical journalist. But you cannot go wrong with a politically correct story about China's failings. This structural preference for the critical approach does not make cultivating mutual understanding any easier.

The pressure to subscribe to this common approach does not just affect journalists. Experts, too, have to fear for their reputation when they say something positive about China in the media. They risk being torn to shreds, not by peer pressure, as with journalists, but by public opinion. And with China experts becoming more cautious, it is the public debate that suffers. 'I've noticed a great reticence towards journalists among my colleagues. As soon as you say something positive about developments in China you run the risk of being pushed into a corner where you don't want to be', political scientist Daniela Stockmann tells me.

The neutral position both she and her colleagues aspire to ('I do not sympathise with the Chinese regime, but nor do I wag my finger like Western pressure groups') is not always appreciated by journalists who like to insert outspoken opinions into their articles. 'We want to retain our independence. Whether you interpret our data negatively or positively depends on your values', she says. In her experience journalists tend to show a clear preference for the negative interpretation.

In turn, the experts have come in for criticism for their tendency to keep quiet. For example, the German journalist Kai Strittmatter, former China correspondent for the *Süddeutsche Zeitung*, attacked the sinologists in his country, accusing them of remaining silent when all over the world protests were taking place against the detention of Liu Xiaobo, the 2010 Nobel Peace Prize laureate. Strittmatter, a sinologist himself, saw it as proof that sinologists had become too dependent on the Chinese government for funding and honorary doctorates. These kinds of serious accusations only increase the pressure on sinologists to be politically correct, thus reducing the chances of a complete and nuanced portrayal of China in the Western media.

# Chapter 7

# Curbing Press Freedom

*The Media's Vulnerability*

'There are agents here keeping an eye on us, so I don't want my family name to be revealed.' In a tea room in Oxford I am talking to a twenty-six-year-old Chinese student, known only as Robert because of his fear of spies. In a city which has been a bastion of academic freedom for centuries, his comment about secret agents sounds a bit unreal. But he is not joking. Some of his fellow students may be reporting to the Chinese authorities, he cannot be sure. And one thing he is sure of is that he does not want to jeopardise his career. After obtaining his doctorate in computer science he hopes to start working for an investment bank in the City or in Hong Kong. It is not hard to picture him in that environment – a quick thinker, bursting with energy and snappily dressed in a sharply tailored grey coat with hip spectacles. In view of that future he says it would be 'unwise' for his full name to be mentioned, especially since he has arrived at some critical insights here in Oxford.

'Initially, I felt insulted when Westerners criticised the Chinese state, because I felt as if it was aimed at the entire population. The government teaches us to love the state, warning that if we don't we might lapse into an older, poorer existence. In primary school you're told that capitalism and greed are bad. In fact, this comes up in the high school entrance exam. But I have come to understand the West's criticism of our system better and I know we have far less freedom to speak our mind.

'And the criticism no longer feels like a personal attack. I've learned to openly disagree with lecturers here. In China we're not taught this, we just listen. Fellow students here dare to write emails to their professors which would be considered disrespectful and insulting in my own country. I can do the same now.'

## Self-censorship Chinese and Western style

More freedom, but still afraid of the state apparatus. There is both a positive and a negative side to Robert's story. After our meeting, the latter was the more dominant of the two for me. I was particularly shocked by the practice of spying on students. But I could not get to the bottom of it. Other students confirmed it nervously, without being able or willing to add anything. The authorities at Oxford University say they are fundamentally opposed to it, of course, but claim ignorance of any actual offences. It reminded me of the Western multinational in China whose CEO I once asked if he knew anything about government spies in his company. We're against it, he answered, 'but we don't know if anyone is writing notes for the party after working hours'.

I never knew China's urge to monitor its own citizens beyond national borders went this far. What I had noticed was the self-censorship among many of the people I spoke to, including Westerners. Who is brave enough to be openly critical of the Chinese government? Western journalists, of course. But you would probably think twice when opposition from the state is a distinct possibility. My impression is that many, both Chinese and foreigners, are walking on eggshells. As soon as 'sensitive' subjects are broached, Chinese people tend to start laughing nervously and shifting in their seats. But at our end too, caution is the watchword. The business people I spoke to do not want to damage their interests; academics waiting for their next visa or hoping for Chinese funding are reluctant to be outspoken. If they are, they will ask me at the end of the interview to be 'prudent' with their statements. Politicians in high offices are careful not to be too critical. Everybody is hyperaware of the thin skin of the Chinese authorities, as evidenced by their detailed intervention when their image is at stake.

Chinese censorship has a long history. Books and later newspapers were first censored in imperial times. There has never been a period of nationwide press freedom. In line with their predecessors and the Soviet model, China's rulers are quite clear about the role of the media: they serve to bolster the legitimacy of the Chinese Communist Party (CCP) and should therefore be seen as propaganda tools. Illustrative is the status of Xinhua, the state news agency. As well as a media enterprise that publishes a range of newspapers and employs ten thousand journalists, it is also a government department. Its CEO is a member of the Central Committee and answers to the country's highest political organ, the Politburo.

An extensive, complex system of censorship and self-censorship has been established to keep the media, and with it society at large, on the straight and narrow. As we all know, government critics run the risk of lengthy detention. The call for freedom of expression and democracy made by Nobel Peace Prize laureate Liu Xiaobo together with 350 other prominent compatriots in their 'Charter 08' petition cost him a prison sentence of eleven years. His case is only one of many who dared to speak their mind and ended up paying a high price for it. Those who voice an opinion on the political system, local corruption cases or environmental issues are treading on dangerous ground. It explains why the average citizen is reluctant to answer questions about 'sensitive' subjects. The censorship has been internalised.

Whether the average Chinese citizen takes as much offence to this curb on freedom of expression as we would do is doubtful. Opinion polls in six major cities indicate that 80 per cent of Chinese people are satisfied with their level of freedom of expression. This is the, for Westerners, baffling conclusion drawn in 2005 by the author of *Public Opinion and Political Change in China*, Tang Wenfang, a political scientist and lecturer in the US. But those who put themselves in the shoes of an ordinary citizen will probably empathise with this position. Issues such as housing, employment and health care are more important to him or her than freedom of expression for many. Besides, because one feels free to express his or her political opinions to friends and family, one does not come up against the limits of that freedom on a daily basis. Those limits come into focus only when a Chinese is in a position to reach a larger audience, for instance in conversation with a journalist. That's generally when they realise it is better to be quiet on 'sensitive' issues.

## 'Out of heaven and into hell'

For a better understanding of the workings of censorship it may be useful to enter the world of a journalist in China. His or her editor-in-chief will receive instructions by phone, email or text message from the party's Central Propaganda Department – or one of its local branches in the case of regional journalism. The department indicates which stories, concepts and words do and do not pass muster. The 'Ministry of Truth' is how some Chinese journalists have mockingly labelled the department, referring to George Orwell's *1984*. Take the instructions issued to journalists when the National People's Congress, a major political gathering, is in session. These were leaked to the California-based *China Digital Times*, which translated them for its fascinating 'Ministry of Truth' column: 'Do not report on or conduct interviews on any sudden incidents. Do not cast doubt on medical reform, the construction of guaranteed housing, food safety or other problems. Do not report on petitioners. Increase the intensity of Lei Feng propaganda.'

The authorities use the word 'propaganda' quite unashamedly, since this is what they believe the media are for. Lei Feng is a soldier from the Mao era who has been worshipped for over fifty years, because he put his personal interests second to those of the state. In the eyes of the government this makes him morally superior to the Chinese of today. The call for more propaganda was successful. According to the *China Digital Times* the number of Lei Feng stories in the papers increased to almost two hundred a day.

Unlike the former Soviet Union, China does not have censors wielding a red pen prior to publication. Nor do journalists need to be given daily instructions. The system works through what the CCP terms 'self-discipline'. Editors-in-chief and journalists do not have to be told exactly what they can and cannot do. They have internalised the fine line between the two.

Chinese journalists in the West are equally familiar with that line. These foreign correspondents were allowed to write to their heart's content about the students who took to the streets of Europe in 2008 to support their government over Tibet. But if the same students were to protest *against* the Chinese government, they could not devote a single word to it, a Chinese correspondent confided in me. Although unwritten, everybody takes these rules for granted.

Journalist and blogger Michael Anti explained to me what this self-censorship can lead to. I spoke to him in a Starbucks in Beijing, the day after Obama's re-election in 2012 and shortly before Xi Jinping's appointment as leader of the party. Anti had just returned from the States, where he had reported extensively on the US elections for Chinese media. Yet he would not be allowed to say anything critical about the 18th National Congress of the CCP, which was to take place a few days later, and where Xi stepped forward. 'Out of heaven and into hell' is how he summarised the transition from one political system to another.

Anti, a pseudonym with which he underlines his pugnacity, has made a name for himself in both China and the West as an advocate for press freedom. In 2005 he consistently pushed the boundaries with his blog on Microsoft's MSN. It made him hugely popular, but the American company decided to remove his posts, presumably to protect its business interests in China. It prompted a worldwide outcry, which earned Anti a lot of publicity and, later on, grants to study journalism at Cambridge and Harvard.

These days he is an international political commentator, informing his Chinese audience in detail about European politics, US foreign policy and developments in the Middle East. But he does not discuss his own country. 'I avoid China. I pretend it doesn't exist. For instance, every week I draw up an overview of the most significant international developments without ever mentioning China.' But how is this possible now that his country's international role continues to grow? 'Oh, it's easy enough. It's the self-censorship you need to function as a journalist over here.'

Equally wondrous is the double role played by some journalists. Working for state media such as Xinhua or the prominent party paper *People's Daily*, they not only write their journalistic pieces but also draw up internal memos for the CCP. Unlike the sanitised reality presented to newspaper readers, these memos outline what is really going on, for instance in local corruption cases. For central government this is a convenient way of keeping informed, while the journalists see the writing of these reports as a privilege. Both media outlets have departments dedicated solely to forming the eyes and ears of the party, and the genre even has its own 'journalism' awards.

## 'Not just propaganda and censorship'

The government's grip on the traditional media is even more extensive. In addition to the system of censorship and self-censorship and the journalists with a dual role, the CCP controls all appointments in the media sector. The editors-in-chief of newspapers, television channels and magazines are all screened. Those who are seen to be pushing the limits too far can forget about their reappointment. This dependence makes editors-in-chief susceptible to manipulation.

The authorities' huge influence on the media explains why China comes 175th out of 180 countries in the World Press Freedom Index of 2014 compiled by Reporters without Borders. 'A model of censorship and repression' is the phrase used by the pressure group for freedom of information to describe China. Since Xi Jinping came to power in 2012, China has 'tightened its grip on news and information considerably, stepping up the daily censorship directives to the media as well as arrests of journalists and cyber-dissidents'. Thirty journalists and a further seventy-four netizens, including Liu Xiaobo, are in jail. According to Reporters without Borders, it makes China 'the world's biggest prison for news providers'.

Journalists who manage to avoid prison are also acutely aware of the increased interference. In the Xi era they are obliged to attend ideology courses, aimed at teaching them the

'Marxist perspective' on journalism. Their knowledge is tested through multiple-choice questions about party slogans. Only if the journalist demonstrates sufficient knowledge will his press credentials be renewed and will he be allowed to carry on doing his job. 'Unlike western countries, the most important function of news media in our country is to be the ears, eyes, throat and tongue for the Party and the people', the course text book reads.

It is a remarkable comeback for Marxist ideology, which had seemed to be on its way out for a long time. Xi is deploying it to strengthen control over the media. This control was quite substantial already by Western standards, but the current president and party leader is keen to put an end to a Western style of journalism which had been gaining ground in the country. This ambition is clear from an internal party memo leaked in 2013, 'Document No. 9', which identifies 'seven dangerous western values'. A Western style of journalism is one of them: 'Some people, under the pretext of espousing "freedom of the press", promote the West's idea of journalism and undermine our country's principle that the media should be infused with the spirit of the Party.' This was underlined with additional legislation. In 2013 a new ban was introduced on 'the dissemination of incorrect information'. The penalty is three years in jail. The authorities claim to have introduced the measure to defend the freedom of the press, which they say depends on accurate reporting. But to investigative journalists this legislation is far from beneficial, worried as they are that revelations about corruption could land them in jail after complaints from the companies or party bigwigs involved. There is no shortage of examples.

There are also new and far-reaching regulations against any form of critical reporting. In 2014, the press watchdog, the State Administration of Press, Publication, Radio, Film and Television, banned journalists from publishing 'critical reports' without 'prior approval' from their employers. Those who do 'must be handed over to judicial authorities' and will lose their press pass. Journalists are not allowed 'to set up their own websites, video sites or write internal reports with critical content'. Since the exact nature of 'critical content' is vague, it boils down to anything the authorities do not like. The predictable outcome is even more self-censorship.

Does this really enable the authorities to put an end to any form of 'critical reporting'? That is the big question, and at this point it cannot really be answered with any degree of certainty. If we take a somewhat longer-term view of developments, it becomes clear that the media landscape in China has become a great deal more diverse since the 1990s, while the quality of the journalism has also improved. At least until 2012 it was a case of two steps forwards and one step back. But since Xi Jinping took office the opposite appears to be true. The best years for Chinese press freedom may well be in the recent past.

## Big litmus test: investigative journalism

Jeremy Goldkorn, a South African journalist who has lived in Beijing since the 1990s, talks of how he became fascinated 'with all kinds of interesting attempts to practise proper journalism' at the start of the millennium. It inspired him to start his English-language blog *Danwei* in 2003: 'I wanted to show a different side to the Chinese media than the one that dominates the Western world. The West has the idea that it is all propaganda and censorship.' Investigative journalism used to be inconceivable: 'This century it got off the ground and has since become more common, even though it's under pressure at the moment. These days journalists don't just hail from schools of journalism, they've got degrees in all kinds of university disciplines. And the fact that more and more journalists have gained experience abroad is another positive development.'

In contrast to what is 'unmistakably a major step forwards' he also paints a picture of increasing censorship. Goldkorn himself encountered opposition in 2009 when, for unfathomable reasons, *Danwei* was blocked: 'I never found out why.' As an explanation for the decline he cites the authorities' increased fear that not only the old, but especially the new media could jeopardise 'the country's stability'. An incident from 2011 reveals that this fear existed before Xi came into power. When the Jasmine Revolution erupted in the Arab world all online mentions of the word 'jasmine' were censored. This included a clip in which President Hu Jintao sang an ode to jasmine blossom.

The big litmus test for Chinese press freedom will be the scope for investigative journalism in the coming years. With its corruption and environmental pollution, the country lends itself extremely well to this type of journalism. In fact it is 'a paradise for investigative journalists', according to Wang Keqin, who is seen as the Godfather of Chinese investigative journalism. In 2011 he had the nerve to write about the mafia practices in Beijing's taxi world for a financial weekly. He has had police protection on a number of occasions and lost his job. Although quite a few media outlets have disbanded their departments for investigative journalism, he remains hopeful. 'In the long term, the number of investigative journalists will increase, because society, the public and history need us', he says, still fully committed. 'But it happens in waves – we take steps forwards, and take steps back again.' One of the core problems, in his view, is the discrepancy between what the authorities and journalists expect: 'The press isn't quite what the government would like it to be. They talk about the press as a watchdog, thinking it can be deployed at moments when it's expedient for them, and that it will back off again after that. But it doesn't work that way.'

Revelations are still possible, even under Xi, as financial weekly *Caixin* proved in 2013 and 2014 with exposés about the network of 'security tsar' Zhou Yongkang. But this top politician was one of the president's political foes, so the magazine may well have been used by the leaders to settle the score with Zhou and his people. Editor-in-chief Hu Shuli is known to have excellent connections with the party leadership. Either way, many young journalists have followed in her wake to practise investigative journalism in recent years, writing about corporate corruption, which the authorities claim they want to tackle, alongside other issues such as poor working conditions.

Felix Lee, a German journalist of Chinese parentage, works for the *Berliner Tageszeitung*. He spent some time as an intern in *Caixin's* editorial offices and was impressed with what he saw. 'The first thing that struck me when I walked into the office was that it was virtually deserted. The weekly employs 150 journalists, and they were all out. Because they don't rely on the official news agencies they have to go out for themselves. They are extremely driven, mostly young journalists who want to work in a Western way, and who have a penchant for investigative journalism. They do a very good job too, for instance with their investigations into the high-speed trains accident in 2011. They revealed how, in the rush to finish this prestigious project, all kinds of safety margins were breached.'

As the darling of Western journalism experts who champion more press freedom, *Caixin* has won a number of Western incentive awards. But it too is subject to increased monitoring to see that the reporting does not overstep the mark. Another Western favourite is *Southern Weekly*, a newspaper with a circulation of 1.6 million and cherished by liberal intellectuals. Tellingly, in 2009 President Obama snubbed state broadcaster CCTV by opting for an interview with this paper.

But two slightly more independent media outlets do not make a spring. Complicating matters further for the written press is the financial position of newspapers and magazines. Until the 1990s they received subsidies, putting the government rather than the readers in charge. In those days, a journalist was a civil servant above all else. When this source of funding fell away, the readers came into the picture. It was a positive development, reckons investigative journalist Wang Keqin: 'In order to make a profit the media now have to come up with interesting stories that tell the truth. Nobody is prepared to pay money for phony stories', he says, alluding to the party paper of choice, the *People's Daily*, which has seen its circulation plummet.

But the rise of the internet and smartphones is a major threat to Chinese newspapers and magazines, according to journalist Michael Anti. 'Nobody is buying papers any more. Everybody reads free online news sites on their mobile. Since late 2013 newspapers have been dying. Only the financial press is doing reasonably well. I fear the press will be dead in China before we've gained press freedom.'

I hope that Anti is a bit too pessimistic and that newspapers and investigative journalists will continue to exist in China. But given the current wave of repression it is likely to be a very small group, like the political dissidents.

All in all, the picture is not exactly rosy for the written press. The internet is threatening the revenue models of old media such as newspapers and magazines, as it does in the Western world. But in China the situation is compounded by the fact that the party leaders see the spread of the internet as a threat, as it has the potential to destabilise the political system. The social ramifications are certainly immense. As we shall see, both the authorities and the traditional media are still in the process of figuring out their response to the internet.

# Chapter 8

# The Internet

*More Openness, More Censorship*

'It's a huge paradox: the government is monitoring the internet more closely, while at the same time internet users feel they can express themselves more freely online. It's an extremely explosive mixture.' Kaiser Kuo, a man in his forties sporting the look of a sixties rocker, whips his long black hair out of his face. In the 1980s he was the guitarist in a heavy-metal band on the American west coast. These days he is the director of international communications at Baidu, China's version of Google. The search engine fulfils a dual role that is hard to fathom for Westerners: it is a cornerstone of the government's censorship machine, but, as Kuo puts it, it also contributes to 'broadening the Chinese people's information horizon'. He plays his own part in this through Sinica, a fascinating podcast in which he reviews current affairs with foreign correspondents and other Westerners in Beijing.

Like Kuo, the gigantic glass head office of Baidu exudes an alternative atmosphere. In the lobby I wait underneath an enormous electronic board featuring a map with the provinces lit up in different colours. Displayed in real time next to the map is the top ten of popular search terms and the day's trending topics. It conveys the message that this is a company that keeps its finger on the pulse of society. In the corridor giant white eggs are lined up side by side, with hundreds of small blue lights on the outside. These, it emerges, are 'nap pods' for employees. Additionally, there are yoga rooms, basketball pitches, table tennis rooms, fitness studios and large amphitheatres for lectures. Plus more than forty gigantic open spaces where employees can 'gather together'. The art of imitation, which the Chinese master so well, has been deployed here to copy a hip high-tech company in Silicon Valley, where Baidu founder Robin Li worked in the 1990s.

But it is also a high-tech company 'with Chinese characteristics'. Critics accuse Baidu of being too keen when it comes to censorship. In interviews Li, a man in his forties, is deferential towards the government. How best to develop the internet market? Through 'socialism with Chinese characteristics', he responds, echoing the party leadership's favourite phrase. He is not above singing revolutionary songs at CCP meetings and often lets the ruling elite cajole him into coming along to the party's historical sites.

He once described censorship to an auditorium full of American entrepreneurs as something 'frustrating' with which he had to learn to live. When he founded his company in 2000, the internet censorship machine had already been in operation for some years. 'My first reaction was: let's move to Hong Kong. But I realised that wouldn't work. If I were to move to Hong Kong, they'd call me some type of anti-government company, and my life would be ruined', he reflected in 2010. Li Yanhong, as he is officially known, decided to stay put. Thirteen years later he is near the top of the Chinese rich list with a fortune of over twelve billion dollars. His company is deriving maximum benefit from the incredible growth of the internet: from 22 million users in 2000 to 649 million by the end of 2014. Of those, some 500 million use mobile internet, which indicates just how sophisticated the market is.

Baidu is by far the biggest search engine, especially after number two, Google, got fed up with being hacked all the time and moved to Hong Kong in 2010. These days around 70 per cent of all searches are done via Baidu. It puts the company in a powerful position, while also making it vulnerable. The government could choose to invoke competition law to make things hard for Li, because of the company's disproportionate market share. It makes compliance with censorship the only option, even if it flies in the face of the company's mission. 'As a consumer-oriented company we want to give our customers the best possible search experience. And not an inferior one, as is the case right now', Kuo readily admits.

Censorship has another disadvantage for Baidu: it is expensive. Kuo says he cannot indicate exactly how many people are working on it. 'But it is very time-intensive, especially for our top-level managers. They're accountable to the regulator at all times.' It is only increasing in scale: 'With hindsight, I think you can say that the internet was most free in 2007. In 2008 there was the Tibet issue and the Olympic Games, which made the authorities pretty nervous. Since then it has only increased.' He adds jokingly: 'The Chinese may not be very good at raising global awareness of their brands, but with the Great Firewall they've done an excellent job.' The Great Firewall is the name the authorities gave to the project, initiated in 1998, to block foreign websites.

But as an American Chinese he can see another side too. 'In the West the Firewall creates the impression of an Iron Curtain, behind which everything is grey and people are always waiting in line. But that picture blinds people to the reality, which is that the internet here is full of dynamism and vitality.' The terrific growth figures corroborate this, but the former political scientist Kuo is more interested in the increased social significance. Excitement takes hold of him when he claims that the internet has given the country a public sphere for the first time in its history. 'China never had one before! Until the internet arrived!' We under-estimate its impact at our peril: 'The top politicians are now constantly monitoring public opinion on things. They do so via blogs and Weibo, the Chinese Twitter.'

## No longer under the carpet

The battle between authorities desperate to control and citizens wanting more freedom, whether for gaming or protesting, can be illustrated by the spectacular tale of Sina Weibo. In the absence of independent media this Twitter variant became a runaway success: launched in 2009, some five years later Weibo has around 600 million users. Of those, 70 million are active. Celebrity bloggers cater to a public of tens of millions, something newspapers and magazines can only dream of. The impact of the discussion platform took both the authorities and official media by surprise.

The events surrounding a high-speed train accident in 2011 illustrate this. On 23 July of that year, on a blustery Saturday evening, lightning struck a high-speed train near Wenzhou and brought it to a halt. Soon afterwards, a later train crashed full speed into its predecessor, resulting in forty fatalities and hundreds of injured people. While the numbers may have been relatively modest by Chinese standards, the accident was shocking in the light of the many triumphant stories about the high-speed rail network that had been dished out to the population since 2007. The speedy construction of 10,000 kilometres of track between 2007 and 2020 would push the country to the world's economic forefront. The accident demonstrated the downside of this haste.

The victims came from the well-to-do middle class that can afford expensive train tickets. A witness explained that passengers began tweeting, phoning and uploading photos right away. It meant that efforts to sweep the accident under the carpet were doomed to fail. This was a common practice in pre-internet times, and although attempts were made in this case, they were unsuccessful. Within no time at all, an emotional debate got underway on internet forums. The fury was all the greater because it was not the first incident. In previous weeks high-speed trains on the prestigious link between Shanghai and Beijing had been brought to a halt by lightning on several occasions, albeit without tragic consequences. Bureaucracy was to blame for things going wrong near Wenzhou: the two trains fell under the remit of different government agencies, it emerged afterwards.

This was not known on the day of the accident, but the disgruntled bloggers did remember that a few months previously the transport minister had been sacked on corruption charges. He had pocketed some 80 million euros in exchange for awarding tenders for the construction of high-speed lines. A selection from the debate: 'How is it possible that there hasn't been a single fatality in France, where they've had TGVs since 1981? And in Japan just one, because someone got caught between the closing doors?' one person asked. 'The minister will have to resign immediately. Don't blame the lightning. The only one to blame is you!' another exclaimed. 'What a large country needs is true strength, not just a pretty façade. Are we toying with lives here? My great mother country, what's wrong with you?'

The authorities made an unsuccessful stab at censorship. The Central Propaganda Department issued instructions to all the media: 'All media outlets are to promptly report information released from the Ministry of Railways. No journalists should conduct independent interviews. Do not link reports with articles regarding the development of high-speed trains. [...] Do not investigate the causes of the accident. Do not reflect or comment.'

But even the state media could not avoid exploring the background to the accident. The debate had been so vociferous on Weibo that the regular media had no choice but to follow suit. The Ministry of Railways was attacked in editorials and even on television. It came under particular fire for the order to destroy and bury the train carriages within twenty-four hours of the accident – a desperate attempt to hush up the affair. According to the authorities, who fired a few rail managers and in a report pinned most of the blame on the already resigned corrupt minister, burial was necessary to prevent 'the theft of technology'. The explanation was met with another wave of scepticism on Weibo. To the embarrassment of the authorities, a two-year-old girl was found after the search had already been called off. 'A miracle' is how a ministry spokesperson described it. He bore the full brunt of the people's anger on internet forums.

On state broadcaster CCTV a well-known anchorman, Qiu Qiming, launched into an exceptional tirade: 'If nobody can be safe, do we still want this speed? Can we drink a glass of milk that's safe? Can we stay in an apartment that will not fall apart? Can the roads we travel on in our cities not collapse? Can we travel in safe trains? And if and when a major accident does happen, can we not be in a hurry to bury the trains?'

## A separate Chinese internet

The internet as a trailblazer for more freedom of information and establishing the truth; as a crowbar for the traditional media, including state television, which then jump into the newly created hole – it is an image of the Chinese internet that people outside China like to cherish. US presidents are inclined to do so. Back in the early 1990s George H. W. Bush once dreamed aloud: 'Imagine if the Internet took hold in China. Imagine how freedom would spread.' His successor Bill Clinton saw the character of the authoritarian state change: 'In the new century, liberty will spread by cell phone and cable modem', he said full of optimism in 2000. Those who think they can monitor information flows on the internet are mistaken; it is like 'nailing Jell-O to the wall'. As Secretary of State, Hillary Clinton also warned that 'governments who have erected barriers to internet freedom will eventually find themselves boxed in'. They will pay moral, political and economic costs, she said in a speech in 2011. 'Countries may be able to absorb these costs for a time, but we believe they're unsustainable in the long run.'

Other optimists point to the successful uprisings of the Arab Spring, in which Twitter and Facebook were thought to have helped the demonstrators get organised. They take hope from the jitters that afflicted the Chinese authorities at the time. When young people used social media to call for a 'collective walk' near a McDonald's in Beijing, a sizeable police presence was mobilised. In the end foreign reporters outnumbered demonstrators.

It is tempting to go along with this kind of optimism about the internet, but if truth be told there is a downside as well. Unlike the US presidents, the Chinese leaders have never aspired to freedom and to linking a global population through the internet. What they do want is a knowledge economy, and while the innovative potential of the internet is seen as an essential tool to that end, it must certainly not lead to a loss of control. The ideal therefore has always been a separate Chinese internet.

To this end they enjoy the topographical benefit of the small number of cables linking China with the rest of the world – the number can be counted on the fingers of one hand. The authorities deploy a double-pronged strategy: the 'Great Firewall' and the 'Golden Shield'. The former serves to selectively admit foreign information, so that certain internet addresses, such as the *New York Times*, Facebook, Twitter and YouTube, are simply not accessible. At the same time software is used to constantly screen for certain terms on web pages which can be blocked in real time.

More significant still is the 'Golden Shield' for domestic information management. The flow of information is kept in check, down to the level of individual messages, by stacks of rules and regulations and a whole arsenal of regulators. Government agencies across the country have invested heavily in software to track and analyse online behaviour. The operators of search engines such as Baidu are constantly issued with instructions to modify search results. The strategy is effective due in part to the flexibility of the authorities, because the internet may be changing rapidly, but the regulators are adjusting surprisingly fast as well. Again, Weibo offers the best illustration.

In 2012 it looked as if the authorities were trying to harness the power of Chinese Twitter for their own political ends. The idea was that it could be used to tackle corruption at a local and provincial level. Citizens joined in eagerly. It effectively sealed the fate of 'Brother Watch'. This local party bigwig, responsible for security, had been rubber-necking with a big grin on his face at a traffic accident in his city which claimed thirty-six lives. Internet users not only took offence at his grinning, but also at his expensive watch. Soon they discovered photos online showing him wearing other, equally expensive watches. The resulting public anger led to his dismissal, removal from the CCP and eventually a prison sentence of fourteen years.

The central authorities in Beijing are more than happy to sacrifice a 'fly' like 'Brother Watch'. But there are very clear limits to the role that internet users can play: the centre of power must remain out of the firing line. Since Weibo's servers are in Beijing, this can actually be controlled. It also means that local and provincial authorities cannot choose to censor accusations and protect themselves, unlike the central authorities.

But central government was forced to intervene when online attacks by the people began to create too much unrest among the lower echelons of the party. In 2013 it introduced new regulations which put a three-year prison term on the spread of 'false information'. Such information can damage a person's reputation after only 500 retweets or 5,000 readers of a blog – levels which are extremely easy to reach in China.

This has had far-reaching, if not disastrous consequences for Weibo: it can no longer serve as a platform for challenging corruption. 'Whistleblowers used to prefer Weibo, but now they are afraid to publish their information there,' journalist Michael Anti tells me, 'because a company accused of corruption or environmental pollution can now go to the authorities and claim it's a false rumour. The person who posted the allegation will then be arrested. These new regulations have effectively given local authorities a blank cheque to arrest anyone who disagrees with them.'

A few years into the Xi era, little remains of Anti's earlier optimism about the internet. When he was in his twenties his internet generation cherished the hope that they could really boost freedom. 'We were convinced that, with the new technology, we could mean something. But the internet has since shown its other face: the face of a monster. It hasn't weakened the government, but strengthened it.'

A well-known metaphor for the relationship between citizens and their government is that of the 'cat-and-mouse game', which sees users exploring the limits of their freedom and trying to outwit the authorities. Sometimes they pull it off and provide amusing stories. There is the example of the netizens coming up with alternatives for the words 'censorship' and 'censored', both of which are censored of course. To begin with, the alternatives were 'harmonisation' and 'harmonised', alluding to the 'harmonious society' which the previous generation of leaders claimed to aspire to. Since they used it to justify censorship, internet users thought it would be funny to substitute 'harmonisation' and 'harmonised'. Meanwhile these words have come to be so strongly associated with censorship that they in turn are censored. Users then switched to 'river crab' and 'river crabbed', because in Mandarin they sound like 'harmony' and 'harmonised' respectively. Now that river crab is no longer safe, 'aquatic product' is gaining popularity. And so it continues.

## The flexibility of the censor

But all throughout this virtual sparring match, with the internet user nimbly avoiding the harsh blows of the censor, the latter keeps learning. Allusions to 4 June, the day of the bloody suppression of the student uprising in 1989, had always been out of the question, but the same now applies to popular successors such as May 35th, April 65th and March 96th. However much sympathy we may have for the mouse, it must be said that the cat is getting better and better at the game. The cat and mice are in a cage that has been designed with the feline in mind.

Jason Q. Ng, a research fellow at the University of Toronto and author of the book *Blocked on Weibo*, remains optimistic. Writing on the ChinaFile blog, he notes: 'One should not underestimate the ability of Chinese Internet users to dig up information authorities are trying to hide.' But he is realistic enough to add: 'One must also acknowledge that China's censors often still have the will and the tools to manage online information effectively to suit the government's needs.'

The next instalment of the Weibo story makes this all too clear. Once the new regulations on 'false information' had effectively undermined Weibo as a discussion platform, many internet users switched to WeChat, a service offered by Tencent and similar to WhatsApp. But whereas tweets on Weibo have the potential to go viral, the debate on WeChat is limited to groups of friends or other social contacts. WeChat became immensely popular: at 270 million, the number of active users has now far outstripped Weibo. Because of its fragmented nature – the groups never number more than 500 members – the authorities were not very concerned about it for a long time. But in the course of 2014 they changed their position. The reason: the terrorist attacks by Uyghurs, who were thought to have communicated with one another via groups on WeChat. It prompted the censors to 'clean up' this platform as well.

Just as China cannot seem to develop into a democracy, despite the rise of a middle class and to the surprise of many Western observers, the internet is not transforming into the free haven Western eyes like to see it as. It is actually showing a different, far less friendly face: that of a great weapon with which to increase control over the people. The Snowden affair brought this 'ugly face' to the forefront in 2013, showing the profound desire of the secret services in Europe and the US to keep an eye on all data traffic. This is no different in China, where these services do everything in their power to unleash the Americans' inventiveness with 'Big Data' on their own citizens. With this difference: under the pretext of combating terrorism and crime, dissident voices are tackled as well.

The Belarusian Evgeny Morozov wrote about this downside of the internet in his book *The Net Delusion*, published in 2011, well before the Snowden affair. For a number of years he worked for a non-governmental organisation propagating internet freedom in his country, but he became disillusioned by the naïve ideas about how wonderful the internet was. In his book Morozov points out that the internet actually makes intelligence work much easier for authoritarian regimes. The much-lauded Facebook, for example, exposes networks of friends to the secret services. 'This is extremely valuable information. In the past people used to be tortured for it', he points out. Censorship can be useful for the authorities, but so can candid online discussions. While these may suggest freedom, they also offer the opportunity to 'identify potential threats more quickly'.

So the authorities in China are constantly adjusting the controls, both old and new, to get the internet to work to their best advantage. They have recourse to a range of techniques with which to manipulate public opinion. On the rise again lately is 'self-criticism', a method the older generation remembers from the Cultural Revolution. Some celebrity bloggers on Weibo have been forced to engage in this. The American-Chinese internet entrepreneur Charles Xue, a billionaire who had 12 million followers on Weibo, is one of the most prominent victims. In his posts this liberal University of California graduate had often spoken out freely against wrongdoings. It made him hugely popular, but all his money and influence could not protect him. He was arrested in 2013, ostensibly for soliciting prostitutes. After a few months in prison he publicly confessed on state broadcaster CCTV. Handcuffed and dressed in a green prison uniform he said humbly about his blog: 'Once I felt like an Emperor when replying to or forwarding online posts. I got so carried away that my vanity ballooned. I overlooked social responsibility.' The confession enabled him to avoid a further prison sentence. His case prompted state news agency Xinhua to speak of a 'warning bell about the law' that had sounded for all bloggers with an audience of millions.

A more modern technique is 'spinning', aimed at letting the 'correct' opinion gain the upper hand in the public debate. To this end celebrity bloggers are approached to join in the debate about important issues with a message that squares with the party line. Since 2005 there has been an army of anonymous bloggers who are paid 'to steer conversations in the right direction'. The collective is known as the Fifty Cent Party, because its members earn half a yuan (around 6 eurocents) per politically correct submission. Allegedly there are no fewer than 300,000 bloggers who are expected to excel at what former President Hu once described as 'the art of online guidance'. The number of these bloggers is just as hard to substantiate as the exact number of censors, with estimates of the latter ranging from thirty thousand to one hundred thousand. A recent study indicated that internet company Sina Weibo employs four thousand alone. These large numbers remain necessary, because despite software a lot of censorship is apparently still done by hand.

But this is gradually becoming more sophisticated. In the past an internet user might have become annoyed when an error message popped up on his screen, but it is now possible for his computer to create the impression that he has shared his opinion with others, when in reality it can only be found on his own computer – the censorship is still at work, but remains invisible. Another refinement is the crackdown on VPN services. For a while the intellectual vanguard was able to access the *New York Times*, Twitter and Facebook via these special connections, but this is likely to become more difficult for the average Chinese user.

The authorities can still conceal important revelations from the population at large. In 2012 the whole world was able to read the exposé about Prime Minister Wen Jiabao's family fortune, which was estimated at 2.7 billion dollars. It was published on the website of the *New York Times*, and soon after on news sites all over the world. But in China the authorities blocked the story:

the US newspaper site went black, all search terms leading to the site were blocked and there was nothing on Weibo. When I was in Beijing several weeks later, many people I spoke to were unaware of the story. Nor did anyone know that for ten days in 2012 Xi Jinping was not seen in public – for as yet unknown reasons. Every now and then speculation about this would pop up on Weibo, only to be suppressed again.

Rebecca MacKinnon, widely held to be one of the greatest experts on China's internet, does not expect it to bring about a Chinese Spring any time soon. In the 1990s MacKinnon was CNN's bureau chief in Beijing; later, as a researcher, she specialised in internet freedom. Like Morozov, she cautions against inflated expectations: 'The role of Facebook in the Arab Spring has been overestimated. It was the young people who caused the revolution, not Facebook.' What particularly strikes her about China is how tight its surveillance of citizens is. 'The government promotes its own internet industry very strongly. This has resulted in large, strong companies like Baidu. They have all grown up with what the government calls "self-discipline". There is even an annual ceremony with awards for companies that best monitor their own customers.' Only lukewarm participation in the system is not an option, for any company. She wholeheartedly agrees with Kaiser Kuo's description of the internet as 'extremely lively', but does not hang any hopes on this: 'In my view the party will be able to hold out for years to come.'

# Part II

# Globalisation

*Collisions and Interconnections*

# Chapter 9

# Why Europe Is Not Being Bought Up

'China is buying up Europe.' This was the rallying cry that opened a 2011 report by the European Council for Foreign Relations, a pan-European, London-based think tank. To qualify their statement, the report's authors added that 'of course, China is not colonising Europe', but it certainly set the tone.

This somewhat hysterical picture reflects public perception. Takeovers involving a Chinese party always receive a lot of media attention, hinting at the dawn of a new era. The purchase of ailing car maker Volvo by then unknown Geely was a sensation in 2010. Three years on, the media were full of car manufacturer Dongfeng from Wuhan taking a 15 per cent stake in PSA, the group behind global French brands Peugeot and Citroën.

The focus on these kinds of spectacular transactions is perfectly understandable, but it is a huge exaggeration to speak of Europe being 'bought up'. More than anything, trade has blossomed since China joined the WTO in 2001. That year, exports to the EU amounted to only 92 billion euros. Thirteen years down the line, 'the workshop of the world' shipped 302 billion euros' worth of garlic cloves, Christmas lights, iPhones, chemicals and associated products to the EU. For many years now, the EU has been China's biggest market.

But investments are lagging. European statistics bureau Eurostat estimates that as of 2013 the Chinese were not yet in the top ten of foreign investors in the EU. At 9.2 billion euros their investment was far less than, say, the Americans who made acquisitions to the tune of 99 billion euros. Conversely, European businesses invested twice as much in China.

Still, the official figures must be taken with a pinch of salt. Chinese investors are known to channel 80 per cent of their foreign spending via offshore centres to conceal the origins of funds. A Chinese investor buying a company in Europe via the Cayman Islands will not be included in his country's investment figures. As a result, an unknown number of investments remain 'below the radar'. Either way, the experts agree that the investments are nowhere near the level that befits China's status of second-largest economy in the world. 'Twice peanuts' is how a top official in Berlin, responsible for German–Chinese relations, succinctly described the Chinese investment level to me.

This modest scale may come as a surprise, since Chinese multinationals have excellent motives for moving in on the EU and buying high-quality technology and globally renowned brands. It would help them compete globally and also bring them benefits on their domestic market. Besides, since 2008 the crisis has lowered the prices of European companies, while the Chinese currency has appreciated in value. And last but not least, if China were to suffer an economic lapse, Western investments would offer the prospect of an escape route. From a European perspective, the advantages are simple: Chinese investments tend to deliver jobs and growth.

Given such a compelling 'win–win' situation, the intriguing question is why investment levels have remained relatively low to date. Could the Chinese enterprises themselves be to blame? The aforementioned German top official suggested they might be. Referring to his talks with German entrepreneurs, he was quite disparaging: 'There are plenty of opportunities here in Germany for anyone with a good nose for a deal. Quite a few family-owned businesses haven't made arrangements for their succession. Yet the Chinese don't take advantage of it. This may have to do with the large role the state plays in their enterprises. It might make them hesitant in Germany, where the situation is completely different. In that respect, the Chinese are quite different from the Indians. Given the choice, a German company prefers to be taken over by an Indian rather than a Chinese counterpart.'

Many of the anecdotes allude to an inability to adapt to European standards, or simple incompetence. There is the example of the Chinese bicycle maker who had the idea of manufacturing bikes in the Netherlands for the Dutch. It launched into production without any kind of market research. The bikes turned out to be too small. Subsequently, Phoenix Bicycles, the 'world's biggest bicycle factory', withdrew altogether.

## Duck on the bone

Equally entertaining was the German adventure of property billionaire Ren Hongbin. In 2005 he planned to build a Chinatown amusement park in the eastern German town of Oranienburg, complete with a Forbidden City, Chinese Wall, pagodas and homes for several thousand Chinese. Initially both parties were enthusiastic, as Oranienburg was keen to benefit from globalisation. But all this vanished into thin air when Ren ignored the repeated requests of local government officials. An environmental impact assessment? Ren thought he would be fine as long as he maintained good relations with the mayor. The occasional visit to an excellent Chinese restaurant 'with duck on the bone' and everything was bound to work out just fine. But unfortunately Ren had 'completely misinterpreted a mayor's power', mayor Hans-Joachim Laesicke concluded in weekly news magazine *Der Spiegel*. The Chinese property tycoon left with his tail between his legs. Not a single brick was ever laid.

A different view of the importance of contracts can also prove fatal to Chinese investors in Europe. This happened to a construction company which had been chosen to build an important motorway in Poland – an essential route for the European Football Championship in 2012. Polish competitors lost out when the China Overseas Engineering Group promised to build the road at half the cost, within no time at all. But a year before the envisaged completion, the Chinese threw in the towel. They had wanted to renegotiate the price after agreeing the deal – and while this is not unusual in China, the Poles were not having any of it. Likewise, the Chinese had underestimated Polish legislation which stipulates that subcontractors should be paid properly. The Vice Minister of Foreign Affairs, Fu Ying, described the crux of the problem in diplomatic, but accurate terms when she said: 'The European market is very demanding and highly regulated and poses a big challenge to many Chinese companies who lack the appropriate experience.'

Just how difficult it is for them to conclude successful mergers and acquisitions is shown by the 90 per cent failure rate on a total of 300 foreign takeovers in the period 2008 to 2010, according to a study by international law firm Jones Day. Following the transaction the Chinese companies lost on average 40 to 50 per cent of their value.

Of course some Chinese companies do achieve success in Europe. The best example is telecoms company Huawei, which is among the world's leaders in its sector. Of its 150,000 employees nearly 8,000 work in Europe, a number the company expects to double in the next few years. It makes Huawei the biggest Chinese employer in Europe. To be successful in Europe it relies primarily on local workers – two-thirds of its workforce in Europe is of non-Chinese origin.

Yet this strategy has its drawbacks too. The company's top management and corporate culture are completely Chinese, producing the curious figure of the Western manager who is not invited to contribute ideas to the company's direction. 'The policy is outlined by those above you and you are not meant to add any critical notes. You're simply told what to do. It takes a bit of getting used to', a European manager at Huawei told me. A Chinese-born colleague confirmed this. Both used to work for a US multinational. The American top-down culture was pretty strong as well, 'but nothing compared to that of the Chinese'.

Can most failures and problems be ascribed to a lack of understanding on the part of Chinese investors? It certainly plays a role, but one would be guilty of a misplaced sense of superiority if that was the sole conclusion. Although harder for us to see, the West plays its part too.

## Fortress Europe

Luckily there is Dato Wong Sin Just, a Malaysian in his forties who works in Hong Kong as an international investment banker. He has Chinese roots and argues Europe is falling short when it comes to openness. His job is to draw European investors to China and Chinese investors to Europe. The latter is proving to be a great deal harder than the former. He blames it on European governments. His clients come up against what he describes as 'Fortress Europe'. Multinationals such as the French LVMH (Louis Vuitton, Moët champagne and other such luxuries) and Kering (owner of luxury brands such as Gucci and Brioni) make his clients' mouths water: 'Interest in French and Italian producers of luxury products is particularly high among Chinese investors.' However, his clients struggle to enter this high-end market. 'It is impossible to acquire those big French brands, because they enjoy government protection. It would be in Europe's own interest to adopt a more flexible approach. Chinese investors think that Europe is too protective of its markets.'

This form of protectionism is as intangible as it is real. There is no legislation barring takeovers of these prestigious companies. But in practice the French government, to name but an example, has certainly used its power to beat off foreign advances. Non-Chinese companies have had similar experiences. One of them, American PepsiCo, showed an interest in Danone (known for its yoghurt and Evian) in 2005. Energised by a possible US bid worth billions, the share price rose by 20 per cent. But then several French ministers rose up in arms 'to defend France's interests' and to protect this 'flower of our industry'. 'France turns yoghurt into a national security issue' was the scornful response from London's City. To the disappointment of investment bankers, the American bid sank without a trace.

This invisible wall, erected by politicians in conjunction with public opinion, is certainly not unique to the French. How would the German government react in the event of a Chinese bid for Mercedes or BMW, or the Dutch authorities to a takeover of Philips? And how would the British government deal with a bid for British Airways?

According to Friedolin Strack, Asia specialist at the Bundesverband der Deutschen Industrie (BDI), the powerful federation of German industries, such a takeover bid would provide a 'proper litmus test' for Chinese investments in Europe. 'I think we should allow them. We cannot let our actions be determined by fear of an end to our comfortable position. But to be honest, I doubt if public opinion in Europe is ready for so much openness.'

Europe has a history of resistance to Asian involvement. In the mid-eighties, a number of European countries, normally champions of free trade, slammed on the brakes when they saw the rapid rise of Japan. Both the US and Europe were seriously concerned that Japan would come to eclipse the West – a fear now aroused by China. Thanks to the combination of cheap exports and a protected domestic market Japan appeared to be unstoppable. At its height, in 1988, Japanese companies invested 30 billion dollars in Europe in a single year. But while their Western competitors may have been scathing about the quality of the Japanese cars, European consumers were only too happy to drive a Toyota. This success prompted a protectionist reflex in Europe. The Japanese car manufacturers were forced to accept 'voluntary export restrictions', both in Europe and the US. The Japanese government agreed in order to avoid a complete ban.

It is a sign of progress that China does not face this kind of open aversion. 'We will not repeat the historic mistake of protectionism of previous eras', the leaders of the G20, the world's twenty major economies, solemnly vowed in 2009, when the full scale of the credit crisis emerged. Memories of the thirties, when US customs barriers were erected to stop European goods, were still sufficiently fresh. It ended in disaster with global trade slumping by two-thirds and the world economy sliding into a depression.

Luckily we have been spared such short-sightedness this time. The official discourse presents China primarily as a partner able to help conquer the economic downturn. So European leaders roll out the red carpet, as President Xi Jinping experienced during his first tour of Europe in 2014. The governments of Germany, France, the Netherlands and Belgium pulled out all the stops to make a favourable impression.

But sometimes those very same European politicians change their tune when Chinese investments take concrete shape. A Chinese–Dutch takeover made headlines across Europe in 2010, when the unknown company Xinmao from Tianjin tried to buy Dutch cable maker Draka for 1.1 billion euros. Italian rival Prysmian was a candidate too, even though at 840 million the Milanese were offering much less. An Italian European commissioner, Antonio Tajani, turned against the Chinese buyer by suggesting that Xinmao was only after the Dutch technology. Europe ought to remain in possession of its high-tech companies, he argued.

But it was not just this opposition that got Xinmao into trouble; its own lack of expertise was to blame too. Its bid failed to specify the role of the Chinese state. The company ultimately withdrew, allowing the 'European solution' to win. This loss of face must have been a real blow to the Chinese.

## Sovereign wealth funds

Suspicion was also evident in France when the national pride of the car industry was at stake. In 2013 President Hollande had travelled to China for the first time in his life to extend a warm welcome to all Chinese investors. France was going to be the most attractive country in the world for them, he suggested. But when, a year later, the Chinese manufacturer Dongfeng showed an interest in the technology of Peugeot and Citroën and was prepared to pay 800 million euros for a minority stake in the ailing car manufacturer, the French government sprang into action. It also paid 800 million euros for an equally large stake in parent company PSA. No more redundancies, the then minister Arnaud Montebourg promptly cautioned his Chinese counterpart, even though PSA had racked up losses exceeding 7 billion in previous years. And so the red carpet which had been rolled out by Hollande was fitted with crush barriers.

Such barriers have been erected all over Europe, blocking for instance possible takeovers in the defence industry in Germany and France in the name of national security. The same applies to the energy sector in Italy and Spain, while the French also have this restriction in place for their pharmaceutical sector. Chinese investors had better not venture into banking either, especially not if it involves 'system banks', as national regulatory bodies are quick to intervene.

A special position is reserved for state-owned 'sovereign wealth funds'. China is using two of them to invest its surplus of foreign currency. The China Investment Corporation (CIC) is making a particular impact. With assets of over 652 billion euros it is the bigger and noisier brother of the Safe Investment Company, which owns roughly 568 billion euros. At the height of the credit crisis there was a fierce debate in Europe about whether these foreign state-owned funds could be the saviour of Europe's troubled banking sector or whether this would amount to selling one's soul to the devil. Fear and scepticism were rife, since both Chinese funds fell directly under the country's Ministry of Finance. As such, they were suspected of serving geopolitical purposes. Their lack of transparency was similarly denounced.

The German government decided to err on the side of caution and strengthened its legislation on foreign investment. Since 2009 the Außenwirtschaftsgesetz has granted the government wide-ranging powers. Should a Chinese investor take a stake of over 25 per cent in a German bank, energy company or telecoms company, the purchase can be blocked on the grounds of 'public policy or public security'.

To date, this law has never been invoked. The debate about the sovereign wealth funds has also calmed down. CIC is now an accepted shareholder in a large number of European multi-nationals. In the UK it owns stakes in household names such as Barclays Bank, Thames Water and Heathrow. It has not sparked any major controversy in this country of pragmatists.

The participation of two Chinese energy companies in the construction of a new nuclear power station in Somerset similarly failed to raise eyebrows. The billion-pound project, led by French multinational GDF, prompted some debate about nuclear energy and the size of energy bills, but not about the Chinese role in the energy supply. More than anything, the investments are gratefully received.

But while they are certainly to be welcomed, some scrutiny would not be amiss. The 'national security' argument may have been abused in the past to justify protectionism, but it can also be valid. Take the successful telecoms company Huawei. In the US the 'Committee on Foreign Investment' has repeatedly blocked invest-ments by Huawei because it would allow the company to penetrate too deeply into US communication networks. This resistance to

Huawei is shared by Australia and Canada. They have a dark suspicion that its founder, former officer Ren Zhengfei, maintains close links with the army. In the aftermath of the Snowden affair it emerged that the US National Security Agency (NSA) had been nosing around on the multinational's computers in search of evidence – much to the anger of the Chinese, of course.

In contrast, the British government has adopted an extremely friendly tone towards Huawei. 'There are some Western governments that have blocked Huawei from making investments. Not Britain. Quite the opposite', said Chancellor of the Exchequer George Osborne almost triumphantly when he visited the company's headquarters in Shenzhen in 2014. The chancellor brushed aside warnings that British internet users might be monitored via the infrastructure provided to British Telecom. Osborne is not alone in this, as Huawei is welcomed with open arms across Europe.

A European investment review panel might not be such a bad solution. Virtually all major power blocs are doing it, especially the US and China. But because reviews are in the hands of national regulatory authorities in Europe, Chinese parties are in a position to play European countries off against one another. The initiative to establish a European 'Committee on Foreign Investment' after the US example has been mothballed. It was the brainchild of French European commissioner Michel Barnier and his Italian counterpart Tajani in response to the Draka affair in 2010. They were annoyed by the 'naïveté' of EU countries in this area. The fact that their plan is now gathering dust can be blamed on a well-known European ailment: dissension among member states. Europe would benefit from a joint approach to China, but cannot seem to agree on one.

This became painfully clear in the course of 2013, when the dumping of Chinese solar panels led to a conflict between Beijing and Brussels. Partly because of a complaint by a German manufacturer, the European Commission had a strong case against the Chinese solar companies. But in this case Germany actually sided with China to be able to conclude other deals. The short-term interests of individual countries trumped in this case Europe's longer-term interest in a joint approach. Britain's Prime Minister David Cameron made the same mistake when, on a visit to Beijing, he promised a trade agreement and in doing so undercut Brussels.

The next test case for Europe's ability to form a united front will be the negotiations over an investment treaty. Both sides agree that investment could and should increase. Since the turn of the century, forecasts have been far too generous. It probably comes as no surprise that they originate from parties with commercial interests in transactions, such as the Rhodium Group. These business consultants believe that by 2020 the Chinese will be investing a total of 250 to 500 billion dollars in Europe. Even in the worst-case scenario Europe can still look forward to an annual 20 to 30 billion dollars, according to Rhodium, significantly more than the 9.2 billion euros it saw in 2013.

Perhaps the optimism is well-founded this time; there is certainly an upward trend. Yet I am inclined to share the concerns outlined to me by the late editor-in-chief of *Le Monde*, Érik Izraelewicz, in 2011, a year before his untimely death at the age of fifty-eight. He published the bestseller *Quand la Chine change le monde* (When China Changes the World) in 2005 and *L'Arrogance chinoise* (The Chinese Arrogance) in 2011. Belying the impression of the arrogant French editor-in-chief, the amiable man was anything but when we spoke in Paris.

He placed big question marks over the positive words of Chinese dignitaries about the importance of European investments. Behind the scenes the story could well be quite different, he believed. To the Chinese leaders the eurozone crisis showed that 'the Old Continent is becoming truly old'. This might 'speed up Chinese thinking' about Europe, he feared. 'They will ask themselves: do we need them at all? They will argue: of course the Europeans form a market for us and possess technology, but they have also ground to a halt, their populations are ageing and they have become less innovative.'

In other words: the risk of Europe being bought up, as the media keeps suggesting, could be less acute than the opposite. Chinese investors could opt for parts of the world that do have the potential for huge growth, such as Latin America and Africa. Instead of worrying that 'the Chinese are coming', Izraelewicz warned, 'we ought to be more worried that the Chinese are not coming.'

# Chapter 10

# Western Investors Coming Up Against Chinese Arrogance

## Or: The Awkward Dance with an Elephant

An interview with a Chinese top banker is far from easy to arrange, but eventually I manage to secure one at the Bank of Beijing, a medium-sized bank with a balance sheet of 32 billion euros. I am asked to submit a detailed list of questions before I receive a firm commitment a couple of weeks later. But when exactly it will go ahead remains uncertain for a long time. Only days before the interview the date is changed again, and the time is only finalised on the morning itself.

The government's careful planning stands in sharp contrast to this apparent improvisation in the banking world. The reason says a lot about the balance of power in China: top-level bankers are at the beck and call of their superiors, especially politicians and top civil servants, at all times. 'From day one I've learnt to work without a diary', explains a Dutch banker who represents the bank ING on the board of directors of Bank of Beijing. It is thanks to his mediation that I have made it through to the banking top, a rare feat for a Western journalist.

On the day itself, I am given a royal reception in a gleaming bank building in the heart of Beijing. After being greeted by two delegations, I am ushered into a gigantic ballroom, where about a dozen large chairs are arranged in a U-shape. A few minutes later the bank's president Yan Xiaoyan walks in, a lively, petite woman in her late fifties, soberly dressed, and sporting a flower corsage on her blouse. In 2010 she was hailed as 'Businesswoman of the

Year'. The accolade captured my imagination, until I discovered that she shared the title with two thousand other businesswomen. A Chinese-style glorification.

Since Western banks are not allowed to have a majority stake, ING owns no more than 20 per cent of the Bank of Beijing. China may have opened up to foreign investment, but there are still plenty of restrictions in place. In all kinds of sectors that are deemed to be strategic, the participation of foreign companies is kept to a minimum or even prohibited. And while the door to the banking sector is ajar, the government is keeping a watchful eye on foreign influence. It is a form of protectionism that does not sit well with the objectives of the World Trade Organisation, which include free trade and free movement of capital.

An interview with a top banker is a perfect opportunity to get the Chinese perspective on these principles, especially since Yan Xiaoyan is also a member of the National People's Congress: she combines her banking role with a high party function, which is inconceivable in the West. When I ask her whether she thinks it is right that foreign banks are not allowed to acquire a majority stake, she expresses her full support for the regulations. 'You must understand that compared to the West our banking sector is still in its infancy. If you were to open it up tomorrow, it would cause a huge shock.' But now that the largest Chinese banks have entered the global top ten, surely they can handle it, I suggest. Mrs Yan disagrees. 'Banks like Citibank or HSBC are much more advanced than our biggest banks in the areas of technology and management. If these Western banks were allowed to do takeovers, our banks could not compete. Our position in the global top ten is also linked to the financial crisis. It is not something we should be proud of. It is not that our banks are that good. They have only a very short history.'

She believes the credit crisis, in which the Western banking sector came close to the abyss, corroborates her theory. 'Luckily, as Chinese banks, we are under less pressure to come up with new financial products than Western banks. Thanks to our protection policy our market remains a protected market, so the pressure to innovate is less acute. And this is a good thing. Just look at what happened on the American subprime market. In my view, that is the result of innovation gone too far.'

## Openness

But there is another side to her story. It is all rather easy for the 'Big Four' – the four major banks that control the lion's share of the Chinese market. They get away with offering the people low interest rates on their savings and lending the money on at much higher rates. They have a big preference for state-owned enterprises, since these credits are underwritten by the state. They also know they are too big to fail. The joint balance sheet of the Big Four is about as big as the national economies of Germany, France and the UK combined. If necessary, the government will bail them out.

Making money like water without any risks, as these banks were doing for years, was no problem as long as economic growth exceeded 10 per cent. But criticism has been mounting since growth has been less abundant. In his final year as prime minister, Wen Jiabao had some harsh words to say. 'With regards to financing costs, let me honestly say that our banks are making a profit too easily. Why is this so? It's because a few big banks are in a monopoly position', he reproached a group of bankers on state television in 2012, before arguing in favour of breaking up their monopoly.

His successors have made a cautious start. The growing unpopularity of the banking sector – a remarkable parallel with the West – has not escaped their attention. Chinese people have been complaining vociferously on social media about the low return on their savings. Entrepreneurs in small and medium-sized enterprises often do not even try to obtain credit from the big banks. Instead they turn to the shadow banking system, which has sprung up alongside the official banking sector and has assumed colossal proportions. It is estimated that since 2009 half of all loans have been issued via this 'grey' circuit. It has presented the authorities with a huge monitoring problem, especially in the midst of the current property bubble. To get the financial sector back on track, the regular banks ought to fulfil their core business of lending better. One way of achieving this is to expose them to more competition. But it is telling that the government is not looking towards foreign banks, which would love to be given more room. Instead the new competitors come from the domestic internet sector. Major players such as Alibaba and Tencent offer their customers financial products that promise a substantially better yield than banks do. Hugely popular, they are forcing the 'Big Four' to innovate.

The fact that the state prefers domestic competition over and above foreigners says a lot about China's current phase of development. For many years the embrace of foreign investors was the key to economic success. The growth of their number was breathtaking: from 100 companies in 1979 to more than 440,000 in 2013. Initially, Western companies were only admitted when they entered into a joint venture with a Chinese company. Even back then the government saw this as a major route to obtaining Western know-how. The American and European investors could live with this, because the advantages were huge: the Chinese employees worked incredibly hard and were dirt cheap. Besides, they benefited from a favourable fiscal and legal regime in the 'special economic zones' established for them. From 2000 they could also set up their own companies, that is to say without the mandatory Chinese partner.

The foreign capital made a huge contribution to China's export model. Despite obvious downsides, it has been one of the cruxes of the country's success, especially since its accession to the WTO in 2001. While export in 2002 amounted to 365 billion dollars, by 2014 it had risen to 2,340 billion. It earned China the honorary title of 'export world champion', which it snatched from Germany in 2009. Although national pride is understandable, this can hardly be called a purely Chinese achievement, as foreign companies are responsible for the bulk of these exports. Of course Chinese businesses export goods too, but they serve primarily as suppliers to Western multinationals. To give an impression of the scale of this phenomenon: US supermarket giant Wal-Mart sources its items from 20,000 different Chinese suppliers, and ships nearly 300 billion dollars' worth of goods annually to the rest of the world, most notably the US.

Now that the economic wheels are turning, a new phase has begun with policy makers wondering just how much their country still needs this foreign capital. The official position remains that all investors are welcome. But in practice foreign investors have to meet more stringent conditions and feel discriminated against while the government is showing a preference for national solutions.

China is feeling stronger, especially after surviving the credit crisis with flying colours. The authorities can certainly be proud of their response to the collapse of Lehman Brothers in 2008, which started the credit crisis. They realised that their export model was at risk: the cranes in the ports ground to a halt, with containers piling up on the quay, thousands of factories were closing and hundreds of thousands lost their jobs when Western demand suddenly fell away. Within two months, the government had launched a sizeable stimulation package, initially worth 580 billion dollars and spread over two years.

Banks were ordered to be generous with credit for the building of homes and offices and the construction of roads. The corporate sector was given some breathing space through fiscal cuts. The American president of the World Bank, Robert Zoellick, said he was 'delighted' with this Chinese sense of responsibility for the global economy. The stimulation programme worked, although some critics claim that the backlash has yet to happen. A lot of bad loans were made at the time, which artificially boosted property prices. Be that as it may, growth in 2009 came to about the 'usual' 9 per cent. The success certainly did not dent Chinese self-confidence and helped change attitudes towards Western companies. The latter complain about discrimination, claiming that Chinese businesses are given preferential treatment on their domestic market. Few have the courage to say this out loud.

## Chinese arrogance

The CEO of American General Electric (GE), Jeffrey Immelt, was a notable exception in the summer of 2010. Fed up with diplomatic rhetoric, he was openly sceptical about China's intentions at a dinner in Rome, in the company of several dozen leading entrepreneurs: 'I'm really worried about China. I'm not sure that in the end they want any of us to win, or any of us to be successful.' He argued that increasing protectionism meant that doing business in China is now harder than it has ever been in the past twenty-five years. He offered to work with resource-rich countries in Africa and Latin America with the words: 'I'm sure they don't all want to be colonised by China.'

This kind of harsh criticism is rarely, if ever, so openly expressed by a Western businessman. In these circles self-censorship is considerable for fear of damaging commercial interests. But Immelt's words clearly echoed the sentiments of many. It goes without saying that his PR advisors vehemently denied the statement – China represented over five billion dollars of GE's turnover after all – but the word was out. After his complaint he received three hundred letters of support from fellow entrepreneurs. This was confirmed to me by the then editor-in-chief of *Le Monde*, Érik Izraelewicz, shortly after he had spoken to Immelt. 'Doing business in China is now far more difficult than it was five years ago', the Frenchman concluded in his book *L'Arrogance chinoise*. The title may sound like an accusation, but is actually meant as a warning to both Westerners and the Chinese.

Izraelewicz did not have any first-hand experience of arrogance. 'In personal contact they tend to be modest and courteous: "We're only a developing nation, we need time" is something you hear a lot.' But after interviewing Western politicians, CEOs and experts, he firmly believes that this modesty is a thing of the past: 'It struck me that almost all of them said: "Don't attribute this to me, but they're becoming really arrogant." Compared to five years ago, the climate has changed considerably.' Why? The economic success goes some way to explain it, but Izraelewicz paints a more complex picture. The arrogance also conceals insecurity and fears over the emerging limits of their growth model. 'They're extremely intelligent. They really don't need us to point out their problems. They are more aware of them than we are.' To illustrate this he quotes former prime minister Wen Jiabao, who judged the Chinese economy more harshly than Western leaders would ever dare to judge their own, describing it when in office as 'unsustainable, uncoordinated, unbalanced, and unstable'.

Western multinationals are experiencing this arrogance at first hand, with Izraelewicz painting a sobering picture of their accomplishments. Major players such as search engine Google, TV mogul Rupert Murdoch and telecoms company Vodafone even decided to leave the world's biggest market, despite concerted efforts including censorship concessions, to achieve commercial success. Murdoch even bought a villa near the Forbidden City, in the heart of Beijing, received members of the Politburo and married a Chinese woman. All to no avail. 'The arrogant men of the western corporate world have met their match in China', Izraelewicz writes, a line that makes him chuckle when I quote it back to him. 'The rise of China as a manufacturer, financier and consumer of resources is so massive it has destabilising effects on the entire western world. It is up to us to dance with this elephant in the china shop.'

Western companies are doing this awkward dance on a daily basis. Two-thirds of them believe it has been getting progressively more difficult in the past two years, according to a survey carried out by the European Chamber of Commerce in Shanghai among its members in 2014. 'Business is tough and is getting tougher' was one of the conclusions. The effects of a decline in economic growth combined with higher labour costs are palpable. Another, more structural issue further reinforces their pessimism: 'European companies still perceive themselves to be discriminated against in the Chinese marketplace.'

## Anti-corruption campaign

One of the things they have learnt is to get out of the way when the tankers of the Chinese economy, the state-owned enterprises, head in their direction. That is when they find that some law or other has been infringed, permits are not in order – in short, things are made difficult for them. The European Chamber of Commerce has calculated the price tag: in 2013 European businesses missed out on 21 billion euros due to various government barriers. It should come as no surprise then that the European firms are sceptical about the 'more market' strategy which President Xi announced in 2013. If it is implemented at all, Chinese companies are likely to be the main beneficiaries. Almost half of the European companies surveyed believe that the 'golden days' are over. The survey also reveals that a growing number of entrepreneurs are looking over the fence, elsewhere in Asia. The Chinese market is still attractive economically, but labour costs have gone up and the political wind is perceived to be unfavourable.

In 2014 Western companies faced a flurry of anti-trust cases, which affected well-known brand names such as Microsoft and Mercedes. According to the authorities this was just a matter of enforcing anti-monopoly laws, but Western companies felt targeted. 'It is because we are foreign', Jörg Wuttke, President of the European Chamber of Commerce in China, pointed out bluntly to me. 'We don't have political protection, unlike the Chinese companies.' He dismissed a comparison with the European Commission which also investigates anti-competitive behaviour. 'Brussels has transparent procedures and gives companies a chance to respond extensively. In China there is none of that, we can't learn from past cases.'

Western companies are affected in various other ways. The Snowden affair, involving espionage, had serious consequences for some major American companies. From 2014 onwards Chinese banks are no longer allowed to use IBM systems. And Microsoft suffers too, as central government agencies are prohibited from using Windows 8 as their operating system.

The anti-corruption crusade, President Xi's trademark, has also hit Western companies, especially in the realm of pharmaceutics. As the former China head of British GlaxoSmithKline (GSK), Mark Reilly is held responsible for the alleged bribery of doctors and hospitals. The prospect of a lengthy term in a Chinese prison for him caused great concern among Western managers in this branch. Many have had visits from the police and regulators. The Chinese media claim that GSK is not the only company guilty of these practices. Whether this is a case of targeted discrimination of Western companies is hard to prove, as there is indeed a lot of corruption in the health business. What is certain is that the consequences of the campaign are considerable, with top managers requesting transfers and potential newcomers suddenly no longer fancying a move to China.

A more clear-cut case of discrimination is the lucrative market of public procurement, such as the building of infrastructure and other construction projects. Thanks to the substantial state sector, this market is worth around 1,000 billion dollars annually. The authorities claim, rather laughably, that anyone can win these tenders, but that the choice for Chinese companies is 'habitual'. As a matter of fact they always win. It is quite obvious that there are no equal opportunities or indeed a level playing field, as world trade regulations stipulate.

Is there anything Europe can do about this? Since Chinese companies are allowed to compete for 80 per cent of European public procurement contracts, there is something to be said for threatening to reduce this to 0 per cent, as long as China keeps its domestic market sealed off. The former French European commissioner Michel Barnier liked the idea of such 'reciprocity', but met with opposition from the 'Big Three'. The UK warned it could result in 'tit-for-tat protectionism', France believed that individual member states should be able to decide these kinds of sanctions for themselves, while Germany feared repercussions for German companies. Friedolin Strack at BDI, the federation of German industries, believes Europe must be wary of insisting on 'reciprocity' towards China. 'A minority of German businesses are in favour of this, among them the construction companies that are barred from the Chinese market for public procurements. But the vast majority rely on free, open markets and every step towards more barriers would not be in their best interest. Instead of getting caught up in a race to see who is best at imposing reciprocity, we should see who offers the most open climate for investments.' If China restricts access to a market, Europe has no other option than to explain why this is not a good idea. Getting tough and demanding reciprocity can have a boomerang effect, Strack fears.

This rather unassertive attitude does not mean he is uncritical of China. On the contrary, Strack denounces the extreme pressure on German companies to part with 'sensitive technological know-how' in exchange for access to the Chinese market. Another thorn in his side is the way Chinese companies compete with their European counterparts in 'third markets', such as Eastern

European, African and Asian countries. Here too government support undermines competition. 'Fair competition is crucial. It determines whether China and Europe can be partners in the future, or mainly rivals.' The signs are not good. The OECD, the Western think tank, has drawn up a whole raft of regulations governing behaviour in third markets, 'but the Chinese show no interest whatsoever. They are happy with the way things are.'

All in all, the emerging picture is mixed. Despite the many barriers that Western companies complain about – and with good reason – there is still scope for success in China. Take the automotive market, for instance, which is the biggest and fastest-growing in the world. Whereas the European market has been characterised by stagnation and overproduction for years, China is the land of plenty for Western car manufacturers. German brands such as Mercedes, BMW and Audi have been unable to keep up with demand in recent years, while American Ford and Japanese Toyota are also doing excellent business. Chinese consumers associate these foreign cars with quality and safety, something the state-owned manufacturers cannot compete with at present. They were once expected to conquer the US and Europe, like the Japanese car makers did from the 1980s onwards. But in actual fact they are losing ground on their own market. With their share still below 50 per cent, they have turned to their government for protectionist measures.

But the state is sending out conflicting messages. In 2014 the government not only started the anti-trust cases, but also removed the necessary red tape in the hope it would prompt public authorities to make faster decisions on foreign investment plans. Nonetheless, Izraelewicz has no doubt that China's policy in the long run is aimed primarily at improving the position of its home-grown companies. He believes this to be 'normal'. In recent years some Western companies have become dominant in certain areas, so a 'correction' is to be expected. Likewise, when viewed from a historical perspective, he is not surprised that China is helping its own industry to conquer global markets by giving them a competitive edge over their Western rivals via subsidies, favourable loans and cheap land. 'Both we and the Japanese did the same in the early stages of our industrialisation.'

But the West cannot continue to just stand by and watch. Izraelewicz believes that the 'hands-off approach' which has become fashionable among European governments is not sustainable now that the Chinese government is giving such firm support to its own industry. A level playing field and free trade are all very good, but they date 'from a period when there was no economic power which was of an entirely different order due to its scale and political organisation'. Europe will have to protect itself through a powerful joint industrial and environmental policy. 'In my view China is the main argument for a united Europe.'

# Chapter 11

# China in Africa

*A Lesson in Modesty*

Westerners travelling to African countries can be a little taken aback by all the Chinese activity they encounter. The Chinese appear to be everywhere, from street traders and shopkeepers to the builders of ports and roads and oil-drilling multinationals. But it should be remembered that while the Chinese involvement in Africa may have risen dramatically, it used to be at an exceptionally low level, especially compared with the European presence.

The following comparison is quite sobering. Chinese trade with Africa has grown spectacularly: from 11 billion dollars in 2000 to 210 billion in 2013, a nineteen-fold increase. The US is lagging behind at 110 billion dollars, but at 437 billion dollars in 2013 the EU remains by far Africa's biggest trading partner. There is no sign of stagnation in the European–African trade flow, which has doubled since 2002. On investments it is difficult to obtain reliable statistics. Chinese statistics are particularly problematic, because investments made by small and medium-sized companies remain regularly under the radar. According to the official figures, China peaked in 2013 at 25 billion dollars. During the period 2008–10, the EU member states jointly invested an average of 20 billion dollars annually, which dropped to 11 billion in 2012. The gap with China is substantial, but with the trade figures included it would be an exaggeration to speak of Chinese supremacy or dominance in Africa.

China's unmistakable rise on the continent is eyed with suspicion in the West. Our historic role as a coloniser may be less than admirable and our development aid may be under fire because of its poor efficiency, but that does not stop us from pretending to know what is best for Africa. Both non-governmental organisations and the media are highly critical of Chinese behaviour. Accusations of 'neocolonialism' are often bandied about, thus obscuring the positive aspects of the Chinese presence, which has helped integrate Africa into the global economy more than ever before.

The list of complaints is long and usually begins with the export of Chinese working conditions. Stories abound of Chinese and African labourers who are forced to work seven days a week and more than twelve hours a day. The enterprising Chinese bosses provide jobs, but they often pay badly and fail to invest in safe working conditions. The Belgian author David van Reybrouck introduces a certain 'Jean' in his compelling book *Congo*. The experienced Congolese smelter worked in a copper mine for a Chinese entrepreneur. One morning a traffic accident caused him and twelve colleagues to arrive a few minutes late. For punishment they were locked up in a container all day. When they were released they were told they had all been fired, as there were 'plenty of willing workers'.

Both the small, independent Chinese entrepreneurs and the large state-owned enterprises tend to be worse employers than their Western counterparts, certainly from a financial perspective. The Western list of complaints also includes corruption, which is widespread in China and which is spread even further in Africa, in keeping with local traditions. It means that Western efforts to achieve 'good governance' are thwarted. Another grievance: the Chinese are largely indifferent to the environment. Ports and motorways are constructed quite indiscriminately, with little regard for their environmental impact. The quality of the work does not always meet Western standards either. But while these criticisms might be fair, they have created a rather one-sided, negative image. The experience of Africans should certainly count for more than our own judgement.

## 'Neocolonialism!'

A look at the biggest contract China has concluded with an African nation to date serves to give us a clear picture of African–Chinese–Western power relations. This 'contract of the century' was signed in 2008 between China and the Democratic Republic of the Congo. The *Financial Times* described it as 'the most ambitious of the minerals-for-infrastructure deals reached' and 'a challenge to the dominance of former European colonial powers.'

Congo, which is about the size of two-thirds of Western Europe, is a paradoxical country to say the least. Underground it is blessed with the greatest natural riches in the world, most notably copper, cobalt and diamonds; above ground are 73 million Congolese people whose per capita income is among the lowest in the world. Since the nineteenth century the country's natural resources have drawn the outside world like a magnet. For a long time, Belgium took a lead in this, but it looks like China will be at the forefront of developments this century. In exchange for the right to extract copper and cobalt for thirty years, the Chinese are building roads, airports, hospitals, social housing and universities. The initial investment was meant to be 9 billion dollars (6 billion for infrastructure, 3 billion for the mines) – a sum the Chinese would lend to the Congolese, who were to pay it back through resources. But under pressure from the IMF and Congo's Western creditors who feared they might lose out, it was reduced to 6.2 billion dollars.

'No sooner was the deal announced than the West screamed blue murder. Neocolonialism! A new scramble for Africa! Predatory behaviour dressed up as a win–win situation!' This is how van Reybrouck summarised the reactions in the Western camp. He sees an irrational fear 'of a new, complex world in which China has acquired the status of a superpower'. He wisely remains non-committal about the financial side of the deal: 'Whether or not it is a fair price depends on the global price of copper. Given the huge fluctuations […] this could be either 14 billion or as much as 80 billion.'

Van Reybrouck shows respect for China's strategy in Africa: 'China is not after the short-term plunder of the Katangese soil, for the simple reason that China's economic policy reflects steadiness and planning. Beijing has no interest in sucking Africa dry and destabilising it. On the contrary […] China has embarked on a long-term, structural presence in Africa.' This assessment puts him on the same line as *The Economist*, which concluded in 2011 that China is not 'a colonialist interested only in looting the land'.

In his book van Reybrouck charts his native country's rather unedifying role in 'the Congo'. From 1885, the Belgian King Leopold II's hunger for Congolese rubber led to such abominable working conditions and such harsh suppression of protest that huge numbers of Congolese people lost their lives. The regime was guilty of a 'perfidious, rapacious policy of exploitation, sacrifices at the altar of a morbid pursuit of profit', he concludes.

This history must not go unmentioned. After all, the experience of colonisation continues to shape the Congolese perspective on the world to this day. The West's prolonged support to the country's self-enriching and utterly corrupt dictator Mobutu has not been forgotten either. He was in power from 1965 to 1997 in what was then known as Zaire. His anti-communism found particular favour with the US. It was not until the end of his regime that the West turned against Mobutu.

But the question remains whether the Western world's apprehension about the mega contract may be justified after all. However great the West's discomfort with its historic role, it does not justify new wrongdoings. Two Spanish journalists, Juan Pablo Cardenal and Heriberto Araújo, are convinced this is the case. As part of a unique project they investigated China's impact in twenty-five developing nations. The results can be found in *La silenciosa conquista china* (The Silent Chinese Conquest), which warns the Western world of 'a new world order dictated from Beijing'. The authors argue that China has something entirely different in mind with the Congolese contract than a 'win–win' situation and a contribution to the country's development. There is a great gap between reality and the official statements, revealing 'very different intentions than those professed by Beijing'. The only winner is China and 'there is very little evidence of any development' of Congo. To substantiate these claims they point out that the total value of the resources is 'many times that of the investment'. The state-owned enterprises may be putting 6.2 billion dollars on the table via China's Exim Bank, but the likely revenue for Sicomines (the joint venture operating the mines) 'will amount to 40 to 120 billion dollars.

In other words: 6 to 20 times the value of the investment. These figures alone make it crystal clear that in the long run China is the major beneficiary of the contract.'

The great variation in projected revenue proves just how imprecise these calculations are. The future copper and cobalt prices are determined by the global economy, but how these evolve is anybody's guess. The price fluctuations could be immense: in 2008 copper traded at 8,400 dollars, but the crisis stripped two-thirds off the price. In 2014 it was back to around 7,000 dollars.

For two French journalists, Philippe Cohen and Luc Richard, the price drop in 2008 was the reason to dismiss the China–Congo deal as a 'lose–lose' situation. Their book is entitled *Le Vampire du milieu*, a play on the words 'L'Empire du milieu' (The Empire of the Middle), China's usual moniker. The pun says a lot about the book's tone and angle, seeking to explain 'how China imposes its laws on us'. According to the authors, China approaches Africa from a 'predatory' perspective, viewing the continent as a 'Chin-afrique', a money-spinning machine.

French journalism is never short on puns, but the two journalists really miss the mark here. Their book is steeped in prejudice against China. And while Cardenal and Araújo may be digging deeper, they are guilty of the same offence. Their conviction that China is the 'major beneficiary' of the contract remains unproven. In addition to the price of copper, the 'proven reserves' can always disappoint in these kinds of deals. That turned out to be the case here: the mines did not contain 10 million tonnes of copper, but only 6.8 million, Sicomines was forced to admit in 2013. The operation of the mine is not proceeding to plan either: extraction should have started in 2013, but has now been pushed back to 2015 and will only be a modest 50 thousand tonnes a year. But in the meantime the Chinese have already embarked on the contractually agreed construction of infrastructure. On top of that they run the risk of political upheaval, which can never be ruled out in this profoundly unstable country. In the event of nationalisation they can say goodbye to their money, as the copper is in the ground and the Chinese army is not going to march into the heart of Africa to protect this investment.

The Chinese themselves seem to doubt that they have the 'world-class deal' Western journalists make it out to be, as the influential planning organisation NDRC expressed its reservations about it in 2012. Following interviews with Chinese participants as well as Western diplomats, two academics, the Danish Johanna Jansson and the Chinese-Canadian Jiang Wenran, cite the project's 'substantial risks' as an explanation for these Chinese reservations. One of the Chinese interviewees believes that his compatriots were so keen to do business they acted in haste. They signed the agreement before enough feasibility studies had been done. The Chinese will most likely net a 'great deal of profits', Jansson and Jiang conclude in the journal *Perspectives on Emerging Powers in Africa*, but the political environment remains risky.

Not only do Cardenal and Araújo ignore this, but they also overlook the profit potential for Congo itself. After all, 32 per cent of Sicomines is in the hands of Gécamines, the Congolese state-owned company. If the copper and cobalt prices go up, the deal will be good for China as well as Gécamines. Hopefully for Congo too, but there is always a risk of the money ending up in the wrong pockets. At any rate, Cardenal and Araújo's conclusion that the country will not benefit from the deal is questionable. Their analysis creates the distinct impression that they were searching for arguments to bolster their 'watch out for the Chinese' message.

## 'Why the attacks on China?'

What is the African perspective on the mega deal? In the spring of 2011, two representatives of the Congolese mining unions, Philip Linza Lukeke and Jean de Dieu Ilunga, delivered a balanced account at a symposium on Congo and China in Brussels. Linza Lukeke placed the deal in its historical context. He explained that mining was given a deathblow in the 1990s, when the West wanted to get rid of Mobutu and stopped buying copper. After the dictator's departure and the years of political instability that followed, Western parties would no longer invest. That's when

China jumped into the gap. 'Before China came along, Congo was completely isolated because of the embargo. The roads were full of potholes and we were desperate for someone to invest. Seeing that the West imposed too many conditions, China pressed ahead with its contracts.'

He did have two points of criticism: the Chinese pay the Congolese workers too little and private Chinese entrepreneurs are heavily involved in illegal copper extraction, something the unions detest. But he was not dissatisfied with the mega deal itself. 'Under earlier contracts the Congolese state received only 15 per cent of the proceeds; now that figure is 32 per cent.' His colleague Jean de Dieu Ilunga struggled to understand why the West takes exception to China. 'Like all other countries, Congo needs a partner and we are open to anyone interested in a win–win situation without too many conditions. Every country is free to negotiate.' Both men expressed surprise at the West's dislike of the Chinese–Congolese deal: 'Why the attacks on the Chinese contract?'

Deborah Brautigam, an American academic who also spoke in Brussels, has an answer. A sinologist and lawyer, she worked at New York's Columbia University for a long time, before taking up the post of Professor of International Development at the American University in Washington. In 2009 she published *The Dragon's Gift*. The provocative title, which labels China's involvement in Africa as a 'gift', reflects thirty years of commitment to the subject. As early as 1983 Brautigam carried out a field study of the Chinese in Liberia. Bringing all of her expertise to bear on the subject, she explains how she sees China's role in Africa. Without obfuscating anything, she tries to balance the negative and the more positive aspects. She takes visible pleasure in holding up a mirror to her Western readership, highlighting various myths that are popular in the West.

Brautigam starts her talk at the Congolese–Chinese symposium as a fairy tale. With an ironic smile the American talks about a poor country with resources and a rich country without that decide to help each other. All those in attendance believe the story to be about Congo and China. But Brautigam is talking about China and Japan respectively, because barely thirty years ago the

Chinese were in the position Congo is in now. At the time China possessed oil, but no capital, and accepted a ten-billion-dollar loan from its arch-enemy Japan. And so Japanese companies helped set up China's infrastructure and enabled the country to buy Japanese industrial machinery. The loans were paid off in oil. The Chinese are now employing the same win–win approach in Africa, Brautigam argues, leaving no doubt about China's motives: 'It's not about doing good, but about doing business.'

Contrary to popular belief in the West, the Chinese presence in Africa is not a recent phenomenon, she stresses. Soon after the decolonisation of many African countries in the 1950s and 1960s the Chinese surfaced in Africa to offer aid. Mao supported the liberation movements that opposed the colonial powers. They could count on his support, especially when they also claimed to be socialist, as did Robert Mugabe's ZANU movement in Zimbabwe.

The kinship was not only ideological. With their 'century of humiliation' the Chinese shared a history of Western oppression with the Africans. Likewise, they are familiar with the fight against poverty. But despite these similarities, the cultural differences remain immense. Among the Congolese he speaks to, van Reybrouck identifies 'a mixture of admiration and suspicion, a paradox that frequently translates into mild ridicule'. The Africans think the Chinese laugh too little and are too detached. The ideological kinship which was important to Mao and the first generation of African leaders plays little or no role these days. But what both have carried over from the past is a less than positive perception of Westerners. Brautigam shows a photo of a beautiful young aid worker by the side of a pool, drink in hand. 'They often lead the lives of pashas,' she sneers, 'which makes it hard to engage with the Africans on an equal footing.' The Chinese, on the other hand, have their feet in the mud, or so she suggests.

There is something to be said against this caricature, as quite a few rich Chinese are now living an equally good life in Africa. But Brautigam is convincing when she sets out the key difference between the European and Chinese approaches to Africa in sobering terms. Europeans view aid and the conditions attached to it, such as 'good governance', as the best way to help Africa. The

West's hostility to the Congolese deal is born of frustration over the other road the Chinese have taken.

China is opposed to political demands, because the principle of 'non-intervention in internal affairs' does not allow it. 'No questions asked' is their motto, which allows them to also fend off meddling in their own internal affairs. Mindful of their own history, the Chinese believe that an exclusive focus on business is an excellent approach to Africa's development. The different approaches were explained to me once with the help of two images: to Europe Africa is a starving child, to China she is a beautiful young woman. It is easy to guess how the Africans themselves prefer to be seen.

The development aid that China provides as well comes second to commercial credit lines from its banks. People in the West mistakenly believe that China is now a bigger aid donor to Africa than the World Bank. Brautigam attributes this misunderstanding to a translation error: Prime Minister Wen Jiabao once mentioned the sum of 44 billion yuan of Chinese aid (approximately 5 billion euros at the time), but this was reported in the Western press as 44 billion dollars. Likewise, Western figures on African land purchases by Chinese businesses are often inflated, as she explains in detail in her fascinating blog *China in Africa: The Real Story*. Sitting at their desks and using newspaper clippings, researchers include in their calculations all kinds of projects that Brautigam, with her field expertise, knows never got off the ground. But because the research into these land grabs is carried out by reputable Western research institutes, this 'zombie story', as she labels it, keeps rearing its head.

Brautigam is highly critical of the Western media, with their 'alarming, extremely negative tone'. They bandy about terms such as 'land grab', 'rogue aid' and 'poisonous aid', and even a reputable publication such as *The Economist* referred to the Chinese once as the 'new colonialists', much to her annoyance. It creates the impression that Africa is simply being rolled up by China, when the reality is far more complex. The Angolan government, for instance, well aware that the oil reserves have made the country an attractive proposition, is cleverly playing its suitors Brazil, China and Portugal off against each other.

The Chinese are also encountering growing political opposition in Africa. Their support to corrupt leaders in Sudan and Zimbabwe has not gone unnoticed and is damaging their reputation in other African nations. As the new presidents of Malawi and Zambia are pandering to anti-Chinese sentiments, these feelings are also coming to the fore in Rwandan and Namibian politics. This backlash ought to give China food for thought.

Important in shaping the country's image are the bankruptcies of African companies as a result of Chinese competition, the importing of Chinese workers who are rumoured to be prisoners, and the 'slave hours' African employees are forced to work at Chinese companies. The honeymoon between China and Africa is clearly over. This is something the major Chinese oil companies have noticed too. In Chad, for instance, they were penalised for 'gross environmental negligence'. In 2013 the Ghanaian authorities deported 4,500 Chinese people who were engaged in illegal gold mining, despite possible repercussions for the Chinese loans promised to Ghana.

Brautigam readily admits that in some cases the criticism is justified. The way Chinese entrepreneurs tend to treat their staff and the environment is inexcusable in her view. She also believes that these entrepreneurs make too little effort to hire local workers, so that unemployment among Africans is falling too slowly. And Chinese production for export, especially in the field of textiles, is done at the expense of local industry and hence employment. 'These are serious problems which rightly tarnish China's overall reputation in Africa.'

But these should be offset against the positive aspects: the railways, roads and ports that may give the economy as a whole a boost; the investments delivering jobs, made by both state-owned enterprises and tens of thousands of private entrepreneurs; and the higher export earnings from resources, in part thanks to the growth in Chinese demand.

All in all, China is making a major contribution to Africa's integration in the global economy. Instead of just criticising, the West might help 'by gaining a more realistic picture of China's engagement, avoiding sensationalism and paranoia [and] admitting our own shortcomings'. The latter include the poor efficacy of aid money and our inability, unlike China, to get major infrastructure projects off the ground. Now that the country has managed to lift hundreds of millions of Chinese out of poverty it also deserves some credit in the development debate. The Chinese development model, with its fairly raw capitalism combined with a powerful state, could well be China's 'ultimate, ambiguous gift' to Africa, Brautigam concludes in her book.

Given the long list of criticisms, the gift certainly is ambiguous. But it is hard to disagree with Brautigam when she pleads for the West to be more realistic as well as more modest. The best course of action would be a dialogue with China about development models. So far the Chinese authorities are refusing to come on board, arguing that as former colonial powers the European nations are not in a position to talk. However, they are pragmatic enough to compare notes with countries such as France and the UK.

This could be the first step towards a proper dialogue. The challenge for the West is to let go of the conviction that its own 'solutions' are best for Africa. There is no point in lecturing China, however morally satisfying this may be. The country is too big, too powerful and too well developed. If China is to become a 'responsible stakeholder' in Africa's development, the West will have to become more open to its involvement.

# Chapter 12

# Resources

## *Chinese Appetite, European Dependence*

On 7 September 2010, at 10 o'clock in the morning and in good visibility, Captain Zhan Qixiong rammed his old, blue fishing boat, the Minjinyu 5179, against a Japanese patrol vessel, thereby unleashing an unexpected chain of events. The US foreign minister, Hillary Clinton, later described it as a 'wake-up call' for the Western world.

Zhan and his vessel were at a disputed location in the East China Sea, around what the Japanese refer to as the Senkaku Islands and the Chinese as the Diaoyu Islands. They form 'no more than five rocky, Japanese outcrops', in the words of a Western diplomat. But China is laying claim to the territory, because it would greatly increase its territorial waters and there is thought to be natural gas under the seabed.

The filmed arrest of Captain Zhan, surrounded by surly-looking Japanese police officers, caused a great public uproar in China – a nationalist chord had been struck. Throughout the country, Japanese buildings had to be placed under police guard, while Prime Minister Wen Jiabao warned that 'Japan will have to bear the consequences'. The next day those words were put into practice: China would stop supplying Japan with 'rare earth minerals'.

This group of seventeen elements, with exotic names such as neodymium, cerium and europium, are globally seen as important 'industrial vitamins'. They are used in the likes of laptops, mobile phones, electric car batteries and wind turbines. The export freeze was a huge shock to Japanese politicians and entrepreneurs alike. The Chinese captain was released within two days. Nevertheless this Japanese–Chinese dispute filtered through to the upper echelons of Washington and various European capitals, as China seized on it as an excuse for comprehensive trade restrictions: it imposed rare earth export quotas, causing prices to soar worldwide.

'The Middle East has its oil, China has rare earth', leader Deng Xiaoping said in the early nineties. Less than twenty years later, China made an attempt to assert its dominant position. On the face of it, its position is fairly modest: the country boasts 36 per cent of global reserves. While this is a lot, it is not enough for domination. But this all changed in the 1990s when other producers began to lose out to Chinese competitors. Not only were the latter able to produce far more cheaply, but they were also more readily prepared to accept the environmental damage that comes with extraction.

As a consequence, by 2010 over 95 per cent of global production was taking place in China – a quasi-monopoly that lends itself extremely well to price manipulation. Yes, the quota system was meant to boost prices, China admitted, to compensate for the environmental costs that the rest of the world had passed on to China. So instead of placing 50,000 tonnes on the global market, the country would now restrict itself to 30,000.

Foreign companies sounded the alarm when their 'industrial vitamins' had suddenly become either completely unavailable, as in Japan, or fifteen times more expensive than for Chinese producers. Their governments' response was three-fold: a complaint was lodged with the WTO, objecting against this 'unlevel playing field'; companies sought to use the metals more efficiently, or tried to find substitutes; and a search got underway for producers outside China. Just how seriously this was taken is illustrated by the fact that in 2011 German Chancellor Merkel twice flew to the Mongolian capital of Ulan Bator. Siemens faced an acute shortage of neodymium for its wind turbines and the Mongolians were in a position to help. In Japan Toyota found a substitute for the neodymium and dysprosium it thought it needed for its hybrid darling, the Prius. It managed to do without. Until then fully dependent on China, in 2013 Japan announced that henceforth it would be obtaining 14 per cent of its demand for rare earths from India and Kazakhstan. Around the world low-energy light bulbs and smartphones were stripped of their rare earths for recycling.

In short: the Chinese strategy backfired. Prices collapsed by a third in 2011 and have not regained their old level since. Chinese takeovers of international rare earths companies are off the cards for now – the wake-up call has seen to that. And in 2014 China lost the procedure which the US and the EU had initiated at the WTO. Countries have a sovereign right over their natural resources, but that does not allow them to manipulate international markets, the WTO panel ruled.

## 'Resource nationalism'

The rare earths case is a cause for optimism. The lesson to retain is that China, even in a market where it is controlling 95 per cent of global production, is incapable of price manipulation. Moreover, other players, when cornered, are capable of finding creative solutions to their resource needs. Does it not prove them wrong, those prophets of doom who envisage a future in which China is such a big player that the rest of the world will lose out, both in 'hard resources', such as metals and minerals, and 'soft resources', such as grain and other food?

Before we can answer this, we need to look at the broader picture. It begins with China's voracious consumption of raw materials. Every year, 54 per cent of all iron ore, 47 per cent of coal, 53 per cent of cement, 40 per cent of aluminium and 39 per cent of copper makes it way to 'the workshop of the world'. Chinese consumption of oil, by far the most important resource economically and geopolitically, currently stands at 12 per cent, or some 10 million barrels of 159 litres a day. By 2020 this may have risen to 14 million barrels.

All countries are more or less in the grip of 'resource nationalism'. After all, raw materials are necessary to keep production lines going and mouths fed. All countries are prepared to go far to obtain them, if necessary at the expense of others. History is rife with territorial conquests for resources. They are the exception to the general rule of globalisation, which is that international trade and investments are in principle beneficial to all parties. If it results in growth of the global economic pie one party's growth need not to be at the expense of another's. But there is no such win–win situation with resources: the barrels of oil going to China will not be coming to Europe. One party's profit is another party's loss.

China occupies a special position on the scale of resource nationalism, concludes a Western energy expert who has extensive negotiating experience with the Chinese. Wishing to remain anonymous, he told me: 'Make no mistake, in this area China only acts in solidarity with itself. The CCP's legitimacy depends on economic growth. Resources, oil especially, are a necessary condition. The supply has to be secured, whichever way possible.'

The Western world is dealing with the fallout. The price paid by Western drivers at their petrol stations cannot be seen in isolation from the sharp upsurge in Chinese demand for oil. Alongside supply-side factors, it explains in no small measure why the oil price has increased from 16 dollars per barrel in 1999 to an average of 96 dollars in 2014. Upward pressure on gas prices has also been caused by Asian demand.

This is only the beginning, warns the Zambian economist Dambisa Moyo in her book *Winner Take All* about the Chinese 'race for resources'. In the long term, she believes, a resource crisis is inevitable, given that the global population is expected to reach nine billion people by 2050 – and especially because of the additional three billion middle-class consumers by 2025. Their demand for accommodation, transport and electricity will have to be met. By that year the earth will be home to five billion urban dwellers. The Chinese among them will, when it comes to energy and water, need respectively four and three times as much as their rural counterparts.

The resulting extra demand for resources will inevitably lead to shortages, in Moyo's view: 'Demand for everything, from copper to corn, outpaces supply', with higher prices and a lower standard of living as a result. The escalation of tension surrounding resources could lead to famine and war, she predicts.

The only country which is preparing strategically well for this commodity scarcity is China, Moyo believes. The commodities-for-infrastructure deals the country is concluding all over the world, not just in Africa, as well as the billion-dollar takeovers of mines are proof to her that China is pursuing this strategy with 'precision, execution and foresight'.

Moyo, listed by *Time* as one of the '100 Most Influential People in the World', cannot be accused of China-bashing. At home she sees both Zambia and China benefitting from Chinese investments in mines. In fact, she is full of praise for the Chinese government for its 'very friendly and very symbiotic' attitude towards other emerging countries. She is annoyed by the negative coverage of Africa in the Western press and its tendency to ignore Chinese efforts to reduce poverty. But above all, she urges the West to come up with a strategy in response to what she calls 'the most aggressive campaign' in the history of resources.

## China Inc.

China is exploiting two of its special characteristics, according to Moyo. First of all, it is using its huge wealth, reflected in the immense state reserves, by investing elsewhere. In the hope of obtaining Chinese money, other countries are throwing themselves at China's feet, happy to part with their raw materials. It makes the Chinese increasingly powerful and ultimately gives them price-setting powers over commodities, she argues. China might even be able to start foreclosing parts of the market via exclusive deals and so lock out other parties. Secondly, China has what Moyo terms internal discipline: 'Ultimately they all pull together, public and private, under one unifying force with a single agenda: the betterment of China.'

It is this close cooperation within a state capitalist system that puts the West, with its faith in democracy and the free market, at a disadvantage in the fight for resources. It could have political ramifications too. The state capitalism of 'China Inc', typified by 'one for all and all for one', could start to appeal to more and more countries, she predicts.

These big claims by the often provocative Moyo do not reflect reality in my view. It is fair to say that China's purse has many countries angling for investments, but certainly not at any cost. The advance of the Chinese is also meeting with resistance – not just in Africa, as we have already seen, but also in Latin America and Asia.

Take neighbouring Mongolia, for instance. It is largely dependent on China for foreign investments and for its export of raw materials, yet according to a survey only 1 per cent of the population thinks China is 'the best partner' for their country. The widely shared aversion has resulted in legislation aimed at curbing the number of foreign (mostly Chinese) workers.

Or take Brazil. Following the credit crisis, China had high hopes for the Brazilian market. In 2007 the governments of the two nations agreed a whopping 70 billion dollars' worth of projects, including some major 'commodities-for-infrastructure' deals. China had bigger plans for Brazil than just buying its oil, iron ore and soya beans. But in 2013 reporters from Reuters worked out that only a third of the projects had come to fruition and that few if any roads or railway lines had materialised – to the frustration of both the Brazilians and the Chinese. Chinese entrepreneurs complained about 'outdated ideas' and protectionism on Brazil's side. But the Chinese are part of the problem too. The resistance they encounter is linked in part to the poor working conditions at their companies.

The Brazilian case also teaches us that the working relationship between the Chinese government and its own enterprises is far from exemplary. This goes a long way to explaining why the billion-dollar projects failed to get off the ground. The government's intentions were not always implemented by the state-owned enterprises, as they tend to pursue their own agenda.

The fact that the public–private machine is not as well-oiled as Moyo suggests is clear from the fieldwork carried out by the American scholars Elizabeth Economy and Michael Levi. For their book *By All Means Necessary* the two researchers from the Council on Foreign Relations assessed China's impact on a large number of commodity markets. Their findings are surprising. The book's subtitle ('How China's resource quest is changing the world') emphasises China's impact on the rest of the world, but the global markets appear to have at least as significant an impact on China. In fact, sometimes developments are the opposite of what one might expect under the influence of a state-capitalist superpower.

The iron ore market is a case in point. For a long time, a few large parties on the supply and demand side were able to dictate prices on the global market. Then, in 2006, Chinese state-owned company Baosteel thought it could exert its influence over negotiations. However, it failed to consider the dozens of small Chinese mills that started buying their iron ore on the spot market. This new demand resulted in free price formation. So rather than upsetting the market, these small mills actually allowed it to function better. 'They pushed in precisely the opposite direction', Economy and Levi concluded.

Iron ore is no exception. There has been a great deal of speculation about China's strategy of 'locking out', i.e. placing resources outside the global markets, but these claims cannot be substantiated. There is certainly no separate world of Chinese oil, the most important of all resources. Like their Western competitors, Chinese oil companies want to sell to the highest bidder. There is 'no evidence that China is regularly removing large volumes of oil from world markets', Economy and Levi write. 'Most overseas production is sold on world markets.'

Moreover the tanker-like Chinese oil companies appear to determine their own course, accepting as little intervention as possible from their government. 'The set-up is often portrayed as an orchestra,' Economy said about public–private relations in China, 'but we identified something more akin to a cacophony.'

In the case of other resources too, Chinese state capitalism is incapable of changing the global rules of the game. The world markets are quite resilient. 'Far from locking up global resources and steering the world away from free markets, China is dependent on – and being drawn ever deeper into – the market arrangements that preceded its rise', Economy and Levi write. 'It has been China and its companies that have had to change most.'

Given the resistance they evoke, it is not that strange that Chinese companies have had to adjust more than most. Their record on environmental issues and working conditions has not only attracted criticism, but has at times also been an obstacle to their business. This was the experience of state-owned enterprises investing in copper mines in Zambia; one was even subsequently nationalised. The Chinese companies draw from these kinds of fiascos the conclusion that they have to start meeting international standards. There is no evidence of the much-feared race to the bottom.

The incentive to meet higher standards comes from more than one direction. When Chinese companies not only invest in emerging economies but also want to extract raw materials in Western countries such as Canada and Australia, they have to meet much more stringent demands than on their domestic market. It marks the start of a learning process that the Chinese are usually happy to embark on.

On top of that, there is increased political pressure in China to eradicate corruption and meet good governance principles drawn up by, for example, stock exchange authorities. It must be noted, however, that compliance monitoring is still falling considerably short. Nevertheless there is a good chance that in future Chinese resource companies will start behaving more and more like their North American and Japanese rivals.

Finally, while their role on the world markets is substantial, it should not be overestimated. As Economy notes: 'What we found is that China is still a second-tier investor in much of the resource world.' Despite public perception, China only ranks fourth in Africa; third in Latin America; and in its own region, South East Asia, a distant third behind Japan and the EU.

Economy and Levi's prediction that in years to come China will have less of an impact on resources than it had in the past decade also provides the necessary nuance. 'Fear of a never-ending price spiral is unfounded', they argue.

## Strait of Malacca

In my experience these kinds of price forecasts need to be taken with a big pinch of salt. The number of pricing variables is enormous, and anyone with the power to correctly predict the market would make a fortune. If the conflict on the Senkaku/

Diaoyu islands between China and Japan were to get out of hand, it could disrupt trade and hence price outlooks. It is also a question of time: with her apocalyptic prediction about rising prices and falling standards of living, Dambisa Moyo could be proven right, albeit at a much later stage.

The truth is that prices have barely risen in recent years, and nor are they likely to in the next few years – at least not as a result of the 'China factor'. The drop in economic growth to around 7 per cent means that demand will not be unexpectedly high. Besides, various government plans have a moderating effect on the use of raw materials. Efforts are underway to make more economical use of resources, and there is a lot to be gained in this area. The Chinese government also intends to tackle overcapacity in the industry by closing surplus factories. And finally, the government's main target is to steer the economy towards fewer investments and more service industries. This too is expected to lower demand for raw materials.

However, these reassurances do call for some qualifying remarks. At present, China still relies on the US for protection of the international shipping lanes used for transporting the resources. The bottleneck is the Strait of Malacca, a 750-kilometre strait linking the Indian Ocean and the Pacific Ocean, through which 75 per cent of all Chinese oil imports are carried. The Americans currently guard this transit route.

The question is whether the Chinese leaders can continue to live with this dependency. Rising tensions with Japan and other neighbouring countries suggest that China is strongly inclined to take on a greater maritime role. This is prompted in part by nationalistic considerations and in part by ambitions that befit a country like China. Other emerging superpowers such as the UK and the US did the same in their time.

This brings us back to the incident around the Senkaku/Diaoyu Islands in 2010, when nationalism and the politics of commodities were inextricably linked. Commentator and analyst Robert Kaplan, who argues in his book *Monsoon* that in the course of this century the Indian Ocean will take over from the Atlantic Ocean as the locus of global relations, does not expect China to resort to violence to exact a greater role: 'China's military rise is wholly natural and non-threatening in my view.' I am inclined to agree with him on this point, as the leaders will want to avoid a war in order not to undermine the economic development of their country.

Kaplan understands that, with its past of Western colonisation, China does not want to trust the US navy to forever 'protect the shipping lanes that carry oil and raw materials from the Middle East and Africa to China'. The challenge for the US lies in allowing China a greater role without alienating its allies in the region – Japan especially. No easy task.

American energy expert Daniel Yergin is not unduly alarmed. In his book *The Quest* he stresses the common interests of the US and China. Together they are responsible for a third of the world's daily oil consumption: 'Both benefit from stable markets, open trade and investment, and improved energy security.' Europe plays a subordinate role in his account. A century ago, Great Britain and Germany fought for global control of the shipping routes. With a view to the supply of resources, the battle is just as important today, but the main protagonists are now China and the United States.

# Chapter 13

# Is China Becoming a Knowledge Economy?

With China already an economic powerhouse, it is crucial to get an idea of what the country's reach will be in the coming years. One of the most pressing questions for the West is: will China become a proper knowledge economy, with a prosperous middle class capable of creating innovative products? Or will the country remain stuck in its role of 'workshop of the world', with a strong profile in cheap products but little added value?

To date, Chinese competition with Europe has primarily impacted the small manufacturing industries in southern European countries. Since China's accession to the WTO in 2001, products that are relatively easy to produce, such as shoes, clothes, furniture and bicycles, have flooded the global market, presenting its European competitors with a choice: bankruptcy or innovation. Better products with greater added value have been the key in the battle with cheap Chinese merchandise.

But what if China follows our example and also manages to climb up the value chain? What if it develops the capability to produce the high-tech products that are such good money-spinners for Europe: the cars, the machinery, the luxury handbags and all the other little gadgets that European companies are famous for and have been able to export? What if Chinese companies start selling these products on 'our' domestic markets and elsewhere at reduced prices?

We must begin by asking: will it ever come to this? China certainly has the ambition, as the government's five-year plans testify. From both an economic and social perspective this makes perfect sense. The current model for success, based on low labour costs and export, is finite. It has brought prosperity to hundreds of millions of people, but the beginning of the end is in sight. Labour costs have already gone up so much that Western clothing and shoe manufacturers are starting to move their factories to Vietnam and Bangladesh. This, interestingly enough, is also true for the Chinese manufacturers of those goods. We are also beginning to see the first reports about Western multinationals moving their production back home, because they believe the labour costs are too high and the appreciation of the renminbi has gone too far. The stagnation of the Western economies puts further pressure on the export model, as the prospects for growth in the main markets, the EU and the US, are bleak.

But China has another strong motivation for wanting to transform its economy. Its current manufacturing role has only limited financial appeal. Take US giant Apple, which has its iPads and iPhones assembled by Taiwanese Foxconn in China. Hundreds of thousands of young people do extremely monotonous work six days a week, ten hours a day, to deliver these gadgets in perfect order. But the bulk of the money goes to Apple. The Chinese estimate that only 1 per cent remains in China; the lion's share is transferred to Cupertino, California, where Apple has its headquarters. It is seen as unfair, and understandably so.

Apple is no exception. While more than half of all Western consumer goods have 'made in China' labels, those responsible for them are usually Western manufacturers. Non-Chinese companies account for no less than 60 per cent of export: of the nearly 1,900 billion dollars' worth of goods that were shipped out of the country in 2011, some 1,100 billion dollars were made by foreign companies. The bulk of the profit was theirs.

An additional reason why the government is eyeing these revenues with envy is that the consumers who are served are no longer only Westerners but increasingly Chinese as well. In order to obtain the key to these earnings, i.e. Western technology, it is tightening the conditions Western companies must meet. You can have access to our markets if you hand over your know-how, Western companies are told. 'Of course they can't come over here thinking they can just sell products. That's unacceptable', a

Chinese with a long international business career once told me. He did not think any further explanation was needed.

Not only from an economic but also from a social perspective, the aspirations for a knowledge economy make sense. There has been an explosive growth in the number of students: in 2010 a whopping 31 million young people were at university, 10 million more than in 2005. It must be added, however, that the term 'university' is much broader in China than it is in Europe. Either way, these relatively highly educated people do not relish the prospect of low-paid work at a multinational such as Foxconn or the local shoe factory. Their higher standard of education is in itself progress, of course, but without suitable jobs this will lead to social problems, especially in the major cities. Every year, new employment must be found for more than six million graduates. It is difficult to overestimate the importance of this challenge. Keeping the student population happy and under control has been one of the main objectives of the country's ruling elite since the uprising on Tiananmen Square in 1989.

Finally, environmental costs – the unpaid debts of the export model – are a motivating factor for achieving a knowledge economy. A high-tech economy with a relatively large service sector, like the one we have in the West, has less of an impact on the environment – another good reason for wanting to replace 'made in China' with 'made by China'.

But scepticism about the feasibility of this ambition is justified. China embarked on this journey under the tenth five-year plan (2001–5), and it was given great emphasis in both the eleventh (2006–10) and twelfth (2011–15) plans. Yet the export model continues to dominate, as evidenced by domestic consumer spending, a good barometer for the transition. It remains well below that of Western countries as it amounts to only a third of the national income, compared with nearly double that figure in Western countries.

The Chinese are great savers, putting aside a third of their income, in contrast to the Europeans and Americans who save only 12 and 5 per cent respectively. Although seemingly virtuous, it is prompted first and foremost by poor pension and health care provisions. The big banks reward these savings with relatively low interest rates. They then lend these billions to the big state-owned enterprises, giving them access to an extremely cheap source of financing. The government can expect opposition from these vested interests if it directs its policy towards encouraging consumer spending. Given its proven success, companies are inclined to continue the export model. While both the government in Beijing and many economists may argue that persisting in this strategy will eventually result in lower growth, as long as things are going reasonably well this will provide insufficient impulse for change. Besides, companies enjoy the support of local or provincial party bosses, who often share in the company profits or are kept sweet in some other way.

Nor do these companies feel any incentive to spend money on research and development, as the government, in its pursuit of a knowledge economy, would like them to do. Compared to their Western counterparts, Chinese firms still only do this in piecemeal fashion. Former Prime Minister Wen Jiabao may have been right when he complained that the economic growth model is unbalanced and unsustainable, but that does not inspire companies to behave differently. Such attempts at 'management by speech' do not get through to small and medium-sized enterprises, even though American and European examples suggest they are the ones that should generate innovation. It is not really happening on the Chinese shop floor. What is going wrong here?

## Entrepreneurs with a penchant for copying

To get an idea, I visit Jsure Healthcare, a small internet company in Shanghai, one Friday evening. Despite the late hour, everybody is still hard at work. Around fifteen young employees are sitting closely packed together in a neon-lit room. They are glued to their computer screens, oblivious to their foreign visitor. On the wall is a sign saying 'Merry Christmas', even though it is now April; the tinsel hanging next to it looks a bit tired. Founder Kevin Lin, in his thirties and wearing a smart navy-blue jacket and hip trainers, escorts me into the garden, where he tells me about the fate of start-ups. It is not easy for them. His company is based, typically, in a somewhat dilapidated villa from the early twentieth century. Now that he has managed to keep his head above water for three years, he may finally get some proper office space. A start-up with an innovative concept cannot count on preferential treatment from either the tax authorities or the bank, he explains. The banking sector is known for its preference for state-owned enterprises. 'I did go to the bank, but they're not interested unless you generate a turnover of three million euros or more. So there was no point in outlining our business ideas.'

But it is through those plans that Lin's business distinguishes itself from the majority of start-ups. By bringing together online pharmaceutical companies and patients, his company offers a different way of organising clinical trials. But it is not a proven business model and therefore at odds with the approach of the average start-up, which wants to be assured of success before it gets going. This explains why the American internet company Groupon attracted over a thousand Chinese competitors in just a few months. 'The people here love to copy. Innovation takes time and people don't want to take that time', Lin tells me. 'Our economy used to grow by 10 per cent annually. With a lot of low-hanging fruit it was pretty easy to earn money. Why make things difficult for yourself with risky innovations?'

Entrepreneurs with a penchant for copying and banks with a habit of ignoring private entrepreneurs – although they claim to have changed their ways – are two reasons for scepticism about the country's ambition to become a knowledge economy. Over a cappuccino in a Starbucks in the heart of Beijing, the American David Wolf supplies me with a few more arguments to feed my scepticism. The forty-six-year-old consultant, with his Michael Moore-like diction, has been advising Western companies for years. He starts by pointing to the education system. 'It's all about learning existing knowledge, not about creativity and experimentation. True, every year vast numbers of engineers qualify, but these kids are not at all prepared for the real world. And the government is, let's put it this way, ambivalent about stimulating independent thought.' The annual budget earmarked for education is impressive, but does nothing to remedy the lack of attention to creativity.

It explains why those familiar with the system are pinning their hopes on the growing number of students abroad. They can learn to think more freely. But that leaves the question whether they want to come back – earlier I noted the reservations among the students in London. The official statistics for 2011 indicate that six out of ten remain abroad, although the number of students returning has been rising: from 86,000 in 2011 to more than 300,000 in 2013. The government stimulates the return of scholars by providing better research facilities. But does it really appreciate the Western, more liberal way of thinking? The authorities have a tendency to transfer returnees to the provinces to see if they are welcoming back too much of a freethinker.

Wolf views the deep-seated fear of freethinking as yet another obstacle on the road to becoming a knowledge economy. 'One of the great mysteries is how the country has been able to grow so much, since culturally there is no incentive to start your own company. Bankruptcy, for example, is something to be ashamed of.' Last but not least, he mentions the poor legal system, which does little to protect intellectual property. This too puts the brakes on innovation. Why bother inventing something if someone else can reap the benefits with impunity? It is a problem that Western companies do not like to talk about, but which they constantly run up against in business with the Chinese. At the centre of it is a fundamental cultural difference.

Dutch China expert and entrepreneur Henk Schulte Nordholt knows the Chinese perspective on intellectual property inside-out. 'They are suspicious of the fact that Western politicians and companies take umbrage at their copycat behaviour. They see themselves as victims: "You only established this system of international law to retain the lead, which you established at our expense." They have the idea that everybody copies, but that they are the only ones who are called to account over it. The same with human rights.'

Schulte Nordholt has been involved in China for nearly forty years. He has seen the copying on all levels. At the bottom level are the local factories that copy CDs, watches and mobile phones. 'As far as this illegal trade is concerned, the saying goes: the sky is big and the Emperor is far away. Sure, they can issue a law in Beijing, but if you and your company are located at a great distance and you enjoy the protection of the local party bigwig, who has a clandestine stake in your company, you can just carry on manufacturing.' Occasionally this protection comes from the army, a 'state within the state'. There are stories about products being copied on military sites, where inspection by other authorities is out of the question.

Among the most incredible and striking examples of copycat behaviour are the 'Western' stores that are sometimes discovered by chance in remote parts of the country. A Western photographer stumbled across an Ikea lookalike in Kunming, the capital of Yunnan Province in the south-west. You could not tell from the outside, but on the inside '11 Furniture' was a perfect replica, including the blue and yellow colourscheme and the small pencils for jotting down the details of products. Only the salmon had been replaced with pork in the restaurant. Similarly, there are plenty of fake Apple Stores, where real Apple products are sold. How the stores get hold of them is unclear. What is clear, however, is that it happens on a large scale. Again in Kunming, the authorities came across no fewer than twenty-two stores that had copied the look and feel of Apple, including the helpful whizz-kids in blue T-shirts with white logos. Then there are the Nibe shoes decorated with the Nike swoosh and you can buy coffee in Star Fucks (no kidding), which boasts a logo that is virtually identical to that of Starbucks. By copying these formulas for success, the owners seek to minimise their business risk.

It is not only at the level of shops that respect for intellectual property is conspicuous by its absence, Schulte Nordholt notes. The major state-owned enterprises, the 'national champions' which are trying to strengthen their competitive position in the field of technology, seem similarly 'unaware that they are meant to do it under their own steam', as he puts it diplomatically. 'They know they can count on assistance from Western multinationals. After all, who wants to be excluded from the world's fast-growing second economy?'

On paper there has been significant progress on the protection of intellectual property. 'There is legislation now and a patent office, where there was none before.' And since the accession to the

WTO, the authorities have spearheaded frequent campaigns, with piles of CDs and other illegal copies going through the shredder in front of the television cameras. So efforts are being made to raise awareness. The government is serious about this, as no other WTO country spends as much money on compliance as China. But coming down hard on offenders is risky because of the huge economic interests. The illegal activities do create jobs and profits.

In practice it is still extremely complicated to protect inventions, although the courts are starting to become a bit more effective. Chinese companies are also beginning to bring charges against one another, especially with the rapid increase in the number of patents. It is seen as an issue of national prestige and the figures are closely monitored. But it means that the bar for a patent is not set high. The fact that the more patents they approve the more the patent offices earn is not exactly conducive to critical scrutiny either. The turning point will probably come when enforcement of intellectual property yields more than turning a blind eye to illegal practices. But legal certainty in this area will take years, which is why some Western companies prefer to be based in other countries, such as Singapore.

## 'National champions'

Despite his criticisms, David Wolf is optimistic, citing what he sees as China's two greatest assets: mass and capital. With over 1.3 billion inhabitants 'it would be strange if there wasn't at least one Steve Jobs or Mark Zuckerberg among them'. Moreover, with financial reserves of roughly 4,000 billion dollars in 2014, the state should be capable of kickstarting innovation, he reckons. 'But they'll do it Chinese-style. That's to say, it won't be the garage innovation of an individual genius, which is the US model.'

'Chinese-style' means a key role for the 'national champions' with global ambitions. They know they can rely on long-term financial support from the state. Leading the way are sectors like defence, aircraft construction and telecommunications. 'In these areas the drive towards independence of Western technology is immense. They'll be making it all themselves', Wolf predicts.

Support for this thesis comes from Frank Sieren, correspondent at German newspaper *Handelsblatt*. In his book *Angst vor China* (Fear for China) he identifies aircraft construction as the field in which the West will lose its technological monopoly. In 2016 aircraft manufacturer Comac plans to launch the C919, which is expected to compete with Western flagship models such as the Boeing 737 and the Airbus A320. The symbolic trickle-down effect of this will be immense, Sieren expects. 'Chinese aircraft can make a substantial contribution to liberating the country of its cheap image.' Wolf anticipates an advance in the defence industry, where substantial investments are made every year for reasons of national security as well as innovation. China's ruling elite, for the most part men with engineering degrees, like to emulate the Americans in this area. 'They have seen how investments in defence lead to lots of innovation elsewhere. They want to follow suit.' Wolf puts their predilection for state-owned enterprises in a political perspective: 'They like them because innovations by these companies can be influenced and directed. There's no need to worry about unexpected chain reactions.'

Surprisingly, a governor of the University of Beijing expresses serious reservations about Wolf's optimism. On the condition that I do not mention his name, he is prepared to share his views with me. He has no faith in the seemingly powerful union of government and state-owned enterprises, because they lack efficiency and corruption is too widespread. The amount of money the government pumps into the heart of the knowledge economy certainly looks impressive, he acknowledges. The latest five-year plan stipulates that 2.5 per cent of the gross national product must be spent on research and development, an increase of 0.7 per cent. While this may seem rather modest, it actually amounts to an extra 45 billion dollars annually. The difference from Western nations, which are actually cutting back on this kind of spending, is striking. But the big question, he argues, is whether the money ends up in the right place.

The facts do not speak in China's favour. To date there have been no major home-grown innovations, game-changers in the vein of Google or Facebook. And while figures show an official increase in the research and development budget in the past eight years, the university governor believes it effectively amounts to a drop of 10 per cent when looking at basic science alone. Add to this the fact that companies also spend hardly any money on this, and China is not catching up at all in his view. 'The US still spends three times as much on basic science.'

More significantly, the R&D funds are not spent wisely, he continues. Corruption and opportunism are doing China a disservice: 'The bureaucrats who manage the flows of money have no idea who the future winners are. When presented with two projects, one of which is about fundamental and therefore uncertain research and the other which has a fairly concrete application that guarantees a fast buck, it is not hard to guess where the money will go. Those same bureaucrats are also the recipients of company gifts. Unfortunately, it often leads to the wrong decisions.' Of course his country is going to deliver innovations, but, he predicts, 'we won't be the powerhouse many people expect us to be'.

Remarkable words from a man who must be extremely frustrated with the levels of corruption. His distaste for it merits respect, of course. I also agree with his view that bureaucrats are incapable of determining which companies will come out on top – Western experiences corroborate this. But is he right to doubt China's future powerhouse status?

## Failing industrial policy

Educated at MIT, Andy Xie is a thorn in the Chinese establishment's side. A thorn with foresight no less, because the man – who is in his forties and lives and works in Shanghai – has already correctly warned of two bubbles: the Asia crisis of the late 1990s and the credit crisis of 2008. At present he anticipates a risk in the housing market. 'I have never called something a bubble that turned out not to be a bubble', he writes with typical strength of conviction in his column for financial weekly *Caixin*.

When it comes to innovation, the government should not concentrate on state-owned enterprises, Xie believes, but on private companies. He points out that foreign businesses dominate many sectors. The automotive industry is a well-known example, but in the pharmaceutical industry foreigners also have the edge over their local counterparts, whether or not via joint ventures. 'In this respect China is quite exceptional.' The explanation is simple: the country's leaders have an unshakable faith in state-owned enterprises, even if they are cumbersome and inefficient.

This faith is tied up with their need for control, which is much easier to implement in the public sector than in the private sector. But Xie is acutely aware of their shortcomings and cannot see a single one of them growing into a global player. 'The results indicate that the industrial policy has failed.' The focus should therefore be on stimulating private enterprises, he believes. They appeared to be doing fairly well in the nineties, before becoming enthralled to the 'get rich quick' mentality. Their focus shifted from core activities to stock exchange quotations, cashing share options and property development. The sums they could make from speculation were simply irresistible, analyses Xie: 'Because of these distractions the Chinese companies got behind, overtaken by their Taiwanese and Korean competitors.'

Xie may be on the right track with his plea for the private sector, but that is not the same as being proven right. Afraid to lose control, President Xi Jinping continues to back the state-owned enterprises. If Andy Xie is right, it signals a dead end for innovation. But if David Wolf is vindicated, the knowledge economy can also come about in this way.

My own view is that China will eventually succeed, but that it will take longer than many observers and perhaps the Chinese leaders themselves anticipate. In the long run, the country, with all of its manpower and financial reserves, should be able to make the leap. But the greatest stumbling block remains its inability to reform, economically and otherwise.

The fact is that the knowledge economy has been writ large in the five-year plans since 2006, but the results so far have been poor. This is reflected in the annual Global Competitiveness Index drawn up by the World Economic Forum in Switzerland. A country's innovative strength is an important indicator in the index which covers a variety of criteria. China is not listed among the 'innovation driven economies', nor is it among the second group of countries that are 'in transition'. Instead, it is classified with the third group of 'efficiency driven economies' alongside the likes of Serbia and Peru. Equally painful is its lack of progress: in 2008 the country was in 29th position, where it remained in 2013.

Looking more specifically at the businesses and universities that are meant to be making a qualitative leap towards a knowledge economy, the results are nothing to write home about either. In the field of science, the Chinese universities have long failed to break through to the world's top, which has been dominated by American and British universities. Only two Chinese institutions made it into the top 100 of the *Times Higher Education* World University Rankings of 2013–14: Peking University at 45 and Tsinghua University at 50. It should be a wake-up call.

The business sector does not show any signs of great innovative strength either. The embarrassing statistic here is that the world's second economy still lacks global brands. A few companies are starting to make headway, most notably telecoms company Huawei, but right now there is not a single Chinese brand in *Businessweek*'s top 100. Indicative of China's failing is that in one of the world's biggest markets, the automotive industry, the domestic manufacturers are still incapable of competing with European, American or Japanese cars – despite the joint ventures. In fact, they are outperformed on their home market. So Xie is certainly right when he claims that the domestic industry is lagging behind.

What does this mean for Europe? I would not put my money on Xie's forecast. Europe will have to take into account that sooner or later China will develop into a knowledge economy. The economic performances of the past few decades suggest that the country must not be underestimated. But there is no need for Europe to cower: it should have faith in its own innovative strength and in the time factor. A Chinese knowledge economy will be a while in the making.

# Chapter 14

# 'How China Steals Our Secrets'

'Admit Nothing, Deny Everything, Make Vigorous Counter-Accusations.' Signs with this text adorn many a Washington office dedicated to counterintelligence, if we are to believe James Mulvenon. The American cyber-espionage expert, affiliated with the consultancy firm Defense Group, gave this glimpse behind the scenes of espionage when testifying to the Congressional-Executive Commission on China. In 2013 the members of Congress were keen to hear his views on the practices of Chinese hackers, a phenomenon Mulvenon has been studying for years.

China is the undisputed star in this opaque and mysterious world, claims his 2013 book *Chinese Industrial Espionage*. By resorting to the theft of industrial and scientific secrets via cyber-espionage the country has opted for an illegal shortcut to becoming a knowledge economy. The scale of the phenomenon is unprecedented and seriously underestimated, according to Mulvenon and his two co-authors.

At the same time, the Snowden affair gave us ample proof in 2013 that his fellow countrymen are no angels themselves when it comes to espionage. The former NSA worker revealed that his employer not only amassed data on US citizens, but was also active in the rest of the world, not least in China. By penetrating China's telecom network the NSA gained access to the text messages of private citizens. Likewise, the agency entered the networks of companies such as Huawei. And applying the tactic of outright denial and counter-attack in response to accusations is as American as it is Chinese, Mulvenon argued.

The sheer scale of both Chinese and American intelligence activities was something Europe's most powerful woman, German Chancellor Angela Merkel, experienced in person. In 2007, weekly news magazine *Der Spiegel* revealed that Chinese hackers had bombarded her department and various German ministries with Word documents containing 'Trojans'. The Chinese embassy in Berlin reacted, as was to be expected, with categorical denial, speaking of 'irresponsible speculation without a shred of evidence'. But when Merkel turned to Wen Jiabao in Beijing, the Chinese Prime Minister implicitly admitted the intrusion as he promised measures 'to prevent attacks'.

Six years later it was President Obama's turn to offer his excuses to Merkel for the NSA's conduct. The agency had been tapping her mobile phone since 2002 – for more than ten years. The Germans were furious and even recalled their ambassador from the US.

To intelligence experts these anecdotes are not exactly shocking. Spying is of all times and everybody is doing it, even on allies. The so-called 'no spy' agreements between some countries should be taken with a substantial pinch of salt. Even the Americans and the British, who are adamant about their friendship, keep a close eye on each other. Everything has to yield when 'national security' is at stake. The same applies to European nations, regardless of their cooperation within the EU. Thanks to WikiLeaks we know that Germany sees France as a prime threat to German industrial secrets.

But however widespread the phenomenon may be elsewhere, the Chinese deserve special attention. In China, espionage is part of a range of efforts to acquire better technology. Other, legal methods for doing so include forcing Western companies to transfer their technology in exchange for market access, entering into scientific partnerships with Western universities and approaching Chinese employees of Western universities and companies with the request to hand over their knowledge. In the latter case, the line with espionage is easily crossed. Chinese legislation formally prohibits intellectual property theft, but that need not be an obstacle in practice.

To the Chinese such a legal ban and a flourishing trade can quite happily co-exist, as the business in fake goods, the cheap imitation of well-known brands, testifies. The tradition of copying and the associated failure to recognise the need for relying on one's own resources reflect the same mindset. This lack of awareness eases the step to industrial espionage. Another tradition is the authorities' habit of spying on the people, a long-established custom going back to early imperial times. In the sixth century BC, General Sun Tzu devoted an entire chapter to it in his renowned military-strategic treatise *The Art of War*. He distinguished five types of spy.

The first type, the local spies, operated in hostile territory. They still exist and tend to keep the American courts busy with frequent cases of industrial espionage. The sums of money involved are considerable. The Pangang Group from Chengdu, for example, transferred 28 million dollars to Malaysian-born consultant Walter Liew for supplying a secret formula for a white pigment from chemical giant DuPont. Every year, the substance generates revenues of 14 billion dollars. The US Justice Ministry, which managed to secure a jury conviction for Liew in 2014, claimed to know of twenty comparable espionage cases. Biotechnology, telecommunications, clean technology and nanotechnology are among the favourite areas of the Chinese. But this old-school form of espionage has been overtaken by its cyber-equivalent, which makes it possible to spy from the comfort of one's own home. A variant not known to Sun Tzu, Chinese hackers have now gained notoriety for it.

## Ransacking the *New York Times*

'China is widely known to be the most aggressive cyber state in the world today', China expert David Shambaugh states in his book *China Goes Global*. In support of his claim, he points to the large number of governments and companies that have owned up to being Chinese hacking victims. Among them are practically all US government bodies, including the White House; the British Foreign and Commonwealth Office and the security service MI5; German and French ministries; and a long list of government institutions in China's neighbouring countries. The pestered multinationals certainly include all major defence and energy companies and media powerhouses such as Google and the *New York Times*. The successful attack on Gmail was one of the reasons for Google to leave China in 2010.

The ransacking of the *New York Times* computer system in 2013 put the topic high on the US political agenda. Needless to say, the Chinese authorities vehemently denied it (the reporting was 'totally irresponsible', containing 'baseless conclusions'), but they misjudged the nature of the spied-upon company. Multinationals who fall victim to cyber-espionage tend to keep it quiet, reluctant to acknowledge the vulnerability of their network. If they do go public, they generally refuse to submit evidence for fear that the outside world will get an insight into their systems. This reticence makes it easier for the attackers to deny involvement outright.

But openness is essential to the *New York Times*, which is why the newspaper began to disclose in detail how Chinese hackers had tried to gain access to confidential information using phishing techniques. It emerged that the hackers wanted to identify the sources behind the story on Wen Jiabao's family fortune which was published in 2012. The Chinese could not believe that its author, Shanghai desk editor David Barboza, had relied exclusively on public sources for his scoop, as he claimed.

The *New York Times* report on the hostile incursion from China caused quite a stir. Other media companies revealed that their computer systems had also fallen victim to Chinese hackers. Having written about President Xi's family fortune, news agency Bloomberg also admitted that its sources, the media's most treasured assets, had been probed.

Up until this point, industrial espionage by China had been a particular cause for concern for specialists and right-wing Republicans. Richard Clarke, chief advisor on cyber-crime to the Bush administration from 2001 to 2003, wrote an alarming piece in the *New York Times* in 2012 under the headline 'How China Steals Our Secrets'. He cites the compelling example of a company that saw the results of ten years of work and a billion-dollar investment copied by hackers overnight. Fighting this kind of misconduct ought to become a top priority, because it 'destroys our competitive edge', he argued. But Clarke did not manage to stir much interest.

This changed after the series of articles on theft at leading media outlets and the exciting follow-up in the *New York Times* about 'Unit 61398' in 2013. Operating out of a run-down neighbourhood on the outskirts of Shanghai, surrounded by small restaurants and massage parlours, it turned out to be a People's Liberation Army base for cyber-espionage. The newspaper had 'digital forensic evidence' proving that the bulk of the attacks on US enterprises, organisations and government agencies originated from '61398'. A detailed report by information security company Mandiant arrived at 140 proven attacks since 2006.

Politicians could no longer skirt around the issue and established a heavyweight commission led by the former ambassador to China, Jon Huntsman. His report was clear: Chinese government policy encourages 'intellectual property theft', so much so that it costs the US more than 230 billion euros annually. This roughly equates to US exports to Asia. 'An extraordinary number of Chinese in business and government entities are engaged in this practice', the report noted. How to hit back at this Chinese threat? Huntsman proposed some draconian measures, including a levy on all Chinese exports to the US and sweeping powers for companies to 'hack back'.

## Moral high ground lost

The US government kept its distance from those drastic measures, but intended to put the issue high on the agenda in future discussions with China. That plan backfired when, in the course of 2013, Snowden fled to Hong Kong. His revelation that the NSA had been spying on businesses, universities and citizens in China for years robbed the American diplomats of any trump cards. Besides Huawei, the prestigious Tsinghua University in Beijing had been a key target – the alma mater of many top politicians.

Snowden enabled the Chinese government to throw the American accusations right back at them. Obama's warning to his counterpart, Xi, that cyber-espionage might become 'a very difficult problem in the economic relation' could be met with a big smile on the Chinese leader's part. Had his country not been the victim of US practices? The impasse put the issue on diplomatic ice. In a subsequent report, Mandiant made it clear that the Chinese attacks on Silicon Valley, energy companies and manufacturers of military equipment were continuing after the talks between Xi and Obama. What's more, after a brief pause 'Unit 61398' stepped up its activities.

What complicates matters for the US is that following the Snowden affair they lost the 'moral high ground' in this debate, if they ever had it to begin with. That is not to say that the conduct of the Americans and the Chinese can be seen in the same light, as some commentators on the subject tend to do for the sake of convenience. It would not do justice to the differences, which I believe are considerable.

The Chinese have a much broader aim, targeting not just national security, like the Americans, but also access to the knowledge economy. 'To the Chinese, this isn't first and foremost a military weapon, it's an economic weapon', wrote Laura Galante, a former cyber specialist working for Mandiant in the *New York Times*.

To the Americans, on the other hand, the acquisition of technology is not an objective for the intelligence services; it is the job of the business community. When the NSA breaks into Huawei's systems it is not to find and pass on advanced inventions, but to ascertain the links between Huawei and the army; to find out whether the telecoms company's equipment is also used for espionage; and whether the NSA can hack them back to keep an eye on other countries.

In his defence of the NSA, Obama placed great emphasis on these different objectives while denying that the security agency passes information on to US businesses or universities. To be honest I am sceptical about this. The temptation to keep the upper echelons of the American scientific and business communities informed of what the Chinese are up to must be huge for the NSA. Some degree of information transfer is bound to occur.

But I see this as fundamentally different from Chinese practices in which, according to the experts, this kind of collaboration is common. This is tied up with a second difference: the circle of hackers sanctioned by the authorities is substantially smaller in the US than in China. In the US, hacking is done by specialist departments within the intelligence services, whereas in China the circle is made up of military personnel as well as private citizens, such as students and scientists, all working under the auspices of the Chinese army. What remains unclear is how much control the ruling elite has over the army, which is known as 'a state within a state'. But that should not stop Western governments from raising the issue with the leadership.

This brings us to the question: what position should Western governments adopt vis-à-vis these Chinese practices? Looking at the reaction of the West to date, it is characterised by not wanting to rock the boat. With good reason. The bilateral relationship covers so much more than just industrial espionage. Trade interests, investments, scientific cooperation – countries are reluctant to jeopardise all this to address an abuse that is difficult to prove. And no government has a clear conscience on espionage.

What happened in the UK is illustrative in this respect. In 2011 Sir James Dyson, the inventor of the bagless vacuum cleaner, rang the alarm bell: he suspected some Chinese students of 'stealing technological secrets'. He claimed to have evidence that they were leaving software on British computers, allowing them to carry on stealing information after their departure. His rather caustic allegations were met with a deafening silence; the topic received no attention whatsoever. On the contrary, that same year Prime Minister David Cameron took another step down this path by agreeing with his Chinese counterpart Wen Jiabao to step up scientific cooperation.

On his trip to China three years later, Cameron took the issue more seriously. Prior to his visit he had received signals from various companies and ministries about an increase in cyber-espionage, especially from China. This prompted him to ask Prime Minister Li Keqiang for a 'proper cyber dialogue', because 'it is an issue of mutual concern and one that we should be discussing.' It was certainly 'mutual' as far as the Chinese were concerned, because the British intelligence services GCHQ had also been exposed in the Snowden scandal. Li agreed.

The British interpreted the Chinese pledge as a success, but it remains to be seen whether the talks will yield results. Judging by the GCHQ report, which the *Guardian* managed to obtain, we should not expect too much: 'Allegations of Chinese involvement in cyber attacks are unlikely to deter China from carrying out similar attacks in future', the report stated. After all, following Obama's attempt at dialogue the Chinese hacking activities only increased. His attempts to raise the issue with Xi during the APEC summit in 2014 bore little result. Where Obama wanted to discuss intellectual property rights, Xi was only interested in cooperating with the US on fighting cyber-terrorism, a different ball game altogether.

The West will have to respond, at least in part, by bolstering its own defences. As Cameron acknowledged in Beijing, there 'is an enormous amount of work to be done' in this area. He thus implicitly agreed with the experts in the US and Europe who believe that for years the matter was not taken seriously enough on a political level.

## Sanctions against China?

By better protecting their own networks, Western nations and businesses can not only defend themselves against Chinese hackers but also against attacks from Russia, Iran, the Arab world, Eastern Europe and – let us not forget – home-grown attacks. But, as James Mulvenon points out, we must not expect miracles: those on the defensive have to defend themselves against all possible attacks, whereas the aggressor needs only a single successful strike. In other words: the many billions spent on firewalls in the coming years will not beat the hackers. Higher walls only lead to higher ladders.

Western countries face a dilemma when tackling this issue. One option is to stick with the defensive strategy, complemented with years of dialogue that will probably garner as much success as the human rights dialogue. It would be naïve to think that the Chinese government will take measures in response to the moral argument that industrial espionage boils down to undermining mutual trust.

The Chinese will defend themselves by saying that Western countries and Westerners also engage in espionage. Statistics on the subject doing the rounds in China suggest that the US is responsible for a third of the attacks that brought down 10,500 websites in China in 2011. Another statistic indicates that China is particularly vulnerable to attacks from outside. A government think tank calculated that there were only 40,000 cyber-security professionals working in China's information security industry as of late 2012, but that actual demand is more than twelve times that number at 500,000. A dialogue between these conflicting perspectives soon turns into a dialogue between the deaf.

The second option for Western countries is to start playing hardball as the Huntsman Commission proposed. Measures can be taken on both a micro and macro level. Individual companies which have resorted to espionage, such as the aforementioned Pangang Group from Chengdu, could be blacklisted, boycotted and their employees denied visas. Another sanction would be the suspension of scientific partnership. By ratifying the Wolf amendment in 2011, the US Congress blocked a limited number of scientific contacts – only those that came directly under the federal government – on account of Chinese espionage activities.

The efficacy of those micro measures is debatable; they are little more than drops in the ocean. Higher up the escalation ladder more draconian measures will come into the picture, such as the threat of export levies. It could herald the start of a trade war in which everybody loses.

Perhaps China can be made to toe the line a little when Western countries manage to persuade them that in the long run the benefits of espionage do not outweigh the costs, neither economically because of the threat of sanctions nor politically because of China's image in the world. In that respect the fight against espionage is no different from the enforcement of intellectual property rights discussed above. But to arrive at that position and to credibly threaten with sanctions we need to act in unison, preferably via a joint US–EU approach. A British–Chinese dialogue, as proposed by Cameron, is pointless, whereas a European–Chinese conversation might have some effect.

I do not have very high expectations of eliminating this problem. In the Western camp the EU member states will struggle to agree on sanctions, so China is unlikely to take the threat of punitive action seriously. The West, not wanting to rock the boat, will probably focus on the first option, the defensive strategy.

Over on the Chinese side there does not seem to be enough impetus to address home-grown wrongdoings, especially not while the cost–benefit analysis is in their favour. The American Mike Rogers, chairman of the House Permanent Select Committee on Intelligence, was probably right when he said: 'Right now there is no incentive for the Chinese to stop doing this. If we don't create a high price, it's only going to keep accelerating.'

# Chapter 15

# The True Cost of an iPhone

*On Working Conditions and the Work Ethic*

Showing open contempt for Westerners is not in the nature of the Chinese, but there is one area where even the Europhiles among them cannot contain themselves: the work ethic. The idea that Westerners are 'lazy' is widely held, although it is often couched in more diplomatic terms such as 'working less hard'. Westerners want to go on holiday every three months and refuse to work six days a week, the Chinese are surprised to note. Their conclusion during the euro crisis was that those who work so little only have themselves to blame.

Conversely, there is mostly admiration for the Chinese work ethic. Ask a Westerner to list the positive characteristics of the Chinese and 'hard work' will almost certainly feature in the top three. But the criticism is never far off. It centres on the 'exploitation' of the Chinese employee who is widely held to do his work under bad conditions and for a pittance.

The French journalists Philippe Cohen and Luc Richard, who studied the fate of the *mingongs*, the migrants who have swapped the countryside for the city, even speak of 'the slaves keeping the Chinese economy afloat'. It is up to Europe to raise a 'barrier of civilisation', the Italian writer Edoardo Nesi reflects in his acclaimed book *Storia della mia gente* (The Story of My People) after witnessing a police raid on illegal Chinese sweatshops in his hometown of Prato. Western multinationals in China see themselves as disseminators of that civilisation, claiming to bring with them lofty values regarding environmental issues and workers' health and safety. The gap between Europe and China appears to be at its widest when it comes to labour. But zoom in and the picture is not quite so black-and-white.

## Unmistakable progress

It still makes Stephen Frost's blood boil. At the beginning of this century the Australian, in his forties and looking like a rugby player in a suit, took the immense task upon himself to popularise 'corporate social responsibility' (CSR) in China. Based in Hong Kong, Frost and his organisation CSR Asia tried to get Chinese and Western companies to practise it. During that ten-year period he developed a fairly thick skin. But do not get him started on Western multinationals lobbying against a new Chinese law to transfer more rights to employees. He struggles to rein in his anger.

The episode kicked off in 2006, when the government announced it was ready to take the next step towards a 'harmonious society' by introducing a progressive new labour law. For the average employee the progress brought by globalisation had been a mixed blessing. Once upon a time socialism provided security from the cradle to the grave. The 'iron rice bowl' policy offered wage and housing guarantees, especially for civil servants and the employees of state-owned enterprises. This was under Mao. In the 1980s and 1990s many of those employees lost their privileges, or their jobs altogether. In the graphic wording of a Western union leader, they were 'used as raw material' – a resource to be maximised.

According to Frost, this situation has improved a little in the past decade, but abuses remain the order of the day. To cite just a few from the long list of complaints: much longer working hours than officially agreed – often ten or more hours per day, six days a week; overtime that is not or not sufficiently remunerated; lack of safety in the workplace, sometimes with fatal consequences; unhealthy working conditions. And although there are official unions, these tend to side with the management and do little or nothing to address these complaints.

As a consequence, the social unrest in the workplace is expressed through less than harmonious behaviour, such as wildcat strikes. There has been a sharp increase in the number of demonstrations, including strikes: from 6,000 in 1995 to 75,000 in 2006, after which the authorities stopped publishing the figures.

This is why, in 2006, the government tried to extinguish the social fire with new legislation. An employee could no longer be fired without an explicit reason, the labour law stated. His employer would also have to make a contribution to his social security, including potential healthcare costs. And last but not least, especially given the work ethic, the hourly wage would have to increase for working weeks exceeding forty hours. To a Westerner these are no more than obvious steps towards a 'normal' legal position. In China some lawyers argued that the bill did not go far enough, as the state's stranglehold over the unions continued. But nobody disputed the fact that the law represented progress for the average employee.

## Threatening multinationals

Yet Western multinationals in China were strongly opposed to the bill. Both the European and US Chambers of Commerce began to demur that this really was not an option. Without blinking an eye the European Chamber of Commerce, with members including Shell, Total, Daimler, Philips, HSBC and practically all the other big names, explained that their rank and file had left Europe because its labour legislation was proving too costly for them. If China were to head in that direction too the country would face 'the same challenge' as the European nations who had lost their investors, the warning went.

The American Chamber, boasting companies such as Dell, Ford, General Electric and Nike among its ranks, was on the same line when it concluded that the law could reduce 'the employment opportunities for Chinese employees'. The barely veiled threat was that other, neighbouring countries were becoming more attractive propositions. Some concerned multinationals started lobbying the authorities on their own, independently of their Chambers of Commerce. Prior to the introduction of the new law, the French supermarket chain Carrefour even forced a new contract on all of its 40,000 employees in order to avoid the consequences.

The multinationals were treated to a chorus of disapproval both inside and outside China – from the Chinese official unions and employment lawyers to Western unions and pressure groups. In the eyes of the Chinese the Western business community was showing its true colours. 'China as a colony' may be a distant, nineteenth-century notion to us, but a large section of the population is convinced that this is what Westerners are ultimately after. Any hint that Westerners are only interested in profiting from cheap, disenfranchised workers rubs salt into the wounds of the 'century of humiliation'. This is exactly what the multinationals' lobby against the proposed labour law did.

The Western critics of the multinationals echoed similar scepticism. American pressure groups wondered how the US Chamber of Commerce could oppose this bill when its statutes boast fine words about improving the position of employees. The high-minded multinationals like to claim that they behave better abroad than they really have to. But now that the government was proposing basic employee protection they opposed it.

The lobby of multinationals failed miserably: the law came into force in 2008. But it did not lead to more social harmony, as the government had hoped. The courts saw a drastic rise in the number of employment cases, while the industrial unrest did not ease off. A handful of Asian companies operating at the lower end of the market left for neighbouring countries as a direct consequence of the law.

But despite threats to the contrary, the Western business community stayed. What's more, it increased its investment. In 2011 the European Chamber of Commerce even went as far as to say it was pleased with the law from 2008. 'The multinationals were hypocritical', Stephen Frost concludes. 'At home, in their reports and on their websites they always take the politically correct line on corporate responsibility. So they should not complain about the costs if the government wants to protect its people and the environment. But they did.'

But Frost remains nuanced. However hypocritical the lobby may have been, it would be unfair to reduce the conduct of Western multinationals to such behaviour. Some of them certainly do their best to achieve practical improvements for their employees. Curiously enough, employees do not always want them, as electronics company Philips discovered. It encountered strong resistance when it proposed to close a particular factory on Sundays. The employees were furious and threatened to run off to the competitor. Why? The seventh working day boosted their savings. In the end the two parties reached a compromise: not only were the employees given the Sunday off, but they would also be paid.

As far as 'corporate social responsibility' is concerned, Frost is still pinning his hopes for China on Western companies. The Chinese government may have embraced the concept in 2004, expecting it to contribute to 'social harmony', but it has always been rather vague about what it actually entails. Some Chinese companies are sceptical, some over-enthusiastic about the concept, says Frost: 'In certain circles there was and still is the feeling that it is a "wolf at the door", a ruse by the Americans and Germans to incur unnecessary costs for Chinese companies and bring jobs back to their own countries. Others are over-enthusiastic, thinking it may be *the* way towards even greater export success. Both extremes are wrong.'

All state-owned enterprises are now expected to draw up an annual CSR report, but many of them have no idea what exactly it is supposed to include, since the government never properly defined the concept. It makes the reports extremely sketchy. In fact, university research has shown that 95 per cent of them are inadequate, because of unverifiable content. Transparency is a major problem. Frost sees better results at Western companies with a long-standing familiarity with the concept: 'They put pressure on their suppliers, because they want their products to be made in a responsible way.'

The standards are higher for Western companies than for their Chinese counterparts, as consumers expect more from them. 'Their reasoning is: "Since we're paying extra for these foreign products, and they're making a bigger profit, things ought to be just right." That's the tacit agreement. If it's broken, they become furious.' Companies such as McDonald's, Nike and Carrefour have been at the receiving end of torrents of criticism when it looked as if they were not keeping their end of the bargain. The consumers tend not to distinguish too much between American and European companies: 'American companies such as McDonald's and Apple are among those the Chinese love to hate. European companies generally enjoy a good reputation. But their lives can be made difficult too.' This is what happened to Carrefour, as we learnt before, when the rumour spread that it would be giving financial support to the Dalai Lama. The French only barely avoided a lengthy consumer boycott.

## Ambivalent attitude

The Western companies that urge their Chinese suppliers to work responsibly are not by definition friends of Frost. There is something perverse about their approach when it is coupled with equally strong pressure to supply both faster and more cheaply. 'It is untenable in the long run. As a Chinese company you end up between a rock and a hard place. The Western company thinks you should let people work less overtime, but at the same time it wants its products to be supplied faster and cheaper. What choice do you have? It gives the suppliers the impression that Western companies do not think corporate social responsibility is important enough to warrant extra money.'

Frost has seen this ambivalent attitude spreading, and there is nothing Chinese companies can do about it. 'They won't complain for fear of losing a big client. But they are extremely frustrated of course, because they feel that their efforts to comply with corporate social responsibility are ultimately not recognised.' The fundamental solution would be a readiness on the part of consumers to pay higher prices. 'I can see the first signs of such preparedness.' But on bad days he thinks there has been no headway. 'When I visit factories that are proper death traps, for instance, I think we haven't moved any closer in the past ten years.' At the high end of the export market, in which the large Chinese businesses supply Western multinationals, he regains his belief in progress. 'A tremendous amount has improved in the past ten years.' But other than that it is a constant battle of 'two steps forward and one step back'. A couple of months after our interview, Frost threw in the towel.

## Routed out of bed by Jobs

It certainly is a long-term process, as the most high-profile case of recent years, the Foxconn–Apple case, illustrates. This was 'a marriage made in hell', as Frost put it, between one of China's largest foreign employers and one of the world's most successful companies. This mouth-watering combination for pressure groups demonstrates the effects of the ambivalent attitude of Western companies.

With its 1.2 million employees, Foxconn from Taiwan is unimaginably big to Europeans. Measured by wages and working conditions, the companies from the island, along with those from Hong Kong, have the reputation of being among China's worst employers. Foxconn produces highly successful products such as the iPad and the iPhone for Apple. The two are condemned to work together, because Foxconn is one of the few capable of supplying what Apple demands: maximum flexibility in tandem with large-scale production. Together they are at the helm of 'one of the biggest, fastest and most advanced production systems in the world', the *New York Times* wrote. The financial difference between the two is huge: Apple's profit margin on its products is 30 per cent or more; Foxconn's a mere fraction of that.

In 2012 the *New York Times* devoted two thought-provoking reports to the partnership. A month before the launch of the first iPhone, Steve Jobs, the late Apple CEO, decided that the screen ought to be made of glass instead of plastic. His decision meant that on the other side of the world eight thousand Chinese workers were routed out of bed to start a twelve-hour shift 'on a biscuit and a cup of tea', attaching glass screens to the telephone frame. We can no longer demand such flexibility and dedication from American workers, Jobs explained when President Obama asked him why Apple only has 43,000 employees in the US. Most jobs have been transferred to suppliers, most notably Foxconn.

Jobs defended the Taiwanese company in 2010 on US television by painting a rosy picture of a company site complete with restaurants, cinemas and swimming pools for its employees.

He was responding to the news that had made Foxconn notorious: eighteen suicide attempts in the space of ten months had taken fourteen employee lives. Foxconn, which also assembles laptops and printers for Dell and Hewlett-Packard, reacted with a substantial wage increase for its personnel: from 900 to 2,000 yuan per month, more than double and the equivalent of almost 250 euros. Nets to deter jumpers were suspended everywhere, and employees had to sign contracts to stop their families from launching legal claims against the company in the event of suicide. That seemed to settle it. Until the *New York Times* followed up on the issue of working conditions.

In 2011 an explosion took place at a new Foxconn factory in Chengdu in the south-west of China. Two employees died at the scene and sixteen were injured when accumulated dust caught fire during the assembly of iPads. The newspaper also looked at length at the excessive overtime and the standing work that made it difficult for some employees to walk back to their crowded dormitories. This stood in contrast with Apple's claims that for the past six years it had been pressing the importance of corporate social responsibility on Foxconn. According to Steve Jobs, Apple is better than anyone at doing this: 'We do more than any other company on the planet', he wrote in an email in response to the Foxconn affair.

Nonetheless, calls for a boycott of Apple briefly reared their head in the American media in 2012. Jobs' successor, Tim Cook, grasped the severity of the issue and hired an external, independent watchdog, the Fair Labor Association (FLA) led by Auret van Heerden. The South African sociologist has been an independent authority in the field of workers' rights since the 1970s, first in his own country fighting against the apartheid regime, later focusing on working conditions in the 'special zones' in China for the UN organisation ILO.

Van Heerden and his team left no stone unturned in the Foxconn plants and encountered dozens of violations. Topping the list of problems was a lack of safety, with nearly half of all employees reporting accidents in the workplace. A majority complained about pain after a day of standing and carrying out the same brief, machine-like operations thousands of times. Then there was the overtime: while sixty hours per week may have been the contractual maximum, breaches were the order of the day. In fact, some employees wanted to work more, because they thought the basic salary was too low. Some employees were working shifts of eleven consecutive days.

Foxconn was forced to make substantial concessions. A ban on working weeks exceeding forty-nine hours was agreed, with the salary kept at the same level. The concession was expected to cost the company hundreds of millions of dollars, as it faced the prospect of having to hire tens of thousands of new workers. Nonetheless van Heerden believed Foxconn would keep its promises. 'I think they have crossed the Rubicon', he told the *New York Times* in 2012. Eighteen months later, in his final assessment, he remained positive about the company, despite ongoing problems with curtailing the number of working hours.

I personally do not see cause for too much optimism. The attention to Foxconn has certainly had an impact, but it has also created a waterbed effect, with the problem being passed to other suppliers. Research by China Labor Watch, an organisation comparable to the FLA, corroborated this in 2013. At the Pegatron factory in Shanghai, for example, it is not unusual for the approximately ten thousand young employees to work eleven hours a day and six days a week. It goes to show just how difficult it is to eradicate these kinds of problems root and branch.

Besides, it remains to be seen whether Foxconn will start flouting the regulations as soon as the spotlight of publicity has disappeared. The solution they opted for appears to encourage it, as the Taiwanese company is forced to spend considerably more and saw its operating margins more than halve to just 1.5 per cent in 2012. In contrast, Apple managed to maintain its generous profit margin of 30 per cent. There are no signs that the Foxconn affair has caused a financial setback for Apple.

The pressure on Foxconn's profit margins does not strike me as a sustainable solution, which is something Apple ought to be concerned about. For the time being the company is happy to conclude that despite the potentially damaging affair, both Chinese and Western consumers are still queuing up to buy its products. The 'marriage made in hell' with Foxconn remains intact; witness the fact that the Taiwanese company recruited a further 100,000 employees in 2014 for the next generation of iPhones. Another Foxconn affair would not come as a surprise to me.

More generally, a rise in the number of clashes over working hours and working conditions is on the horizon now that China has been confronted with a drop in economic growth. The activists of China Labour Bulletin, another Hong Kong-based NGO in the field of labour relations, registered no fewer than 1,171 strikes and other protest actions between June 2011 and the end of 2013. The weakening economy was to blame according to them, because 'many manufacturers in China sought to offset their reduced profits by cheating workers out of overtime and cutting back on bonuses and benefits. These cost-cutting tactics proved to be a regular source of conflict with the workforce', the NGO said in its report *Searching for the Union: The workers' movement in China 2011–13*.

A telling example of this activism was one of the biggest strike actions of 2014, which took place at shoe manufacturer Yue Yuen. This large supplier to the likes of Nike and Adidas saw its 45,000 employees going on strike to demand decent pensions. They were inspired to do so when an older manager retired and discovered that her pension was a shambles. She managed to get other members of the management on her side, and after being mobilised via WeChat the big mass of twenty-somethings also sprang into action. The strike action eventually cost Yue Yuen – like Foxconn, a Taiwanese enterprise – a total of 65 million dollars: some of it as a result of the strike, and some of it for higher pension payments. The government has mixed feelings about these kinds of strike actions, most of which tend to take place in the southern Pearl Delta. While the new labour law was meant to create more social harmony, it is now used to enforce better working conditions – with great social unrest as a result.

## A new ethic

The strikes are also significant as they highlight a changing work ethic among the younger generations. The strike leaders are mostly in their twenties, part of a new generation unwilling to work six days a week and twelve hours a day, for 150 dollars per month – all the more so when they realise that on such a salary they will never be able to afford their own flat. They are growing increasingly assertive: 'They are shaking off the mantle of individual victims and are emerging as a strong, unified and increasingly active collective force', China Labour Bulletin states. This is in part wishful thinking by an activist organisation, but it also contains a grain of truth, in my opinion. A new approach to work is emerging among young people. In his book *Chinese Whispers* Ben Chu, a British-Chinese journalist, describes them snidely, but not inaccurately, as 'China's little emperors and empresses, spoiled rotten by their doting parents'.

The first to draw my attention to this new mentality is an Italian manager working for a European recruitment giant in China. He talks the frustration off his chest about 'the young generation, those in their twenties and early thirties, who have been treated like princes their whole lives because they were the only child at home'. Another reason the work ethic of those born after 1978 is so different, according to him, is 'because they have never lived through a crisis, they experienced only growth. Their parents remember how bad things were during the Cultural Revolution, but they have no idea.'

A Dutch manager at a large insurance company charged with managing four hundred Chinese employees also puts the world-renowned work ethic into perspective. 'In our office the eight-to-six mentality reigns supreme and nobody works at the weekend.' Deduct the lunch breaks and the working week of these white-collar workers adds up to no more than forty-five hours. Within that timeframe they show far too little enterprising spirit for their Western boss's taste. 'I've worked in India as well, and there the attitude is very enterprising: "How are we going to solve this problem?" The Chinese are much more likely to ask: "Why is this going to fail?"'

This view is common among Western managers. Especially young professionals with a university degree are no longer prepared to work as hard as their parents, are extremely good at making wage demands and often lack a realistic sense of their skills. 'If they are genuinely good, they know damn well how scarce they are. They are extreme job-hoppers', my Italian spokesperson comments. 'They might change jobs every two, three months and do so at the prospect of the tiniest improvement. They have no company loyalty whatsoever.' The Dutch manager agrees: 'They don't go in for career planning. They leave for a little bit of extra money. The result is a war for talent.'

It is true that the market is extremely bullish for talented employees. Western companies are acutely aware that highly educated young people are essential for making it on the Chinese market. You are not going to succeed with Western expats. The thinking these days is that a handful of those will do, complemented with as many Chinese as possible. And so both Western and Chinese companies engage in this 'war for talent'.

Paradoxically, unemployment among the well-educated in the cities is high. The reason is that the more than six million annual graduates are, on average, at a much lower level than their Western counterparts. They are extremely ill-prepared for the labour market. In line with the mandarin tradition, their degrees are entirely geared to knowledge, not to skills.

Training young graduates within the workplace might seem like the obvious solution, as they should be able to participate fully after a couple of years. But that fails to take the jungle of the labour market into consideration. The European Chamber of Commerce complains about this, saying graduates lack 'soft skills' such as presentation and communication. But teach them these and a Chinese rival will be ready to lure them away. Turnover of staff at Western companies is considerable: 30 per cent per year is not uncommon.

Looking at the multinationals' grievances, you cannot help but notice how far removed their problems are from the stereotypical image of the exploited Chinese worker, doing his job under appalling conditions. Western multinationals chasing after Chinese graduates – it represents a decisive break with the traditional image and underlines the shift in the balance of power. Equally interesting is the decline in workaholism among young people. The renewed interest in Buddhist monasteries reflects this. The reserve of the aged in the 1980s and 1990s, these days the monasteries are also attracting young people in search of something more than material satisfaction. It goes without saying that compared to the masses, these youngsters are relatively few in number. But it is a trend which, alongside the increasing labour unrest and the decline in working spirit among young people, is a symptom of dissatisfaction with society. It puts the disparity between the Chinese and Western work ethics into perspective.

Will this cultural difference remain intact as prosperity increases? Many of the members of the one-child generation I spoke to eyed our lifestyle with a degree of envy. They would love more leisure time. And they will grab it when they can. In the past few decades increased prosperity in Europe has also led to shorter working weeks, enabling us to abandon the strict work ethic of the postwar reconstruction years.

The Chinese could well be heading in our direction. Their readiness to work incredibly hard is tied in with the poverty and hunger that used to be so widespread and which they were keen to escape. As their prosperity increases, the Chinese will also weigh up whether they think leisure is more important than work. Change the socioeconomic conditions and the work ethic will change as well.

# Chapter 16

# A Fragile Economic Superpower

'We really don't care whether you're afraid of us in Europe. We'll carry on down our path no matter what. You'd better make the best of it.' This well-intentioned advice came from a Chinese businessman after he had shown me around his gigantic solar panel factory under construction just outside Shanghai. Assessing the global balance of power, he reckoned he would be having his hands full with his Chinese competitors, but did not see European and American manufacturers as a serious threat.

Afterwards, his comment ('we really don't care') kept echoing through my head. It was confrontational: you can either be scared at the thought that the Chinese do not care about our feelings (then again, do we care about theirs?), or you can let go of your fear, since it will not get you anywhere ('we'll carry on down our path no matter what'). I am inclined to do the latter. Europe, scared or not, will have to learn to 'dance with the elephant' which China has become within a short space of time.

As a manufacturer, financier and consumer of resources the country has become so important during this century that it has reconfigured all fundamental relationships in the global economy. It would make more sense to learn this undoubtedly awkward dance than to harbour fears.

How much effort we are prepared to put into this depends on the answers to some of the most pressing questions: should we see the country as the future and only superpower of this century, far surpassing the United States in economic terms? And if so, should we be worried about this supremacy? Or are we dealing with a country that still faces so many political and economic challenges that we ought to view it as merely one link in a multipolar world, alongside the US, the EU, Japan, India and Brazil?

Someone who has pondered these million-dollar questions at length and has written an influential book on the subject is the Indian Arvind Subramanian. I spoke to him in Brussels, where he was visiting to promote *Eclipse: Living in the Shadow of China's Economic Dominance* to policy makers. The book earned him a place in the 'Global Thinkers' top 100 published by *Foreign Policy* journal.

## 'The most dominant economy in the world'

Subramanian, in his early fifties but with the energy of a man in his twenties, is an economist with an impressive record of service. He currently works as The 5th Chief Economic Adviser to the Indian government. After obtaining his doctorate from Oxford he embarked on an international career working mainly for the IMF in places like Rome, Geneva and Egypt. In 1997 he settled in Washington, where he established a reputation for explaining the worldview of the emerging economies to the political elite in the US. With his Indian roots he has both the ability and the credibility to do so. Given the growing interest in these perspectives, he makes frequent appearances in the columns of the *New York Times* and the *Financial Times*.

His particular bête noire is Larry Summers, Obama's chief economic advisor until late 2010, who downplayed the impact of the emerging economies. 'Predictions of America's decline are as old as the republic', Summers stated, referring to popular predictions that the US would be overtaken by other superpowers, in particular China. In the late fifties the Soviet Union was thought to have that capacity, and in the late eighties it was Japan. Both predictions proved incorrect. Summers attributes this to the US, saying: 'We have the most flexible, dynamic, entrepreneurial society the world has ever seen. If we can make the right choices, our best days as competitors and prosperous citizens still lie ahead.'

This self-assurance inspired Subramanian to draw up a model for the economic dominance of countries. Gross national income is only one of the three criteria, alongside a nation's role as either an international creditor or debtor and its share in global trade. It will not come as a surprise that China scores well on the latter two. According to Subramanian's calculations the country overtook the US already back in 2010 as the 'most dominant economy in the world'. He speaks, provocatively, of a future 'G1', where more cautious others stick with a 'G2', a world dominated by both China and the US. His book cover features a photo of Obama bowing deeply for a smiling Chinese president.

China is already making its economic might felt in various ways, he believes, pointing to the ease with which the country continues to keep its currency artificially low, despite years of fierce criticism from the US. 'There is nothing the rest of the world can do about it.' China benefits from globalisation here: many American businesses export from China and therefore profit from a cheap renminbi, whereas others are disadvantaged by it. So the American business community has mixed feelings about the Chinese currency. 'Thus, the United States bark, but cannot bite', Subramanian concludes. Other Western nations are not even barking, as they prefer not to spoil their relations with China.

One of the other symptoms of China's growing power is its ability to force Western companies to hand over technology in exchange for market access. Another expression is the high level of protection of its domestic market. 'Economic dominance of China relative to the United States […] may already have begun', he concludes. In the long term, no other country will come close to China, he reckons. With its young population, his native India is often seen as a challenger to China and its ageing population, but Subramanian does not agree. As the main advisor to the Indian government he knows what he is talking about. 'The state is so weak. The political system precludes any decision making, so India is incapable of exercising power, neither internally, nor on the world stage. I don't see this changing in the next twenty-five years.' China and the West may have extremely disparate systems, but one thing they have in common, according to him, is that they have powerful governments. Unlike India, they are capable of leading and organising their societies.

His calculations, done with an econometric model which is quite inaccessible to the uninitiated, take him up to 2030. In that year China's dominance will be comparable to the huge lead the US had on the rest of the world in the 1970s. To give an idea of the practical consequences, he opens his book with a scene set in 2021. It shows the newly elected US president heading over to the IMF one cold, stormy February morning – cap in hand. The US, buried in debt, needs a billion-dollar credit to satisfy the financial markets. The IMF's Chinese director hands him a list of demands in exchange for the loan. The wish list, strongly influenced by China, includes the reduction of US defence spending, through the decommissioning of expensive naval bases in Asia, and a tax rate of at least 40 per cent. Since he desperately needs the money the US president capitulates – effectively for China.

## 'Dominance is not a terrifying spectre'

It is an entertaining, provocative piece of fiction, but how realistic is it? Subramanian, whose words have trouble keeping up with his stream of thought, laughs. 'Of course it's fiction, but I don't rule it out. What I'm trying to say is that it is no longer in the hands of the US whether they can remain the biggest or not. It's naïve to think so. Even at conservative estimates the US's gross national income cannot keep ahead of China's.'

His conservative estimate puts Chinese growth at 7 per cent, substantially lower than the 10 per cent achieved during the past three decades, but on par with the current level. He puts US growth at an average of 2.5 per cent, which he describes as 'optimistic' in the light of the period 2006–11, when only 0.7 per cent growth was chalked up. So China will automatically draw level and head unchallenged towards a 'G1' over the next fifteen years. Its dominance will be reflected in the position of the Chinese currency, 'which in ten years' time will have knocked the dollar off its international perch', Subramanian happily continues his provocations.

But could China not meet with the same fate as Japan in the 1980s?, I interject. In those days everybody was convinced that this Asian competitor was destined to eclipse the US. Instead the Japanese property bubble burst and decades of stagnation followed. The parallels with China are all too evident. Both countries opted for an 'all for export' development strategy, based on cheap industrial labour and an artificially low currency. Are the increase in labour costs and the upward pressure on the renminbi not signs of the decline of the Chinese model? And does the 'property bubble', with its infinite number of empty offices and apartments, not constitute another parallel with Japan?

Subramanian thinks I am mistaken. 'What you are losing sight of and what plenty of forecasters at the time failed to see is that the Japanese economy had already peaked by the late eighties. The income level per capita had almost reached that of the average American. But the income of the Chinese is nowhere near that. With its gross national income per capita still four times lower than that of the US, China has a lot more room for growth than Japan at the time.'

He also believes the Chinese leaders have learnt from Japan's mistakes. At the time the Japanese government yielded to Western pressure by appreciating the yen and accepting 'voluntary export restrictions'. This happened under the notorious 'Plaza Accord' agreed with the US and Europe in 1985. In the eyes of the Chinese this marked the beginning of the end for Japanese growth. According to Subramanian, Chinese policy makers are keen to stress they are not up for such a hara-kiri.

But he acknowledges that the property bubble is a major problem. With houses and offices significantly overvalued, banks and other financiers have tens of billions' worth of bad loans on their books. But he believes these problems are not insurmountable. 'China will rise through trial and error. It is safe to predict that their financial system is in for a major shock within the next five years. The question is: can they pull through? With a powerful, efficient state such as China's there is every chance they can and I think that after the shock they will be able to return to their former level of growth.'

Subramanian is not alarmed by the spectre of dominance. If China does indeed become the 'G1', other nations will find it increasingly difficult to exert influence over the country. Besides, the Chinese will always put their own interests first. But Subramanian expects China, whose economy is more open than Japan's, to remain positive towards globalisation, given that it has been one of its greatest beneficiaries. The system of free trade, as historically conceived by Western nations, is not under threat – not so much because it has been laid down in the WTO statutes, but because China is reaping so many benefits. But that does not alter the fact that conflicts, like those about the rare earths, will continue to occur. In fact, given the prospect of a more powerful China, fewer resources and relatively low economic growth, they will probably be more frequent. The biggest challenge for other countries will be to keep China 'anchored' within multilateral alliances such as the WTO. Because, again according to Subramanian, no other nation will have sufficient bilateral power to stand up to China, not even the US.

## China 2030

Subramanian's analysis, delivered with plenty of verve and self-confidence, sounds quite persuasive and the clarity of his vision is appealing. But does he not underestimate the obstacles en route to Chinese dominance? Fond as he is of his econometric model, he tends to skim over all social and political peaks and troughs. Looking ahead up to 2030, he shows little sensitivity to the potential problems. Couldn't political upheavals and economic recessions during this lengthy period lead to less growth than the 7 per cent Subramanian predicts?

To measure China as an economic superpower let us first look at the figures. In 2014 the US economy was still considerably larger at 17 billion dollars compared with China's 10 billion. If the US is to grow 2 to 3 per cent and China 7 to 8 per cent, China will not become the biggest until halfway through the next decade. Nor is it likely that the twenty-eight EU member states, constituting the world's biggest economic zone in 2014 with a gross national product of over 18 billion dollars, will be overtaken by China in this decade.

A comparison based on purchasing power produces a different picture. It is fair to do so, because the real cost of living, known as purchasing power parity (PPP), is recognised as the best way to compare the size of economies. Since goods and services are relatively cheap in China, the country's economy becomes a lot 'bigger' using this measure. PPP calculations by the World Bank suggest that China became the world's number one economy in 2014. The report attracted quite a bit of attention ('World Bank shocker') and was coupled with a grand, historical sweep in various media: in 1872 the British lost their global lead to the Americans, but in 2014 the 318 million Americans with their joint purchasing power lost out to over 1,365 million Chinese people. This historical fact has come about much sooner than anyone thought possible, as an earlier purchasing power comparison suggested 2019.

Funnily enough the Chinese government was not at all pleased with the success. 'They hate it', an insider told the *Financial Times*. The Chinese state media ignored the milestone completely. At first glance this seems astonishing, because isn't the global number one position the goal that the party leadership secretly dreams of? Sure, but the World Bank figures were inconvenient for various reasons. To begin with, the leading position might result in increased responsibilities. When you are the biggest you have to bear the equivalent burden: regarding $CO_2$ emissions, for example. The leaders are not exactly keen on that. They still prefer to 'lay low' on the international stage, in accordance with Deng Xiaoping's old adage: 'Hide your brightness, bide your time'.

A second, equally important reason is the avoidance of loss of face. Claim to be number one now and you run the risk of sliding down to number two one day. And no political leader wants to lose face, especially not a Chinese president. One day China will proclaim itself the biggest economy in the world, but not before the time is really ripe. This might well be 2021, the centenary year of the CCP and near the end of Xi's tenure. Various China experts predict that the president wants to prove by then that the CCP has been able to lead China back to the top.

Even if Xi succeeds in proving in 2021 that China is indeed the biggest economy in terms of nominal GDP, it has to be noted that size says little about strength. The eighty-five-year-old economist and independent thinker Mao Yushi hit the nail on the head when he responded to the World Bank's PPP calculation by saying: 'It is not a surprise that China's economy is big, but this is just because its population is big. China is big, but not strong.'

Criteria such as innovative strength and the standard of living come into the picture when we want to determine the strength of an economy. I already outlined a number of reservations in connection with the former when I addressed China's bumpy road towards a knowledge economy. As for the standard of living, the usual criterion here is per capita income. According to the afore-mentioned World Bank calculations, China is placed no higher than 99th with 8,000 dollars, roughly on the same level as Peru. The average American is four times better off. The fundamental question in the coming years is whether China will manage to achieve progress in this area: can it manage to swap its middle-income status (defined by the World Bank as incomes of up to 12,000 dollars per annum) for the club of countries with high incomes, which includes most Western nations?

## The unpaid debt of China's growth

The step from 'low' to 'middle', which China has taken in the course of the past thirty years, is much easier than the one from 'middle' to 'high'. Of the more than one hundred countries which have tried the latter since 1960, only thirteen have succeeded. This low success rate has produced a general fear of what development economists refer to as 'the middle-income trap'. The Chinese leaders are all too aware that this poses a threat. To avoid it, structural reforms are necessary. Before I consider their content more closely it is important to have a look at the overall context in which they have to be implemented.

Viewed from the US or Europe, China's economic successes generally draw most attention, thus concealing the country's problems. Those who are aware of their scale will understand why the leaders are cautious about a model-based (Subramanian) or statistical (World Bank) top position. The country's international behaviour also makes more sense when we understand these problems. It is no wonder that China creates the impression of being internally focused – or, as an expert once put it to me succinctly, 'a dragon chasing its own tail'.

For the Chinese themselves, 'inequality' comes first on their list of troubles, more so than environmental pollution or corruption. In the past decade, more than 500 million people have been lifted out of poverty, which is a formidable achievement. No country in the world has done so much to combat poverty. Yet nearly a third of the population, roughly 400 million people, still live on less than two dollars a day; 13 per cent earn no more than 1.25 dollars a day, according to the United Nations Human Development Report of 2013. Out of 187 countries surveyed in this report, China ranked 101st in the overall index.

This level of poverty is particularly shocking now that the upper echelons of the urban elites, including the country's leaders and their networks, live in extreme luxury. The gap between these elites and simple factory and farm labourers is growing year on year. The Gini coefficient, a measure used by the World Bank for the disparity between rich and poor, is not only higher than that of the US, but even approaches that of notorious countries such as Brazil and Mexico. The to-be-expected result is more social tension.

Air and soil pollution is another downside of the sole focus on economic growth. The Chinese have first-hand experience of it: food quality is a source of fear and on bad days the air quality in the cities is many tens of times above the level deemed safe by the World Health Organisation (WHO). On several occasions both children and the elderly have been advised to stay indoors. Despite this well-meaning advice air pollution is causing great harm to health. According to an estimate in the Global Burden of Disease Study published by the WHO, 1.2 million Chinese died prematurely as a result of it in 2010. Life expectancy in the heavily polluted north of the country has even dropped by 5.5 years.

The price of progress is not only high in terms of human lives. It is also having a significant impact on economic growth.

In 2010 alone air and soil pollution cost 230 billion dollars, or 3.5 per cent of gross national product, the Chinese Academy of Environmental Planning, a government body, estimated in a study.

In the long run water shortages will probably constitute the most serious threat. By nature China has relatively little water; despite having a fifth of the world's population it has access to only 6 per cent of its fresh water resources. But the rise in prosperity has brought a sharp increase in water consumption: think of showering and bathing, not to forget the construction of golf courses, despite an official interdiction. Agriculture, with the cultivation of rice as its main focus, has traditionally been a water-intensive sector, but the industrial sector will also need more, especially when the extremely water-intensive process of shale gas extraction gets going.

If environmental costs are seen as the unpaid debt of the growth strategy, the ageing of the population is referred to as the unpaid debt of the one-child policy introduced in 1979. China initially benefited from this policy, simply because there were fewer mouths to feed. But more than thirty years on, the adverse effects are materialising in the shape of a diminishing workforce. In 2012 it shrank for the first time: by only three million to the still respectable figure of 937 million, but even so. According to UN estimates, by 2030 this number will have dropped by a further 67 million. The deteriorating ratio between active and inactive people raises the question: who is going to pay for the pensions and the extra healthcare when they are needed? In ten years' time nearly one in five citizens, a total of around 240 million, will be over sixty-five. Many of them carried out hard physical labour in the past, which is bound to give rise to a relatively high number of physical complaints. Their only children can hardly be expected to take care of both parents when they have their own children to look after. Meanwhile, the birth rate has spontaneously plummeted as a result of the growth in prosperity, so there are serious doubts whether the promised relaxation of the one-child policy will be in time. 'China is growing old before it is growing rich' is a frequently heard warning.

In order to settle all of these unpaid or yet-to-be-paid debts, high economic growth is indispensable. But it is not as easy to achieve as before. Higher labour costs are making China less attractive compared with other Asian countries. Most of the 'low-hanging fruit', in the form of higher labour productivity as a result of migration from the countryside to the cities, has been picked. These factors explain, in part, the drop in growth to 7 per cent, after decades of 10 per cent. The difference may seem comparatively small, but is actually quite significant. The country needs at least 6 to 7 per cent growth to create enough jobs to absorb migration to the cities. The Chinese leaders are looking at small margins.

So given this background, how can the country make the leap and start moving towards a 'modern, harmonious, and creative high-income society', as the leaders would like? The answer can be found in the World Bank report 'China 2030', published in 2012 in collaboration with a government think tank, the Development Research Centre (DRC). Through its Chinese partner the World Bank economists gained access to data from the horse's mouth. Interestingly, the DRC researchers took the lead in drawing up radical plans, in the hope that the report might serve as a lever in the fight against the vested interests: the state-owned enterprises, banks and lower levels of government that are thwarting reforms which they suspect may damage their interests.

'China 2030' can be read as a call to arms to the party leaders. If they do not enter the fray, China can forget about its transition to a high-income society. The state's role in the economy has to change and the private sector must be given more space. At present, it is getting a raw deal, with credit from state banks a particular problem area. The state banks prefer to give state-guaranteed loans at bottom rates to their friends at state-owned enterprises. The report may not actually use the word 'friends', but the description certainly implies it.

While allusions to corruption are avoided, the message is that the state-owned enterprises must be tackled. Excessive credit loans have created overcapacity in various sectors: there are too many factories, as well as an office and apartment bubble in the property sector. The answer should be more market forces, but local governments and state-owned enterprises tend to shudder at the thought.

The government too will have to bite the bullet: its central role in the economy will have to be reduced. The party leadership's total control over the banking sector, in particular, is no longer tenable. Banks ought to serve their customers, not the state. At present they are not really responding to what is happening on the market, which is detrimental to the dynamism of the economy. So here too the recipe ought to be: more market forces and independent monitoring. The latter, especially, is entirely at odds with the current system.

'China 2030' contains a whole raft of recommendations: the party leadership ought to properly tackle social inequality by expanding the social safety net; the system's shortcoming is slowing down consumer spending and with it people's standard of living; farmers need to be given greater legal certainty over their land, or at least adequate compensation in the event of dispossession. The list is much longer, but the gist is clear: fundamental reforms are unavoidable.

## 'More market' for China

In the ten years assigned to them, from 2002 to 2012, the previous generation of leaders proved incapable of implementing such reforms. The economic engine rattled on, but when they stepped down in 2012 it was widely concluded that their era had been a 'lost decade' in terms of reforms. The vested interests had been too strong, and the leaders too fearful that rocking the boat would undermine the economic success.

Initially it looked as if the World Bank report was destined to languish in a desk drawer, but President Xi is keen to make up for lost ground. After eighteen months the report was dusted off and various recommendations have now been included in Xi's reform agenda. The president has received a fair amount of praise for this – deservedly so in some respects, as he acknowledges the scale of the problems. A single quote, in dry Chinese government prose, should suffice to illustrate this: 'The lack of balance, coordination, and sustainability in development is still outstanding. The capability of scientific and technological innovation is not strong. The industrial structure is not reasonable and the development mode is still extensive. The development gap between urban and rural areas and between regions is still large, and so are income disparities. Social problems have increased markedly.'

Xi deserves praise for trying to provide a comprehensive response. He certainly shows more ambition than his predecessors. But unfortunately his response is still vague on many points. His intentions are not always clear and when they are, he appears to be similarly susceptible to the 'don't rock the boat' virus. Take the state-owned enterprises, those bulwarks of vested interests. Privatising or splitting them up is out of the question and their role is still described as 'fundamental' to the economy. That said, they will have some of their privileges curtailed. By 2020 they will have to hand over three times as much profit, up to 30 per cent, to finance the social system. It is a sign that things will get a little bit harder for big business. But Xi is not tackling their dominant position, despite adopting the World Bank's 'more market' credo. As a result, his drive to economic reform remains ambiguous. It certainly does not bode well that since the hype around the announcement of the reforms at the Third Plenum in November 2013, more than a year later not much has actually been done. It could still happen, of course. But with the vested interests by no means beaten, it promises to be a tough fight.

Threats to the economic reform agenda may also come from a different direction. I am thinking here of the crisis in the financial system that Subramanian anticipates in the coming years. Since 2008 there has been speculation about a Chinese version of the American property crisis. It is a distinct possibility given the scale of the debt burdens and the bubbles. Should it occur, I believe the authorities are perfectly able to cope. If the worst comes to the worst, the system is capable of defending itself – the credit crisis has shown us as much. But fighting these problems could take up the energy needed for structural reform. You can trust the leaders to combat an acute crisis, but the reform of the economic system itself, from investment and export-led to consumption- and innovation-driven, is another matter entirely.

Europe can only watch this internal fight from the sidelines, just as China was mainly an observer during the eurozone crisis. Nonetheless, the two worlds will be coming into ever greater contact. Europe will have to take due account of greater competition from China following its successful transition to a knowledge economy. Because the obstacles on that road are substantial I have reservations about the speed with which this transition will come about, but in terms of manpower, capital and work ethic China should be able to avoid the 'middle-income trap'. Yet it strikes me as unlikely that China will turn into the 'G1' Subramanian predicts. The sixteen years of 7 per cent growth on which his calculations are based seem to me too wildly optimistic for a country with that many internal problems and rising production costs. If growth proves to be structurally lower, for instance as a result of a drop in global demand for Chinese products, I foresee more outbreaks of social tension in response to the country's extreme social inequality. Economic chaos is a greater threat to the West than China's G1 position.

In addition, the unpredictability of international events makes me wary of this kind of long-term forecast. The traditional end-of-year analyses in December 2010 are all too vivid in my mind: not a single Middle East expert predicted revolutions in the Arab world. A month later they started happening. The fall of the Berlin Wall seemed to most observers unthinkable, yet it happened. China's future is especially hard to predict, because its internal processes of power are impenetrable, possibly also to Chinese in high offices. And while experts may be perfectly happy speculating away in response to questions about the future, their honest answer should be: 'No idea.'

Unlikely though Chinese supremacy in the global economy may be, China's influence is certain to increase. This, in itself, is no cause for panic in my view. It is only natural that under the influence of globalisation and technological developments the country will become more closely integrated in the global economy. Politically, this is an incentive for cooperation instead of confrontation. This has been borne out by events in recent years; despite the credit crisis and the subsequent economic downturn, Western and Chinese leaders have not gone down a confrontational route. Since 2008 there has been a slight increase in the number of trade restrictions, but overall global trade is not suffering from protectionism. This is admirable, because it means that the process of establishing closer ties can continue, which reduces the chances of conflict.

That said, the risks of regression and a resurgent nationalism, both in China and Europe, are never far off, especially when economic growth on both sides is less than robust.

Moreover, both China and Europe face fundamental and urgent reform challenges. For Europe, the question is 'more Europe' or not. For China, it is 'more market' or not. In both cases success depends not only on the strength of the leaders who happen to be in power, but also on the political system in which they operate.

**Part III**

Politics and Values

# Chapter 17

# A Soviet-Era Engine Block

*On Democracy and 'Socialism with Chinese Characteristics'*

Ask a random selection of Westerners whether they still see China as a communist country and the opinions will almost certainly differ widely. Since it yielded to a fairly rough-and-ready form of capitalism in the late 1970s, Western confusion about the country's system has been considerable. A still largely state-led economy, governed by the CCP which describes itself as a communist party but readily admits capitalism – it is confusing to say the least.

The only indisputable consensus in Western pubs and parlours is that China is not a democracy. Whether or not that ought to be deplored is up for debate. Some believe that 1.3 billion people simply cannot be governed democratically – prompting the entertaining counter-question whether 1.3 billion Americans would warrant the same view. Others praise the system for its perceived efficiency. 'It's incredible how fast they can get big projects off the ground' is a commonly heard argument. The Chinese capacity for long-term planning, symbolised by successive five-year plans, is often compared favourably with Western politicians' inability to transcend their breathless four-year election cycle. The grass is always greener on the other side.

The belief that democracy remains the superior – or certainly 'the least bad' – political system has not disappeared, but is subject to erosion. The period of recession and accompanying loss in purchasing power which started in 2008 and lasted five years planted doubts in the minds of many citizens. Many feel remote from the political process, especially the proceedings in Brussels.

Citizens in eurozone countries watched their leaders at a never-ending series of summits going down the road of 'more Europe' without being asked for consent via a referendum. Mindful of the trauma of 2005, when the people of both France and the Netherlands rejected a European constitution, national governments are fearful of such referendums. Moreover, they frequently depict 'Brussels' as the bogeyman, when European resolutions they have previously agreed to force them to take painful measures on a national level. The cuts needed to meet Europe's 3 per cent budget deficit target are the most striking example of this.

The ambivalent attitude of national politicians only increases people's lack of understanding, to the pleasure of the populist parties that have been on the rise across Europe this century. A bigger gap between voter and politician is grist to the mill of their key message that 'the political elite' is not fit for purpose. It undermines confidence in the democratic system.

## 'Not a single communist!'

The economic prosperity and political stability in China seem to present an immense contrast at first glance. While the European economies have been stagnating, the Chinese growth machine has been slowing down somewhat, but growth percentages of 7 per cent are still a source of envy in the West.

With results failing to materialise here but continuing over there, some are finding the old contradiction between a good democracy and a bad dictatorship less convincing than before. Various commentators even wonder whether state capitalism may be the future. Western businessmen, especially, have a tendency to extol the efficiency of the Chinese system of planning, talking of their good experiences with politicians. The latter tend not to refer to socialism, which prompted Rupert Murdoch to exclaim after talks with representatives of the CCP: 'I didn't meet a single communist!'

The appreciation of political systems changes with the economic climate. In the EU, after a slight economic recovery from 2013 onwards, democracies seem under less pressure than at the height of the eurozone crisis when countries such as Italy and Greece required technocratic governments to impose painful austerity measures – something elected politicians had been incapable of. Still, the contempt for the failings of the democratic process remain widespread.

Conversely, in China the slowdown to a growth path which is substantially lower than what the country had known for decades has led to more urgent calls for fundamental reforms. Yet the political system has shown a great inability to enact them. The most fundamental problems identified by the previous leaders when they took office in 2002 were the gap between rich and poor, the corruption of party members and environmental pollution. More than a decade later, those three issues are still at the top of the political agenda. In his farewell address President Hu Jintao highlighted them as the great challenges facing his successor. Many commentators have therefore described the era of the fourth generation of leaders as a 'lost decade'. The political system is a lot less effective than many in the West, looking at it from a distance, are inclined to think.

Alongside envy, mutual contempt between China and the West tends to rear its ugly head. Both political systems have a habit of criticising each other. Since the start of the credit crunch, the Chinese state media have been able to indulge in something they have always enjoyed doing: exaggerating the shortcomings of Western democracies. Conversely, Western politicians and opinion leaders cherish their belief that a democratic system is superior and therefore something worth aspiring to for China. Consciously or not, the country is always measured by democratic standards. The hope that sooner or later the political system will be heading in our direction is deep-rooted.

In the spring of 1989 it looked as if those hopes might finally come true, when student demonstrators occupied Tiananmen Square in Beijing and demanded democracy. Following a heated internal debate, hardliners within the party, led by Deng Xiaoping, decided to crush the student rebellion. The army opened fire on the students and their supporters, resulting in hundreds if not thousands of fatalities. There are no official figures and it is still forbidden to talk openly about events on that day.

In the twenty-five years that have elapsed since then, there has been no prospect of a Western-style democracy. In fact, the debate among intellectuals these days is no longer focused on this issue. Wen Jiabao, who represented a more liberal current within the CCP, liked to allude to the need for democracy, but he never actually specified whether he meant the Western 'one man, one vote' principle or just more democracy within the party. No leader is prepared to go further than the latter, thus upholding the one-party system.

Likewise, ordinary citizens steer clear of advocating Western-style democracy, since the CCP would view it as an attack on its very nature. When they do, the authorities bare their teeth, as Nobel Peace Prize winner Liu Xiaobo experienced. In 2008 the poet and literature teacher was one of the authors of *Charter 08*, which called for Western democracy and freedom of expression. Following a show trial, in which his lawyers had no more than fifteen minutes to argue his case, he was handed an eleven-year jail sentence.

## 'Democracy with Chinese characteristics'

How to make the case for democracy without landing in jail is shown by academic Yu Keping. As Professor of Politics at Peking University he caused a stir in the West with his essay 'Democracy Is a Good Thing'. It was particularly well-received in US academic circles. Yu follows the essay's appealing title with a clear, but rather cautious argument. He explains that his country has no choice but to become a democracy, but that it will be different from the West's understanding of that term.

He is enthusiastic about the concept, because it forces those in authority to take citizens into account. When elected, 'officials cannot simply do whatever they want' (read: be corrupt). A political democracy 'is the trend of history, and it is the inevitable trend for all nations of the world to move towards democracy'. His viewpoint is less remarkable than it seems – party officials have been known to adopt it.

But Yu is vague about the implementation. What is certain is that the road cannot be travelled too fast. Adopting a foreign system and imposing it on one's people is out of the question, because it amounts to 'national tyranny masquerading as democracy'. He stresses it will have to be the people's choice, thereby overlooking the fact that communism itself came from outside and was imposed from above.

How the population can express its choice is something Yu leaves open. He also warns other countries that they must not try to impose their 'so-called democratic system', because it would amount to 'international tyranny'. A Chinese democracy would have to reflect the country's own history, i.e. 'a socialist democracy with unique Chinese characteristics'. In fact, some believe China is already a democracy, because the president is formally elected by the National People's Congress. Except that its 2,987 representatives are not elected by the people, but screened by the CCP. Some 70 per cent of them are also party members. The nearly 600 members who do not belong to the party are the so-called 'technical experts' and the representatives of eight small parties. And although they are formally independent of the CCP, they are closely monitored as well. Both their choice of leader and their finances are subject to ratification by the CCP. This means there is no opposition in the Western sense of the word. Nor is there any need for it, Xi Jinping underlined during his tour of Europe in 2014. In a speech in Bruges he gave short shrift to Western democracy. 'It would not fit us and it might even lead to catastrophic consequences', he said.

In Western public opinion, his country is politically about as grey as the former Soviet Union, with only a handful of political dissidents injecting a note of colour. We are inclined to see authoritarian China as a monolithic block without any political movements. The lack of transparency on the part of the Chinese does little to remedy this misconception. The CCP likes to maintain this image to prevent 'enemies' taking advantage of its disunity. But the Westerner who meets the policy makers on their own terms will find more variation than he ever thought possible.

This was the experience of the Brit Mark Leonard, who published the book *What Does China Think?* in 2008. As the director of the pan-European think tank ECFR he makes a brave attempt at answering this impossible question. He became fascinated by China because 'for the first time since the end of the Cold War, a non-Western power is in the global premier league: China has joined the United States and Europe as a shaper of world order'. Leonard decided to take the country seriously as 'a powerhouse of ideas' and carried out some 200 interviews with leading minds at universities and think tanks between 2006 and 2008. These 'insiders', as he calls them, 'have chosen to live in mainland China [...] in their quest to push for change within the system'.

Some got into trouble with the CCP during the course of his project, while others still have the ear of the ruling elite. While political movements may have no formal organisation, that is not to say they do not exist, he concludes. Their debates take place behind the scenes. The party may be trying to convince its people and the rest of the world that it is an impregnable bulwark, populated by interchangeable leaders wearing the same suits and dyed black hair, but the reality is more varied.

Leonard identifies two main movements, the 'New Right' and the 'New Left', whose views are at opposite ends of the spectrum. The first movement, inspired by American ideas, has quite a few economists among its ranks. They had the momentum in the 1990s. Their plea for a more market-driven economy led to, among other things, large-scale redundancies at inefficient state-owned enterprises, which cost tens of millions of workers their jobs.

In the past decade, the 'New Left' supporters have been making headway. They advocate more social security, greater environmental awareness and more democracy, at least within the CCP. Their movement left a great mark on the eleventh five-year plan (2006–10), which was full of allusions to 'common prosperity' and a 'sustainable economy'. That is not to say that the 'New Right' is finished, as evidenced by the enthusiasm for a smaller role for the state in the economy – something championed by government think tank DRC in 2012.

A comparison with left and right in Europe may be tempting, but is tenuous in my view. The more modest state role envisaged by some 'New Right' adherents can also be dubbed 'leftist' in the Chinese context, since it jeopardises various vested interests in both industry and politics. If a 'New Right' disciple were to add a plea for a constitutional state with truly independent judges, he would be facing an even more antagonistic establishment. On the other hand, the 'New Left' movement envisages such a strong role for the state that it is justified to ask if anything would really change if its adherents were to have their way.

## A fall from grace

If it is to maintain its supreme position, the CCP is probably best served by the ideas of the leftist movement. That would explain why its representatives have managed to gain influence in recent years. The movement grew noticeably stronger in 2011, when the party secretary of Chongqing, Bo Xilai, achieved great success with his 'red campaign'. In China's harsh society, in which social security is deficient, Bo cleverly tapped into people's need to belong to a larger collective. He attracted attention with the singing of traditional 'red songs' and with 'red commercials' on local television. Besides this renaissance of the old, communist culture, the basic elements of his 'Chongqing model' were large-scale social housing and better welfare for migrant workers, attracting foreign investors and a tough campaign against corruption and crime. In 2011 policy makers were drawn into a serious debate about whether Bo's model could be a recipe for the rest of the country. In response, another political movement emerged: the champions of the 'Guangdong model', named after the southern province where one of Bo's greatest rivals was in charge. This model is more in line with the 'New Right' and sounds a lot more appealing to Westerners as it calls for improvement of the rule of law, more balanced economic growth, transparency of public expenditure and more space for civil society in the form of unions and non-governmental organisations. It must be noted, however, that this civil society is not seen as independent from the CCP.

In 2012 the ambitious Bo fell from grace with the ruling elite, and he was sentenced to life imprisonment for corruption and abuse of power. This also marked the end of the debate about the Chongqing model, a term nobody dares to use any more. Likewise, little has since been heard of the Guangdong model.

The Bo case teaches us a lot about Chinese politics, which is, as Leonard suggests, more about the exercise of power than about ideas. In his enthusiasm about the diversity of political ideas he encountered Leonard significantly overestimates the scale of the political changes, in my view. In fact, he even concludes that in the past thirty years Chinese politics 'has changed almost as much as the economy – just not in a direction the West is comfortable with'. He agrees with the 'New Left' thinker Wang Shaoguang, Professor of Political Economy in Hong Kong, whom he quotes as saying that 'the analytical framework of authoritarianism from the West is completely unable to capture these deep changes in politics'.

Today's political system is supposed to have changed beyond recognition compared to the 'strong men' era, when leaders such as Mao and Deng Xiaoping took their decisions alone. These days, a five-year plan is drawn up after extensive consultations, while scholars travel the world to arrive at the best possible policy options. Leonard concurs with this line of reasoning, arguing that those he spoke to have more influence on Chinese policy than their counterparts in many Western countries: 'Paradoxically, the power of the Chinese intellectual is amplified by China's repressive political system.' In the absence of other dissenting views, from the media or the unions for instance, intellectuals are frequently consulted by the CCP leadership. 'The intellectual as king', he describes their role.

## Return to the 'strong men' era?

Of course Leonard is right in saying that the variety of opinions he was able to record would have been unthinkable in Mao's time. It points to an increase in freedom for policy makers and academics, which in itself is significant progress. But ultimately what matters is what happens to those ideas. For the CCP any proposal is negotiable, as long as it helps the party stay in power. Any changes in the exercise of power have been far less profound than Leonard would have us believe. In fact, since Xi Jinping came to power, one might wonder whether we are witnessing a return to the 'strong men' era. The extensive powers of Xi, who is the subject of the next chapter, have already been compared to Deng's and even Mao's, which in my view is an exaggeration.

Historians specialising in Chinese history, those who study broader trends than the one charted by Leonard, point to similarities between the emperors of yesteryear and today's party leadership. The country is governed from the centre of power in Beijing, backed by a massive bureaucracy. Every now and then, party officials who have gone too far in the eyes of their subjects are sacrificed. The people are supposed to harbour the illusion that central government only wants the best for them, but that lower-ranked administrators have a tendency to thwart the good intentions of those at the top. It is an illusion the erstwhile emperors liked to maintain as well. According to these historians, this way of exercising power is not so much communist as Chinese.

Another form of historical continuity to substantiate the view that little has changed is provided by political scientists. Despite the Western accessories such as think tanks and focus groups, the bonnet still hides a Soviet-era engine block, equipped with a Politburo, a Central Committee and a propaganda division called the 'Information Department of the Central Committee'. All these attributes were used by Stalin in the mid-twentieth century. The continued use of this Soviet legacy proves that the foundations of the system have not been eroded.

Equally, in its rituals the CCP continues to cling to the old Soviet style, as I experienced during the party conference in 2012. The event, held once every five years, takes place in the Great Hall of the People, a gigantic building bordering Tiananmen Square. The 200-strong Central Committee is seated in long rows on the stage of the Great Auditorium, against a backdrop of a yellow hammer and sickle, also gigantic, while a red star shines majestically at a height of 50 metres. A moment later, the twenty-five-member Politburo, complemented with a few prominent party elders, sits down right in front of them, in an even longer row. Facing them is an audience of 2,200 delegates from around the country, ensuring a rapturous applause as and when the speaker wants it.

Communist ideology continues to play a role at these meetings. While businessmen and politicians tend not to mention it in contact with their Western counterparts, within their own ranks they continue to pay lip service to what is called 'socialism with Chinese characteristics'. Outgoing President Hu Jintao secured his place in the history books by elevating his theory of 'The Scientific Outlook on Development' to the level of CCP dogma. It goes without saying that the delegates accepted it. The party conference ritual, which strikes Westerners as dated, illustrates just how much the party values its traditions – and its inability to effect change. The big question is whether the new fifth generation led by Xi will prove to be different in the years to come.

# Chapter 18

# Xi Jinping

*Tough Manoeuvres at the Top of the Party*

Xi Jinping looks a bit tired when we shake hands, but he does not come across as unfriendly. His response to my English greeting is a firm Chinese *ni hao*. When I direct those words to his wife on his left, Peng Liyuan responds in English with 'How do you do?' Her charm is in the same league as that of Queen Maxima of the Netherlands who is standing next to her.

This hand-shaking ceremony, in which I am allowed to participate, precedes the state banquet the Dutch royal family is hosting for the president and his wife at the Royal Palace on Dam Square in Amsterdam. A moment later, the party saunters over to the dining tables. As soon as an opportunity for more informal conversations with Xi presents itself, it becomes clear what power can do. A Dutch captain of industry tells him eagerly that his company has just welcomed a big credit line by a Chinese bank. Xi expresses the hope that relations will continue to intensify. 'What a kind man', the CEO beams like a kid on Christmas morning. 'It's great. Even someone in his position is only human in the end, like you and me.' A China expert is equally impressed after a brief chat. 'Really friendly. Absolutely not the kind of party hard-liner I've encountered before.'

The admiration and respect for Xi remind me of the occasions when, as a correspondent in France, I saw how awed people were in the presence of the French president. One can only guess what that does to the individual who holds such power. No doubt Xi sees it as something perfectly normal. After all, he is a princeling, a member of one of the great families who fought on Mao's side. His father, Xi Zhongxun, was a member of the Politburo.

The members of the 'red nobility', as the families are sometimes referred to, sincerely believe that China ought to be ruled by them.

If Xi Jinping stirs such emotion in us, one can guess the effect he has on his compatriots. There are no opinion polls, but we do know he is far more popular than his reserved predecessor Hu Jintao. His more natural style and his ability as one of only very few leaders to occasionally speak without notes betrays his ease in handling power.

Like Western politicians, he goes on the occasional walkabout among the people. Of course, these are carefully choreographed, but that does not make them any less effective. On a day with severe smog he visited a working-class neighbourhood to show that he breathes the same air as any city dweller. On another occasion he ordered fried dumplings in a modest eatery for less than three euros. It made an impact: the place became a tourist destination, with people queuing to eat the same dish as 'Xi Dada', or 'Uncle Xi'.

When he took office in 2012 he was largely unknown, I discovered when doing street interviews, and primarily known as 'the husband of'. His wife Peng Liyuan is a national celebrity, as a singer with the People's Liberation Army and performing on state television. Xi now appears daily on the news and in the papers, and has certainly surpassed her in the fame stakes. And there is no doubt that he is endearing himself with his key programme issue: tackling corruption.

The people's sympathy for this fight stands out against the great fear it arouses among the eighty million party members, which makes the CCP by far the world's largest political organisation. Corruption among its rank and file is widespread; one would be hard-pressed to find a party official who has not been tainted in some way. As a result, millions of Chinese have something to fear from Xi's campaign, which is meant to catch both 'flies' and 'tigers'. With these words Xi deliberately draws on Mao's vocabulary to warn both the lower and upper echelons that with his campaign nothing less than 'the survival' of the CCP is at stake.

The party members are acutely aware of the risks they run. Those who fall in China fall hard. Party exile, imprisonment, confiscation of assets – one bad day it could all happen. It could spell the end not just for the party member himself, but also for his family members, friends, mistresses and business networks. The fear of losing it all is deep-rooted, not least because it happened to the ruling classes in 1949 when the CCP came to power. A process of large-scale nationalisation was initiated at the expense of all owners of private property. The fear of new losses has led to the fascinating phenomenon of the 'naked officials' whose number is estimated to run into tens of thousands. These are party members who have lined their pockets with bribes and, as a precaution, have brought their relatives and possessions to safety. The entire family has obtained a residence permit in, say, Canada, where the wife and children settle into a luxurious villa, while the husband carries on working in China. If the worst comes to the worst, the official with dual nationality can always board a plane. As a countermeasure, some officials are ordered to hand their passport to their superior for safekeeping. It is a telling sign that in a country where political stability is seen as paramount, so many of the elite have so little faith in the system.

To them and all other Chinese, it is vital to know what Xi has in mind for the country. Nobody can see inside his head, but we can infer a fair amount from his words and actions, bearing in mind of course that we have insufficient insight into the machinations at the top. 'Anyone claiming to know what happens in the party's top twenty-five is either deluded or part of that club', says Frank Pieke, former lecturer at Oxford University and now Professor of Modern China Studies at Leiden University. Having spent his life studying the CCP, he qualifies the predicament as follows: 'We're always drawing on indirect evidence to work out what happens in the upper echelons – it's like trying to solve a murder without the murder weapon.'

What we do know is that since he came into office Xi has spectacularly wrong-footed many China experts, both at home and abroad. At the time, it was widely predicted that Xi would be a president in the line of Hu Jintao, i.e. pragmatic and averse to drastic changes, an approach linked to his experiences during the Cultural Revolution.

After his father fell out of favour with Mao in 1968, the young Xi was forced to spend several difficult years in the Northern

Chinese countryside. From the age of fifteen to twenty-two the young man destined for a top-flight career literally lived in a cave, a BBC reporter discovered in Yanchuan County. He spent years transporting manure and coal. Those hardships are thought to have turned Xi and other fifth-generation leaders into pragmatists who espouse the motto 'don't rock the boat'. A historian, Zhang Lifan, whose father was friends with Xi's father, told the *China Digital Times* when Xi took office that the president 'had suffered a lot in his childhood', so once in power he was likely to adopt a cautious approach. Besides, the experts agreed, it would take him years to consolidate his position.

## Xi's concentration of power

Instead, Xi is now referred to as 'the most powerful Chinese leader since Deng Xiaoping' because of the speed with which he seems to have taken control. This might very well be an exaggeration – we just don't know, as Pieke rightly underlined. What is certain is that Xi is not only fulfilling the dual role of party leader and president, but that he also immediately became chairman of the powerful Central Military Commission. His predecessor only managed this after two years. Moreover, Xi expanded his powers by taking on the chairmanship of several committees and 'small, leading groups'. Economic reform, security and internet policy are all areas on which he has the final say. He is in charge of both the newly created National Security Council, based on the American model, and the 'leading group' responsible for overseeing all reforms. Xi has a hand in everything.

Does this signify a break with the 'collective leadership' model, established in response to Mao's regime, which spun completely out of control in its final years? The aim of this model was to stop a single ruler from seizing supreme power, but in practice it had a paralysing effect. The 'lost decade' between 2002 and 2012 had its roots in this model. Xi appears to have drawn the conclusion that he is better off concentrating power in his own hands. It makes his friendship with Russian autocrat Vladimir Putin all the more telling.

It is premature to proclaim Xi as 'China's Putin', even though it could well come to that. For now, it remains unclear how much influence the six other members of the standing committee still have. Four of them are known to be extremely conservative and are thought to have been chosen in reaction to the turmoil of the Bo Xilai affair. What is clear as well is that Prime Minister Li, who is considered to be a reformist, has ended up in a more subordinate position than his predecessor Wen. Even the economic reforms, which are Li's remit, are signed off by Xi.

Despite the self-confidence Xi exudes and the smile with which he greets both heads of state and Chinese citizens, he is also watching his back. The battle at the top is ruthless. Relationships of trust, which can be traced back to loyalties forged a long time ago, are crucial for survival. A cocktail of family background, geographical origins and career path determines the faction to which one belongs: princeling or not, background in the Communist Youth League or otherwise, Shanghai or Beijing, reformist or conservative. Having said that, the word 'faction' suggests that the CCP is made up of co-existing movements, which is not the case according to party expert Pieke. 'In order to create order out of chaos we are inclined to categorise. But there is no "princeling" faction. A shared background is no basis for collaboration. There are networks whereby one official receives patronage from another. They are "one good turn deserves another" relationships, but these networks are more flexible than we imagine', he asserts.

The Bo Xilai affair of 2012 provided a good glimpse behind the scenes of power. The top politician had gone so far as to order fellow politicians, all the way up to the president, to be tapped, the *New York Times* revealed shortly after his downfall. Bo's suspicion formed the rule rather than the exception, if Australian *Financial Times* journalist Richard McGregor is to be believed. In 2010 he published *The Party*, a fascinating book about 'the secret world of China's communist rulers'. He is convinced that all Chinese leaders 'bug each other', he told US broadcaster PBS in response to Bo's downfall. 'They all keep files of dirt on each other. And it is just at different tipping points that they become valuable and are used. It certainly shows that this is how they play the game internally. It is very tough.' In other words, there is a fundamental distrust at the top. As an expert put it succinctly to me: 'However powerful you are, the fear of a knife in your back is unrelenting at that level.'

As well as political interests, the leading politicians have great personal financial interests. Insight into family fortunes has increased since the Bo Xilai affair. After his downfall the media reported that his family had amassed a fortune of 136 million dollars. The leaders who remain in place are no doubt anxious about additional revelations. They confirm the dark suspicion among the Chinese people that their leaders are first and foremost looking after themselves. These reports of self-enrichment undermine their authority and that of the CCP.

What made it all the more painful for the party leadership was that it did not stop with the revelations about Bo. The official story was that he was the only rotten apple in the basket. In reality, says Pieke, 'there are no good, fruity apples in that basket. There never have been. Bo did what everybody does: enriching yourself and boosting your job prospects. Those two can go hand in hand. In the West we have trouble accepting this, because we think of ourselves as morally superior. As if there's no corruption here.'

The next revelation concerned outgoing Prime Minister Wen Jiabao. Helped by his modest background, he had established a reputation as a 'man of the people', but the *New York Times* ran a story in 2012 concluding that his family fortune amounted to no less than 2.7 billion dollars. Compared to this figure Bo's wealth paled into insignificance. Soon after, news agency Bloomberg had the nerve to investigate investments made by Xi and his family. Consulting public sources, reporters identified investments worth many tens of millions of dollars in a wide range of businesses. No evidence of corruption by Xi was found. In his defence officials cited a secret cable from the US embassy in Beijing from 2009, leaked by WikiLeaks, which described Xi as a man 'repulsed by the all-encompassing commercialization of Chinese society, with its attendant nouveau riche, official corruption, loss of values, dignity, and self-respect'.

This moral repulsion ties in with his anti-corruption campaign. But it is simply impossible to eradicate the phenomenon.

Corruption is too closely linked with the political system, which is characterised by a complete lack of external monitoring of the CCP. Power is exercised by officials who hold both a position within the party and a public office – Xi as party leader *and* president is the highest-ranking example of this, with the former function considered to be the more important one within China.

Alongside the absence of external controls, low salaries foster politicians' susceptibility to corruption. Xi's salary has not been made public, but is said to be no more than 19,000 dollars per annum. It goes without saying that officials cannot earn more than their president. Yet they are expected to make decisions involving billions, for instance when granting tenders for building projects, as the market for public contracts is worth more than 1,000 billion dollars annually. A clear case of trusting the cat to guard the cream.

Similarly, CCP officials allocate the most important jobs in the country. The party controls the appointment of all the top executives of state-owned enterprises, all judges and all editors-in-chief, to name but a few. Without transparent procedures, such appointments are also prone to corruption. Besides, taking bribes is deeply embedded in Chinese culture; it was quite common back in imperial times. A single individual with good intentions cannot break this pattern. A telling example is cited by Richard McGregor, when he mentions a local official who was dispatched to a small town near the border with Russia. The man saw no other choice but to accept the gifts which were literally left on his doorstep: 'Otherwise people would think I didn't trust them.'

One indication that Xi is not really interested in fully eradicating corruption is his dislike of the people's initiative New Citizens' Movement. Since 2010 these activists have been campaigning for greater transparency of party officials' assets. This is an important first step en route to a systematic fight against corruption. But several citizens behind the initiative have been arrested and their leader Xu Zhiyong has even been sentenced to four years in prison for an alleged 'public order offence'.

For Xi, the real gains of the anti-corruption campaign can be found on a political level. It gives him a tried and tested tool for eliminating political opponents. It allows him to formulate allegations against anyone. So far he has shown himself more than willing to do so. Among the victims of his first few years in office are high-flying businessmen, especially from the oil industry, high-ranking military men, including some generals, and direct political opponents.

## No political reforms under Xi

The most prominent victim in the latter category is Bo Xilai's long-term political patron, 'security tsar' Zhou Yongkang, who resigned in 2012. It is the first time since the Cultural Revolution that a former member of the standing committee, the supreme party organ, has come under official scrutiny. He is investigated for 'serious disciplinary violation', which is party language for corruption. As chief of intelligence and police, Zhou was used to having all those deemed 'hostile to the state' locked up. Ironically this has now happened to his own network. As of this writing, hundreds of arrests are thought to have been made and 14 billion dollars' worth of assets confiscated.

Two former presidents, Jiang Zemin and Hu Jintao, have reportedly issued a warning to their successor: the anti-corruption campaign must not go too far. Ordinary members may lose faith in the party, Jiang is supposed to have said to Xi. He has a valid point: if the campaign is taken too far it will undermine the authority on which the system rests, the 'every good turn deserves another' relationships between the great families. As a consequence it will ultimately threaten the CCP itself. Bearing this in mind, Xi will want to draw a line somewhere. As Chen Yun, a former party elder, is said to have stated: 'Fight corruption too little and destroy the country; fight it too much and destroy the party.'

What are Xi's plans for China until the end of his tenure in 2022? Much has been made of the 'Chinese Dream' which he has held up to his citizens since taking office. What that dream entails is rather vague, which is both its strength and weakness; everybody can project onto it what they like. Unlike the 'American Dream', it is certainly not about self-realisation, but about a collective effort. It is meant to lead to 'a prosperous and strong country, the rejuvenation of the nation and the well-being of the people'. Jokes and different interpretations on the internet are inexorably censored and removed.

Xi's plans for reform, announced in 2013 following the party's so-called Third Plenum, are more concrete. The programme boasts land reforms, allowing hundreds of millions of farmers to sell land so they can benefit more from increasing prosperity; changes to the *hukou* system, which currently treats farmers who have migrated to the cities like second-rate citizens; and above all it encompasses more space for the free market.

The overbearing role of the state will have to be cut back, in line with the World Bank's 'China 2030' report. Whether Xi will actually manage to implement this and thereby distinguish himself from his predecessors remains to be seen. One year after the Third Plenum the progress is very slow, suggesting political resistance. But the concentration of power in his hands and his tough fight against corruption still make it considerably more likely that he will be able to push through his economic reforms in the years to come.

It is clear that Xi will not be venturing into political reform. If there is any change on a political level, it will be in the direction of strengthening the party's role even further. The CCP is meant to govern the state, but there are no signs of a greater distance between the two entities, despite hopes of certain Western experts when Xi came into office. As party leader, he retains the model in which the separation of the powers of state is no more than a façade. In reality all executive, legislative and judiciary powers are controlled by the CCP; Xi has stated that these powers are meant to work together, thus countering the Western concept of their separation, guaranteeing checks and balances.

As the founder of the People's Republic of China, the CCP has a right to govern the state – on behalf of the people, of course. It explains why, in Xi's view, as president *and* party leader, state and party cannot be separated. Both entities are intimately inter-twined, with the party coming out on top. Tellingly, the armed forces do not fall under the Ministry of Defence but directly under the CCP.

Under Xi there are signals that there is a stronger emphasis on ideology and slogans, although it is yet unclear whether this is more than a superficial change. One can see it in the revival of the old instruments of 'self-criticism' and 'study sessions' for party members. In the former, used extensively in the Mao era, party officials have to point out their own failures. In the latter, ambitious young people swallow old Marxist slogans. Even when they do not subscribe to the ideology, they realise that membership of the party is absolutely indispensable for getting ahead. Xi can rest assured that the ageing of the population which is threatening society at large will not be a problem for the CCP, as ambitious youngsters flock in.

The greater role for the party reflects Xi's distrust of 'civil society', which is difficult to keep in check and therefore suspicious. The members of the New Citizens' Movement and other civil rights activists as well as bloggers and journalists have had first-hand experience of this, coming up against more stringent legislation on 'the spread of false rumours'. The repression has increased, civil rights lawyer Teng Biao told me: 'Before you could be a human rights activist as long as you did not cross a red line. Nowadays they attack you also when you are not crossing a red line.'

The democracy movement in Hong Kong, which figured prominently in world news in the autumn of 2014, has also experienced Xi's unwillingness to make any concessions to civil society initiatives. The principle of 'one country, two systems', which had been agreed when Britain transferred its sovereignty over Hong Kong to China in 1997, does not make him any milder.

Xi's emphasis on the revitalisation and purging of the CCP is closely linked to his determination to avoid the disaster that befell his sister party in the Soviet Union: the disintegration of both party and state. Not surprisingly, he and his friend Putin have expressed a great dislike of Mikhail Gorbachev, a man widely praised in the West. When a seventy-year-old Xi leaves office in 2022, the CCP will just have celebrated its centenary in the preceding year. His primary and overriding goal is that it will be just as firmly in control then as it is now.

# Chapter 19

# 'They Are Human Beings, Just Like Us'

## On the Importance of 'Chinese Values'

We were getting on really well, Robert Wang and I. In the spring of 2008 he guided me around Shanghai and surroundings, where he worked for a Western multinational. He told me quite candidly about his struggles to maintain a work/life balance and his hopes for his young child. As members of the same generation, we could really relate to one another. He had spent a couple of years studying in the Netherlands, which must have boosted our mutual understanding. But I was surprised by how much the two of us, a European and a Chinese man living nearly 9,000 kilometres apart, had in common.

Still, our cultures also clashed. One morning we were walking to a Buddhist temple, as he was keen to show me that his country had more to offer than just an economy. But we were unsure about the route, so he approached a passer-by. He did this so bluntly, without any word of introduction or thanks, that I challenged him. Staring back at me was the Chinese fear of loss of face. He apologised. 'It's the Cultural Revolution. We lost our sense of manners back then.'

A second clash occurred a couple of days later, as we were watching fierce riots in Tibet on state television. Whereas my sympathy lay with the rebels fighting against occupying forces, Robert got all wound up about them. His compatriots were being attacked, even though China was doing so much for Tibet, he exclaimed. Like our political leaders, we failed to reach agreement.

So what is it that defines our relationship: our mutual understanding or those clashes? In other words: how important are cultural differences? I identified two schools of thought among the experts I quizzed on the subject. A traditional school stresses the unique nature of Chinese culture and the national character. The Chinese may be living in the house of mankind as well, but they occupy an entirely separate wing. For thousands of years, their civilisation developed independently of that of the rest of the world. The resulting separation remains palpable to this day. Partly because of this long history, the Chinese feel culturally superior and are very attached to their identity. 'They think very differently from us' was a recurring statement.

The other school stresses similarities. Just look at the huge influence of Western culture to which the Chinese have opened up in the past century, so the reasoning goes. Take individualism and consumerism, with all their advantages and disadvantages, which are booming as they are over here. Or take Mao, the founder of the modern state, who embraced Western Marxism to combat age-old Confucianism.

To my mind the first school often gets the wind in its sails by reports implying that a human life counts for less in China than it does in the West. Take for instance the enthusiasm among bloggers when a patient killed his doctor. 'Serves him right' was their delighted response, as corruption and malpractice among physicians has reached alarming levels. Or take the fate of Wang Yue, a two-year-old girl hit by a car, not once but twice in 2011. Security camera images showed that as she lay in the street, crying and bleeding, eighteen people passed by without offering assistance. A week later she died.

But you can look at this case in a different light. Many Chinese people were truly shocked by the fate of this little girl. The students I spoke to in London were perplexed. Their reaction was no different from that of Europeans after the extremist Anders Breivik shot dozens of young Norwegians. More than four million Chinese people, spouting their indignation about Wang Yue's death via Weibo, were of the same mind. A 'stop the apathy' campaign was launched. The party secretary in Guangdong, the province where the incident took place, described what happened to the girl as a 'wake-up call for everybody'. An opinion poll commissioned by the *China Daily* showed that a majority of those surveyed believe that 'our moral values have declined in the past decade'.

## 'No such thing as Chinese values'

This collective need for reflection on values is just as interesting as the incident itself. It argues the case for the second school, which is inclined to take a more nuanced view of cultural differences. It recognises social dynamics, which is always useful when looking at ever-changing China. In the past half-century, stretching from Mao to raw capitalism, Chinese society has lived through such extremes that values are bound to be affected. My friend's sense of a loss of etiquette confirms this, as does the survey about plummeting moral values.

Someone who represents this second, more nuanced school is Tilman Spengler, a German sinologist and author I spoke to in Berlin. He is as eloquent as he is provocative: 'There's no such thing as Chinese values. These past sixty years society has been busy trying to destroy them. What is or might be Chinese is something that can be redefined over and over again.'

In 2011 the sexagenarian made the news in Germany when the Chinese authorities refused him access to their country. In his capacity as advisor to his government, he was due to travel to Beijing for the opening of an exhibition. However, the authorities claimed he had 'hurt the feelings of the Chinese people' with his eulogy to dissident Liu Xiaobo. When I spoke to Spengler a year after the incident, it did not seem to bother him in the slightest. The large man with the wild curly hair, lopsided spectacles and heavily creased face preferred to talk about China's values and its similarities with the West. 'We have a strong tendency to make them stranger than they really are. I always like to quote the Italian missionary Matteo Ricci, who wrote in the early seventeenth century: "They are human beings, just like us." Of course there's a difference between Berlin and Beijing, and even more so between Beijing and the countryside. But you would be hard-pressed to spin this into a theory.'

Halfway through the 1990s, 'Asian values' such as hard work and obedience were in fashion, Spengler recalls. The prime minister of Singapore, Lee Kuan Yew, was particularly enamoured and used them to explain the success of Asian economies. 'Then the Asian crisis erupted and obedience was singled out as one of the main culprits. The whole concept of Asian values sank without a trace.' Spengler believes that values are far more universal than many people think. The fear of loss of face, a frequently cited characteristic, may be considerable, but surely Westerners aren't exactly itching to feel embarrassed either. This qualification is germane to other so-called 'Chinese values' too.

Take *guanxi*, for example – the way of doing business which is so closely tied up with personal connections. It certainly has a specifically Chinese dimension, but the difference with our business dealings is one of degrees. Don't we draw on our networks? Or take the idea that the Chinese have a more highly developed sense of the collective. Then how can one explain the huge number of corruption cases, all examples of officials putting their own pockets before the public interest? And while family has traditionally played a relatively important role, it does not stop the process of individualisation. This is borne out by the sharp rise in the divorce rate and the problem of spoilt members of the one-child generation who were born after 1979 and who grew up in relative prosperity.

In short, how important are traditional values to understand China? Spengler's quip – 'there's no such thing as Chinese values' – may be an exaggeration, but it is certainly worth pondering. 'Overall, I believe we have plenty in common. When I'm drinking tea with my Chinese friends, there is a lot of shared territory. We all know how to tell a story, for instance. Of course there are differences. A person is likely to be more cautious when he has been beaten up by police after exercising his freedom of expression. But I prefer to stress our similarities, and these are only intensifying thanks to globalisation. If there is a new religion it has to be consumerism. People act as if consumer goods like the iPhone or iPad might offer redemption. It shows how empty their minds are after decades of being cleansed of Confucian, Buddhist, Taoist and Maoist beliefs.'

The government is aware of this emptiness and keen to address it. Shared values can contribute to stability and help the party. Now that Marxist ideology has been largely hollowed out by the adoption of capitalism, a new narrative is needed to explain to the people why this party, more than any other, deserves to be in power. Economic growth provides only a slender basis. The Chinese leaders see the ancient system of Confucianism as a possible solution.

## Crowded churches

For a party that still describes itself as communist, this requires the necessary intellectual flexibility. The key Marxist concept of the class struggle is at odds with the Confucian 'harmony' between the social strata. Likewise, the subordinate role which the philosopher envisaged for women has no place in modern China, where women have acquired far more equality since the time of Mao. That side of Confucianism tends to be obfuscated. Instead, the spotlight is trained on the concept of harmony, which is as beautiful as it is vague. It is applied widely – from ties between countries to the relationship between a farmer and his local official. Harmony demands that the former respects his superior, who in turn is expected to look after the best interests of the farmer.

So much for the theory. Spengler, who describes himself as a 'German liberal', has little but scorn for the Chinese leaders' efforts. 'So the party that did what it could to eradicate Confucianism root and branch from 1949 onwards is now trying to rebuild it because it happens to suit its needs. It beggars belief.' When I put the concept of harmony to Chinese students in London, one of them said sarcastically: 'In the eyes of our government, harmony means toeing the party line.'

Zhou Yongming, a cultural anthropologist researching the values of the Chinese community in the Italian town of Prato, rates the importance of Confucian values more highly. The professor at the University of Wisconsin believes that Confucianism remains at the heart of China's identity. He points to parents who are prepared to sacrifice everything for their children's education:

'Schooling is a core value of Confucianism.' He also believes that people's preference for harmony is deep-rooted, and that includes their relationship to the government. That said, the latter must abide by its duty to act in the best interest of its citizens.

Zhou agrees with Spengler that the Western lifestyle is a major influence, although he is less than impressed with this. 'I sometimes tell my American friends that the Chinese are becoming Americanised. They always laugh, but I'm serious: they are becoming more and more materialistic. It's a real problem.' But besides the 'new religion of consumerism', as Spengler puts it, Zhou also identifies what he sees as a positive development: a greater susceptibility to Western ideas 'such as individual freedoms and democracy'. They are at odds with Confucianism with its emphasis on obedience to the state.

Interest in Western religions is growing sharply too, which is not a source of joy for the party either, as it prefers to see the moral vacuum filled by Confucianism and nationalism. Building on Mao's doctrine that 'religion is poison', schools continue to preach atheism. But in the meantime the Catholic and Protestant churches are welcoming more worshippers on Sunday than those in Europe. Official sources put the figure at 25 million believers; others believe there may be as many as 60 million Catholics and Protestants. Belief in the existence of God, of a power higher than Beijing, is something the authorities are none too pleased about, as people might get their loyalties mixed up. The party is particularly dubious about God's representative on earth in the person of the Pope. Which authority is allowed to appoint bishops, Beijing or Rome, is an endless point of contention. An added complication is that a substantial number of the 80 million CCP members identify themselves as religious. Alongside the rise in Western beliefs, China's 'own' Buddhism is doing well too. The monasteries are popular among young people wanting to add a spiritual dimension to their lives, similar to young Westerners who are open to Eastern spirituality.

Despite the many Western influences and the arguments in favour of the more nuanced school, it needs to be said that the more traditional school, which stresses the unique character of Chinese values, has had the wind in its sails in recent years. With their image of an 'eternal China', its advocates are perfectly in tune with the country's growing nationalism. President Xi likes to tap into that as well, as it may help fill the moral gap. Many bloggers are keen to express their national pride, especially in relation to everything Japanese. But the authorities do not want feelings to run too high however, lest they get blamed for not making enough of an effort. After anti-Japanese protests, especially, it can be difficult to put the genie back in the bottle.

National pride is ubiquitous. British nationalism during the London Olympics in 2012 rivalled China's during the previous Games. But there is a difference: in China it is part of the school curriculum. The student uprising of 1989 prompted the leadership to conclude that the country was lacking in patriotism. Since then the subject has been taught in schools. Imperial times are depicted as glorious, thus flatly contradicting the earlier view of Mao. In the nineteenth century, this golden age was brutally cut short by Western powers responsible for China's 'national humiliations'.

The country's major achievements are also celebrated through cultural expressions, television programmes and pop songs stimulated from the top down. Add the Western shortcomings that are made much of in the media and the picture of a superior China emerges. This sense of superiority goes back a long way. It is at the heart of the arguments of those stressing the unique character of Chinese civilisation.

Contemporary exponents of this traditional school are figures as diverse as Henry Kissinger, whose book *On China* was published in 2011, and former Marxist and journalist Martin Jacques. In *When China Rules the World* he stresses that we should view the country as a 'civilization state'. Its inhabitants firmly believe themselves to be both racially and culturally superior to other races and civilisations, according to him. He concludes that the rest of the world has 'a serious problem' now that China is becoming more powerful. A fifth of the world's population is cursed with what he terms the 'Middle Kingdom Mentality'. Alongside superiority it also encompasses a sense of isolation. While the country 'is fast joining the world, true to its history, it will also remain aloof'. The chance that this mentality can be overturned is, in his view, virtually nonexistent.

Jacques dismisses the possibility of Westernisation through reference to Japan. The latter country's economic development is far more advanced than China's, but it can hardly be considered a Western culture. Besides, a self-reinforcing effect is at work: the more important China becomes the more superior it will feel. It will look for inspiration not to the rest of the world, but to its own past. Unlike Spengler, Jacques sees a key role for Confucianism, saying 'its DNA remains intact'. As a result, the Chinese will always place more trust in their government than Western citizens do. In the Confucian worldview, the state is an end in itself, not a means to personal happiness. 'The state remains venerated, above society, possessed of great prestige, regarded as the embodiment of what China is.'

His firm conviction notwithstanding, I doubt whether Jacques is on the right track. Should we believe in 'the eternal China', superior and impervious to outside influences, or are we witnessing a fundamental transformation of a country and its people brought about by globalisation? A country which is far less certain of its own identity, as well as less Confucian than Jacques suggests?

## Mix of inferiority and superiority

Based on my own experiences, I am drawn to the latter position. The degree to which young people, especially, are open to Western culture is impressive, and this does not just include consumer goods, but also television programmes and pop and sports stars. And although the official statistic that puts English speakers at 300 million seems a little generous, it is fair to say that the language has been embraced. English is now a compulsory subject in primary school from the age of eight. Studying in either the US or Europe is top of the wish list of both smart children and their parents. The ruling elite sets the example by sending its own children to universities such as Oxford and Harvard. And thanks to translations, Western literature has become a lot more accessible.

Interviewing both in China and Europe, I found little evidence of the sense of superiority Martin Jacques ascribes to the Chinese.

Most experts I asked about this believe there is a mix of both inferiority and superiority – that's to say, a far less black-and-white picture. I believe the rough edges are being smoothed out by the increase in business and scientific ties between China and the West. These contacts help create a different perspective on the world, while better control of English reflects a broadening awareness. It is the same in the West, where students also spruce up their CVs with foreign languages and travel experience.

Sometimes the elites in China and Europe understand each other better than they do less privileged members of their own societies. The distance between a farmer and a highly educated urbanite in China is greater than that between the latter and a highly educated Westerner, as Spengler points out. This is echoed by Jean-Baptiste Soula, a viticulturalist running a chateau in the Bordeaux region on behalf of a Chinese owner. Talking about a French employee who refused to listen to him, he observed: 'I was aware of an immense cultural difference with her.' But with the owner, a Chinese middle-class woman, this was 'not an issue at all'.

Every day, globalisation leads to more interaction in all kinds of fields, with Chinese and Western people meeting in lecture theatres, offices and laboratories. The outcome of this far from straightforward process is bound to be more mutual understanding.

# Chapter 20

# 'Western' Values for China

*Megaphone Diplomacy and the*
*Wagging Finger*

'Here in the West we've always tried to tell China what to do. Become Catholic, or Protestant, turn socialist, communist, capitalist – you name it! Leave China alone, allow the country to develop itself.'

Kristofer Schipper, grand old man of European sinology and emeritus professor at Leiden University, says it in a polite but passionate tone. Early in 2011 he was interviewed on Dutch television about a subject which has dominated his life: relations between China and the West. His name reflects this, as he is known in China as Professor Shi Zhouren, or the little man in his boat. He interprets the name, 'given to me by my Chinese friends', as reflecting a mission to bring the two cultures closer together. His lifelong devotion to getting to know the country's culture has earned him the official, government-conferred status of 'Friend of China'.

Schipper, now in his seventies, is not only taking pains to familiarise Westerners with China's culture through translations, but is also trying to make Western culture more accessible in China. In the port city of Fuzhou he and his Chinese wife founded a library specialising in Western literature and culture. His motive? 'Once you get to know something better and learn more about it, you stop being afraid. Knowing is understanding. When you do that, it becomes a part of yourself and you start loving it.'

The erudite Schipper looks at relations from a centuries-old perspective. He notes that European meddling has had mostly adverse effects, reaching its nadir in the nineteenth century with the opium wars and the unfair treaties. This has prompted him to conclude that it is up to China itself to decide on changes to its constitution. It goes without saying that he regrets the human rights violations, but he is also understanding. 'China has been through an incredibly difficult period of revolution. The country became traumatised and developed an obsession with public order. They then take that too far, which is something we all regret. Of course you can't expect them to turn into angels overnight.'

China's rise means that the country 'will finally occupy the place in the world it should have had all along'. This is 'good news for China itself and for the world'. For European countries it is particularly important to learn more about China and not be overcome by fear. 'We really ought to know better than to incite the *gelbe Gefahr* (Yellow Peril) again, as Emperor Wilhelm did in the nineteenth century.'

Schipper's call on the West to take a level-headed approach to human rights and democracy greatly appeals to another grand old man. Now in his nineties, Germany's former chancellor Helmut Schmidt is exasperated with the generations of politicians who have succeeded him and who are taking the country to task. 'Mrs Merkel complains about human rights in China. As if it makes a difference, as if it prompts the Chinese to respectfully lower their eyes', he scorned in an interview in *Die Zeit* in 2006. 'This kind of interference strikes me as offensive.'

Schmidt also points to the bigger, historical picture to explain why human rights do not eclipse everything else. The sixteenth-century principle of sovereignty, which enables nation states to determine their own destiny without the interference of others, 'remains an excellent principle', he writes in *Nachbar China* (Neighbour China). In this book he looks back on his own experiences with the country from the 1950s onwards. Unfortunately, his successors show little respect for the principle. 'Non-intervention in domestic affairs' is now mainly propagated by China itself, especially to counter criticism of its human rights record. 'We interfere in everything, on moral grounds and out of humanitarian idealism. Idealism can be something beautiful, as well as something stupid', he grumbles.

Schipper and Schmidt have the same message for Western politicians: don't spread fear, show respect. In his role as chancellor, Schmidt did so in discussions with leaders Mao Zedong and Deng Xiaoping. His memories of those encounters reveal the tension between practising global politics and standing up for human rights. He met Deng in 1990, a year after the then eighty-six-year-old leader had ordered the quashing of the student protest on Tiananmen Square. Deng's popularity in the West, gained through his open-door policy of the late 1970s, quickly turned to infamy.

Schmidt was the first European leader to go to Beijing after the bloodbath, thereby infuriating the German press. The intention of his visit was to prevent the West from moving on to a Cold War against China after the collapse of the Soviet Union. He feared that the economic sanctions imposed on China on the initiative of the US could result in the termination of the open-door policy. Therefore, he urged Deng to put China forward for the G7, the group of the six biggest Western industrial nations plus Japan.

Deng was right in thinking it would provoke too much resistance, but he did reassure Schmidt: the West's anger would subside and he would carry through his reforms come what may. So he did. In the years that followed, Deng successfully fought the conservative forces that sought to isolate China. 'Thanks to his unswerving pragmatism he managed to integrate a fifth of mankind in the world', Schmidt notes with admiration. It makes Deng 'one of the most successful statesmen of the twentieth century', despite having the blood of Tiananmen Square on his hands. 'It is self-righteous and arrogant to impose Western, democratic values on China and Deng, and to condemn them on the basis of a human rights standard that China simply cannot have attained yet.'

Looking ahead, Schmidt expects rising tensions with the West when China becomes a fully fledged knowledge economy and Western countries start to see job losses. He hopes Europe will be wise enough not to 'pin the blame on China', but to examine its own shortcomings instead. The risk of a Cold War is, in his view, far from over. 'A clash of civilizations is possible, but certainly not unavoidable. The decisive factor will be whether we Europeans, and the West as a whole, acknowledge and respect China's autonomy and equality.'

## Weakening China

Respect rather than wagging our finger over human rights is what both Schipper and Schmidt advise. But is it really wise not to raise the subject of human rights, out of respect for the principle of sovereignty and because we have been so meddlesome in the past?

In an Amnesty International report I read about Fan Yafeng, a man in his early forties who worked at the prestigious Chinese Academy for Social Sciences in Beijing until 2009. As a specialist in comparative constitutional law he wrote about sensitive subjects such as 'the constitution and democracy' and 'the law and freedom of religion'. This went well for six years, but in 2009 he was told his contract would not be renewed 'for political reasons'. In his spare time he also led a group of Christian lawyers, who represented members of the heavily persecuted Falun Gong movement. Fan did not desist, not even after his dismissal. He was arrested on several occasions, once even together with his wife and three-year-old son. He was also beaten and tortured and had his personal possessions confiscated by the authorities. He was released following international pressure, but placed under house arrest. Forced to submit regular reports about his spiritual condition to the authorities, he now keeps as low a profile as possible.

His case is not unique. According to human rights organisations such as Amnesty and Human Rights Watch, civil activists have had a particularly tough time since Xi Jinping became president. 'A journalist, a lawyer or someone working for a non-governmental organisation, in short, everybody trying to change something in society is no longer safe', journalist and blogger Michael Anti told me, sombre after two years under Xi. To illustrate this, he cites the case of Xu Zhiyong. This lawyer advocated the right of peasant children to study in the cities. 'This is a completely non-political activity and yet he was handed a four-year prison sentence on the grounds that with his call to demonstrate he posed a threat to public order. It supposedly hindered traffic. Absurd.' Anti summarises the fate of activists in a one-liner: 'Even the lawyer's lawyer now needs a lawyer.' In other words, those who dare to offer legal assistance to civil activists will get into trouble themselves.

The notorious re-education camps where dissidents used to be held without trial were closed shortly after Xi came to power. This is progress, human rights organisations admit, but the repression of dissenting voices continues unabated. It is hard to believe that it is just a matter of time before individual human rights will come to the fore, as Chinese diplomats tend to suggest. In the past few decades, China's argument goes, we have been preoccupied with fundamental social rights, we have lifted hundreds of millions of people out of poverty: give us a bit of time for individual rights. It echoes the request for calm and respect made by Schipper and Schmidt.

What are Western governments to do about this complex array of forces and interests? Pressure groups such as Amnesty and the like inform them of the fate of activists. Can they respond by saying that it is up to the Chinese authorities to exercise their sovereignty and decide how to handle their citizens? Can they point to all the other interests they share with China, such as reducing $CO_2$ emissions, preventing trade protectionism, combating terrorism, you name it?

One thing is certain: politicians will have to maintain a dialogue on all of these topics. Critical remarks on human rights do little to improve the atmosphere. They may not always show it, but the Chinese are certainly annoyed by it. 'The Chinese genuinely think it is our intention to weaken them in this way', explains Fraser Cameron, a Brit working at the Brussels-based think tank EU–Asia Centre. From the Chinese government's point of view the West uses human rights as a political tool to drive a wedge between the people and their leaders. And this is exactly what the leaders want to avoid at all costs. In conversation with Chinese policy makers Cameron has noticed 'the depth of distrust on the issue'.

As an example he cites the diametrically opposed views on the Dalai Lama. In the US and Europe the spiritual leader of Tibetan Buddhism is held in high regard, but China sees him as a 'traitor' intent on an autonomous Tibet. The views on Liu Xiaobo, the winner of the 2010 Nobel Peace Prize, are similarly divergent. His plea for human rights and democracy, expressed in the *Charter 08* manifesto, incurred an eleven-year prison sentence. To the authorities he is a 'criminal' guilty of 'incitement to subvert state power'. Liu committed to the internet sentences such as: 'Since the Communist Party of China (CCP) took power, generations of CCP dictators have cared most about their own power and least about human life.' It makes him a criminal in the eyes of the authorities, and a brave fighter for human rights and democracy in ours. Schipper's little boat is bobbing forlornly between these two shores.

## 'The Chinese are our brothers'

In order to bridge this gap, the French philosopher and sinologist Guy Sorman makes a suggestion: differentiate between the people and their leaders. Seeing the attitude of the Chinese people as evidence that human rights are not 'Western' or 'relative' but universal, he urges us to 'listen to the cry for freedom of the ordinary people'. Right now, 'a mafia-style organisation' is still in charge, but the Chinese would like nothing better than to 'consign all the apparatchiks to the dustbin of history'.

The Frenchman did not conceive this 'cry for freedom' sitting at his desk in Paris or New York, where he lectures at the Institut de Sciences Politiques and Columbia University respectively. The philosopher of Polish-Jewish extraction likes to travel. He spent the year 2005 criss-crossing China to visit all the places where revolt was brewing. Through strikes, environmental protests, peasant revolts against dispossession and petitions in favour of democracy, Sorman was there to record the anger about 'the tyranny of the Party'. His book *L'Année du Coq* (The Year of the Rooster) from 2006 is one long, impressive indictment.

Ordinary citizens would love to enjoy individual human rights and deliver themselves from 'the suppressive regime', he concludes. Here in the West we ought to realise that 'the Party is not China, but merely its temporary dictator. Just like the twenty-six imperial dynasties that preceded it, this regime will one day disappear.' He also argues that we should not use the term 'dissident' to describe opponents of the regime. They are not a tiny minority, but 'democrats who articulate what the majority of the people want'.

The latter statement suggests that wishful thinking has got the better of Sorman. Most experts are sceptical about the people's wish for democracy. The ordinary citizen's priority is with day-to-day concerns, such as his health and old-age pension. Political desires tend to be projected onto him by Westerners, so the thinking goes. But for want of reliable surveys, nobody can be quite sure.

Tackling China not 'from the top', as the *Realpolitiker* Helmut Schmidt and Henry Kissinger do, but from the ground, speaks in Sorman's favour in my view. The statesmen limit themselves to the leaders who, like themselves, will make it into the history books. Sorman, on the other hand, spoke to people who do not make, but undergo history. 'The Chinese are our brothers' is the somewhat melodramatic closing line of *L'Année du Coq*. When I spoke to him six years after his book was published, he was still of the same mind. While there may have been no large-scale uprising against the regime, he views the estimated tens of thousands of demonstrations annually as proof that opposition to those in power is immense.

Unlike Schmidt and Schipper, Sorman unashamedly forces 'our' values onto the Chinese, and he shows no desire whatsoever to 'respect' the leaders. In order to maintain their dignity, European politicians 'ought to stop overestimating China. Chinese leaders often say: "We're still a poor country." And for a change that's not propaganda, but true! They've got a long way to go before they catch up with us. The adverse effect of our overestimation of them is our tendency to self-censorship in the area of human rights. It's suicide. It's crucial that we stand by our own values.' We ought to help dissidents where we can, 'or else we will lose our dignity'. Sorman himself puts these words into practice by helping Liu Xia, the wife of Nobel laureate Liu Xiaobo.

The French sinologist is less than impressed with the efforts of fellow Westerners in positions of power. Most Western politicians and business people are inclined to, as he puts it, 'look right past the oppression'. A positive exception is Angela Merkel, who was the subject of Schmidt's scorn. 'She's prepared to raise the issue of human rights in Beijing and is the most outspoken of all the European leaders.' Sorman identifies a division within Europe, singling out the northern European countries as considerably more principled than countries such as Spain and Italy 'which care very little about human rights'. He believes it is important for each and every Western citizen not to lose sight of the fundamental difference between democracies and the Chinese system. 'Nowadays you sometimes hear people say that enlightened despotism is better than democracy. That's extremely dangerous. Democracy is not a given.'

Sorman's passion for human rights in China is appealing to me. His 'bottom-up' approach convincingly demonstrates the universal power of human rights. But it remains to be seen whether the Chinese really want a democracy, as he claims. The answer depends on the way you phrase the question, Michael Anti stresses: 'Of course they'll say "no" when asked whether they want a democracy. They have been brainwashed for years that it's a bad political system. But ask them whether they want to help decide who will be in charge in their town or village and whether they want to have a say in environmental issues. The answer will be a resounding "yes". Describe democracy in terms of those individual rights and most people will be in favour of it.'

## 'Meddling' in China

To my mind, Sorman overshoots the mark by stressing the government's totalitarian character and ascribing it almost North Korean characteristics. It does not reflect the developments of the past forty years during which, with the government's consent, freedom has improved in a range of areas: business, travel, studying abroad, science, as well as communication. The internet has given the Chinese access to many more sources of information. Still, their freedom could be so much greater without censorship, which is increasing rather than decreasing.

The move towards more freedom is certainly no linear process. It also involves steps back. In his first few years in office, President Xi is gradually recovering ground on civil society, thus putting pressure on freedom of expression. Everything that is even remotely critical of 'the Party's leadership' is taboo. Prior to the Xi era, a scientist was able to criticise the government's environmental policy, as long as he did not cast doubt on the one-party system. Under Xi, however, the ideological reins seem to be tightening again. A prominent institute such as CASS (the Chinese Academy for Social Sciences) is accused of having 'ideological problems', as its scholars are thought to be too receptive to Western ideas. How far this tightening goes remains to be seen.

Those who cross the 'red line' of criticism of the political system are punished harshly, as Liu Xiaobo experienced. The difference from the old days is that the rest of the world is concerned for his welfare. During the Cultural Revolution countless intellectuals were tortured and murdered without ever causing uproar in Western public opinion.

This leaves the question: how should Western leaders respond to Chinese human rights violations? A synthesis between the positions of the relativist Schmidt and the universalist Sorman seems inconceivable. A choice needs to be made. My preference is for Western 'meddling'. It is important as a matter of principle to subscribe to the universal character of human rights: equality prevails over the principle of sovereignty. It is also important for the West's sense of self-esteem to adhere to this universalism. However exasperating the Chinese leaders think broaching the issue of human rights may be, our relationship will benefit from insistence on this point. Ultimately, the Chinese have more respect for people who do not renounce their values.

Unfortunately, the West's interference has decreased rather than increased in recent years. China's growing power encourages Western politicians to 'look past the oppression', as Sorman notes rightly. Following the 1989 bloodbath, human rights were top of the agenda, along with trade flows. As the latter have widened, the attention to human rights has narrowed.

If we are to address them, we need to find the right tone. Unlike Sorman, I believe that showing respect would be a good starting point. Calls for a regime change to enforce human rights will be counterproductive. We had better refrain from doing so in all the areas where we want a serious dialogue. The suggestion that democracy really is better for China, often made by Americans, comes too close to such a call. It is completely understandable that it antagonises Chinese leaders who regard the one-party state as the foundation of their existence.

Other forms of 'megaphone diplomacy' are equally counterproductive. We must take care not to use China to prove only a point to our own constituency. A member of parliament for the German Green Party, Viola von Cramon, showed me her deep annoyance with colleagues who 'hurl press releases about dissidents into the world without any form of dialogue. These kinds of public statements only anger the Chinese. They are not just ineffective and you end up running the risk of harming the prisoners you claim to be standing up for, because the anger will be taken out on them.'

On the other side of the German political spectrum, the sinologist Eberhard Sandschneider agrees with her. 'Viewed from a human rights perspective, China's Tibet policy is extremely problematic. But change can only come about via a dialogue with Beijing, not via public accusations. A dialogue may not sound like much, but we simply cannot expect instant success.' In his view, governments must not get involved with individual suffering. 'It's good that an organisation like Amnesty does. But as an element of foreign policy it is no longer effective. Now that China has grown so big and self-confident, we have to accept that the time when we could wag our finger at China is over.'

An 'effective division of labour' between organisations such as Amnesty and Western governments may be the solution, Sandschneider believes. Governments ought to focus on structural projects, Amnesty on people. As an example of such a project he cites the German training programmes for Chinese judges. 'In the past they used to be retired army officers, now they will be people with legal training. It may not make the newspaper headlines, but it does contribute to human rights.'

I agree with his point about poor effectiveness, but I am less enamoured of the strict division of labour. I do not see why Western governments cannot stand up for individuals behind closed doors during state visits. Given the status of politics in China, this will carry a lot more weight than Amnesty's efforts. However, it is crucial that it is not done unexpectedly and not made to sound like an indictment. We need an exchange of views, not a monologue. It must be done with respect and with reference to values which the Chinese themselves have included in their own constitution. Freedom of expression is among them, so at least on paper it is a Chinese value. Such an approach is not spectacular, but surely realistic.

# Chapter 21

# Chinese Values for the West

*Investing Billions in 'Soft Power'*

During Xi Jinping's first year in power, a confidential party memo, 'Document No. 9', was leaked. The bland title concealed a hard, anti-Western message, admonishing the party apparatus 'concerning the situation in the ideological sphere'. It turns out there are no fewer than 'seven dangerous western values' currently threatening China. Among them are virtually all the principles that underpin the West's social structure: Western constitutional democracy, including the separation of powers and independent judiciaries; the universal value of human rights; civil society; and last but not least, media independence. It also called on party members to strengthen their resistance to 'infiltration' by outside ideas.

While it is not entirely certain whether the document came straight from the horse's mouth, Xi himself, it is not improbable either. His predecessor Hu also identified dangers from the West threatening China. 'Hostile international forces are westernising and dividing us', he wrote in party publication *Seeking Truth* in 2012. The then president did not specify his accusation, but it seems fair to assume that it was US culture in particular that bothered him. Fear of its attraction is considerable among the Chinese, as Hu's observation suggests: 'The West's international culture is strong, whereas we are weak.'

When Chinese leaders visit Europe or the US, there are no signs of this anti-Western stance. Instead they are all sweetness and light, full of fine words about shared interests and harmony between the respective nations. But a party memo such as

Document No. 9 probably says more about the leadership's thinking than the diplomatic clichés. This seems to be borne out by 'the Chinese Dream', which Xi has introduced as an alternative to the American Dream. By pitting the American emphasis on self-realisation against the collective interest, Xi invites the Chinese to contribute. The main objective is 'the rejuvenation of China'. An index has even been developed: China stood at 65.2 per cent rejuvenation in 2012.

But how does Xi expect to prevent China coming off worst in this battle of ideas with the West? Which values is he deploying? Or put differently: if his country becomes a dominant world power, which values will the West come up against?

These questions are fascinating, like so many other questions about China. But unfortunately the answers are often speculative. The same is true here. What exactly the Chinese Dream entails is vague – and that is probably the whole idea. In a speech addressed to senior party members, Xi indicated that the dream should reflect 'the modern Chinese values'. In the same speech he also explained what he has in mind for China in the ideological battle with the West: more soft power.

## 'Beijing has no idea what it wants'

The concept of soft power, introduced by Harvard professor Joseph Nye in 1990, is often interpreted as 'the ability to produce outcomes through persuasion and attraction rather than coercion or payment'. In the multipolar world we live in, with its growing interdependence in the economic sphere, this is increasingly important. When resorting to military solutions, the traditional hard power, you are likely to shoot yourself in the foot because of those economic connections. China acknowledged the importance of soft power relatively late, in 2007, and has since been trying to catch up. Under President Hu, China began to promote its own culture in response to the West's preoccupation with democracy and human rights. A budget worth billions has been earmarked for media, internet, film and other artistic expressions, with the aim of procuring soft power.

One of the top priorities of the charm offensive is the establishment worldwide of as many Confucius Institutes as possible to promote the Chinese language and culture. Their number is growing fast: from the first in 2004 to more than 450 in 2014. The target is one thousand by 2020. Europe has a significant number, with 129 institutes spread across thirty-four countries in 2012. Although the activities, which include language classes and cultural pursuits, seem innocent enough, the institutes have been encountering substantial problems in practice.

Gilles Guiheux, a cheerful man in his forties, is the director of the Confucius Institute at the Université Paris Diderot where he also works as a professor. Since the university opened in the 1970s its faculty for Eastern Studies has established quite a reputation. In 2005 it was the scene of a minor revolt when it planned to use government money from Beijing to establish a Confucius Institute within its walls. Members of staff protested that opening the doors to an authoritarian regime would amount to an erosion of academic freedom. But the bag of money prevailed over the objections of principle – and Guiheux became director of the institute. 'I'm a bit more pragmatic than my colleagues and could see the potential benefits for our faculty.' Like most universities in France, Paris Diderot is struggling with its finances.

Beijing was prepared to allocate a generous amount of money for lecturers, books and cultural activities. Guiheux was curious to see how much freedom he would have in practice. 'To be honest, I feel quite free to do as I please. I won't finance evenings about Tibet or Taiwan with money from the Confucius Institute. That would be an affront to the Chinese. For such gatherings I use the university's own money. My overriding impression is that Beijing does not have a clue what it wants with these institutes. They only target quantitative objectives, like how many people are taking classes and how many are attending evening sessions. They don't talk about the content of the programming. It's as if they don't care.'

Beijing does not seem to be interested who the students are either. In fact, many of them are senior citizens. 'Why would the Chinese state invest in Westerners whose professional lives are behind them?', Guiheux asks rhetorically. With often only limited resources in classrooms at home, China is making money available in Europe to teach well-off, Western seniors Chinese. Because of this absurdity, the concept of the institutes has come under fire in China.

In the West this has happened for a different reason. The afore-mentioned tension between academic freedom and Chinese funding is seen as problematic, and not only in France. Columbia University in New York initially declined a Confucius Institute in 2011, to the satisfaction of one of its professors, Guy Sorman. Scandalised, the Frenchman pointed out that the Chinese director of each institute 'has a contract stipulating that he has to do his job in perfect harmony with Beijing. Where does academic freedom come into it?'

But in 2013 the Confucius Institute at Columbia was never-theless inaugurated. The same happened at the University of Chicago and the London School of Economics. In Chicago 170 academics declined an institute in 2010, on the grounds that it was 'an academically and politically ambiguous initiative'. And an LSE professor made the case in *The Sunday Times* that such a 'propaganda organisation' had no place in his establishment. In both instances, the power of money prevailed.

Guiheux believes the critics are a bit too principled. He is prepared to admit that 'a foreign power' within the university gates is 'bizarre' and 'potentially dangerous'. But the real test for him is whether there is an actual curb on academic freedom. 'Our Confucius Institute is not a propaganda tool. The world is not as black-and-white as that. But precisely because of this special status I remain extremely vigilant.'

If the promotion of Chinese values is Beijing's intention, Guiheux is not fit for purpose. 'I hate it when people talk about such things as "the Chinese way of thinking" and "the Western way of thinking". As if they are poles apart. I prefer to think about our common ground, for instance on foreign policy. But that's not to say that everything is great.' In that respect he really objects to the name: 'The emphasis on Confucius reinforces the exoticism. It gets in the way of a true under-standing of China.' When asked whether he can think of any specific values which China could showcase internationally, he is quiet for a moment before answering: 'They want to be a huge world power, but what exactly they want to achieve by that, except economic success, they don't quite know. What do they want? As yet China has nothing to offer the world, except consumer goods of course.'

The Chinese answer to Guiheux's incisive comment is rather vague. For years now, Chinese leaders have been saying it is all about 'socialist core values', but ask what those are and you are left with rather vague notions such as 'harmony' and 'progress'. These answers suggests that the Frenchman has a point. It does not come as a surprise to him that Beijing lacks a clear vision of what the institutes are supposed to achieve: 'Here in the West we have a tendency to attribute a "grand vision" to the Chinese government. But there is more amateurism than we think. Take Confucius, who has been dusted off in recent years to solve social problems. But how this is meant to happen, how you can use values to keep society together and restructure it, remains unclear. And so Confucius and his institutes operate in a vacuum.'

Given the continued opposition, the candid director even questions whether the Chinese government should go on with the scheme in this shape and form. 'I notice that both French and Chinese scholars are cautious precisely because it is a government initiative.' It is a debate that continues to rage in other countries as well. In Canada an organisation of university teachers urged their employers in 2013 to end collaboration with Confucius Institutes altogether. As a result two Canadian universities closed their institutes. One year later two American universities, the University of Chicago and Pennsylvania State University, followed this example after American university professors urged them to do so, unless academic freedom would be fully restored. But so far most universities have kept their Confucius Institutes open.

## Alternatives to existing ideas

Do other soft power initiatives that China has come up with since 2007 inspire similar distrust? The best part of the multibillion budget is spent on a 24-hour news channel to rival CNN and Al Jazeera. Beijing is hedging its bets here: both official news agency Xinhua and state-run television channel CCTV launched such an initiative in 2010 to provide 'a Chinese perspective' on world events and national news. The aim is to provide a counterbalance to Western media. Neither strays from the party line.

It remains to be seen whether this 'better view' will catch on outside the mother country. The market for international news channels is far from straightforward, as evidenced by the financial difficulties of CNN, the biggest name in the field. Competition is fierce, because besides China, the UK (BBC World), Japan (NHK World) and France (France24) have also entered the market for 24-hour English-language news channels. They all vie for the attention of viewers, the vast majority of whom watch national channels. Commercial success will almost certainly be limited.

From a journalistic perspective the problem for Chinese broadcasters is that toeing the party line and offering independent information are mutually exclusive. Perhaps they can emulate *China Daily*, a newspaper with a print run of 500,000 which is sold in China itself, as well as in Europe and the US. It cleverly piggybacks on the credibility of major Western newspapers by including its own *China Watch* as a supplement with titles including the *International New York Times*, the *Daily Telegraph* and the *Washington Post*. Experts believe this state newspaper is clearly given more space to practise critical journalism than Chinese-language publications. Here, too, attacks on the party are absolutely out of the question, but abuses such as corruption and environmental pollution receive widespread coverage and critical commentary on aspects of government policy is permitted.

*China Daily* also receives daily instructions from the party, but the newspaper appears to be interpreting them in such a way that, in my experience, the average Western reader is surprised by what it can get away with. In that respect the newspaper does a better job than the *Global Times*, China's second English-language paper, which seems to take pride in promoting nationalism even more than the party line prescribes. Like the TV channels, China's English-language papers operate in a challenging international market.

How much soft power these initiatives can generate for China in the future will depend largely on the freedom Beijing is prepared to give. A serious stab at independent journalism might yield a good reputation and with it significant numbers of viewers and readers. This is borne out by Al Jazeera. The Arab channel, headquartered in Qatar, wants to provide an alternative to 'prevailing views' on behalf of the emerging nations. The station's international recognition cannot be separated from its independent reporting. But those in charge of the Chinese 24-hour news channels still operate under the same party guidance as in the days of Mao, who proclaimed in the 1950s: 'Let Xinhua News Agency span the globe, let the whole world hear our voice.' The media as the mouthpiece of the government – it is a classic Leninist outlook that President Xi likes to propagate. 'Document No. 9', with its explicit condemnation of Western journalism, bears witness to this. Chinese leaders see Western media as 'hostile international forces' trying to divide their country. As if the Western media would have such an agenda. The CCP still does not see the public sphere as a forum for debate, but more as a battlefield that needs to be conquered.

## Negative image

This lack of belief in journalistic independence came to the fore in 2012 when Melissa Chan was deported from China. The Al Jazeera correspondent was the first foreign journalist to be expelled in fourteen years, probably as a result of a critical broadcast about the prison system. The following year other foreign correspondents ran into similar difficulties with their visas. Particularly badly hit were journalists working for the *New York Times* and Bloomberg, after publishing stories about the personal wealth of the ruling elite. Working conditions for foreign correspondents worsened in 2014, compared with the year before, a survey by their professional organisation FCCC showed. They face many hurdles, such as travel bans, intimidation of their sources and difficulties in obtaining working permits. 'China is rapidly eroding the progress it made in "opening up" to the world prior to the 2008 Olympics', the FCCC observed on the basis of its survey. This is clearly at odds with the Chinese efforts to generate soft power.

So how is the country getting on in this respect? Whatever new cultural activities and media are conceived, I believe the big events that attract worldwide publicity for China tend to have a greater impact on the country's image. In the positive corner are events such as the Olympic Games of 2008 and the 2010 World Expo in Shanghai. The elite forum on the island of Hainan can also be added to this list; this 'Davos of China' attracts every year two thousand politicians, CEOs from the international business community and scientists. There is good news too from a number of Latin American and African nations where, according to popularity polls carried out by the Pew Research Center, a large part of the population has a positive opinion of China. But the same polls, published in its Global Attitudes Project, show a downward trend in large parts of Europe, the US and Japan. When asked to express a preference for either China or the US, Europeans overwhelmingly opt in favour of the Americans. Only Greece chooses China.

The spiritual father of soft power, Joseph Nye, attributes this predominantly negative image to human rights. Through persistent violations China undermines its own attempts at amassing soft power, the Harvard professor argued in 2012 in the *New York Times*: 'In the aftermath of the Middle East revolutions, China is clamping down on the Internet and jailing human rights lawyers, once again torpedoing its soft power campaign.' He agrees with the writer and blogger Han Han, whom he quotes as saying: 'The restriction on cultural activities makes it impossible for China to influence literature and cinema on a global basis or for us culturati to raise our heads up proud.' It prompts Nye to conclude that if China wants soft power, 'it will need to unleash the talents of its civil society. Unfortunately, that does not seem about to happen soon.'

The geopolitical consequences of this are considerable. Without sufficient soft power, countries in China's immediate vicinity are looking towards the United States for protection. Soft power explains why Canada and Mexico do not have a similar fear of the United States, which has a lot more military clout. Of course Nye is right in saying that the human rights issue damages China's international image. The many stories of corruption and pollution are not helping much either. Besides, China is increasingly asserting itself as a global power by making territorial claims in the South China and East China Seas. This has certainly not done much for China's public image in recent years.

But to my mind Nye fails to address the impact of the economic balance of power. And this must not be underestimated, because, to quote him, 'there is no doubt that a successful economy is attractive'. Doesn't this tip the soft-power scale in China's favour? Europe's declining activism in the area of human rights cannot be viewed in isolation from China's economic success. Of course 'no protest' is not the same as wholehearted agreement, but it does help. Perhaps therein lies China's future soft power: an authoritarian state that offers its people economic growth by keeping a tight rein on the economy. This is what Mark Leonard, author of *What Does China Think?*, meant when he expressed his belief in the viability of the 'Chinese Model' as an alternative to our 'democracy with free market' model.

## The risks of boasting about the Chinese Model

In 2010 the left-leaning Leonard found support in a right-wing American, Stefan Halper, who served as policy advisor under four Republican presidents in Washington. He is now a professor at Cambridge, specialising in China and US foreign policy. In other words: a heavyweight. In his alarming book *The Beijing Consensus* he describes how the Chinese government is surreptitiously capturing the 'moral authority' in the world.

He attributes our lack of awareness of this to the 'Jekyll and Hyde' character of Chinese diplomacy. Beijing tends to express an interest in cooperation and multilateral partnerships towards Western nations, while at the same time building a network of friendly nations with whom they conspire against the existing world order. The Beijing Consensus is making the West less relevant in global matters, he argues: 'China is shrinking the West'. If the US and Europe fail to meet this 'challenge', both the tone and course of global politics are bound to change in future decades.

The Beijing Consensus revolves around state capitalism under the control of an authoritarian regime, guaranteeing 'growth, security and stability'. It is an appealing recipe for countries that have lost faith in the IMF and its Washington Consensus of deregulation and privatisation. Another benefit of the Beijing Consensus is speed, which is particularly valued by African countries. Beijing's 'no questions asked' approach compares favourably to the Western demands of good governance and compliance with human rights.

China is setting itself up, in Halper's words, as the 'sugar daddy' of human rights violators. The international bloc it is seeking to lead is made up of 'marginal, rogue and autocratic states' that are convinced that state capitalism works. Among those keen to walk 'a path around the West' he identifies Iran, Burma, Pakistan, South Africa, Saudi Arabia, Egypt, Turkey and a number of West African dictatorships. Where Moscow foundered with military hard power, China will succeed 'with the pen', i.e. the ideology of the Beijing Consensus.

While Halper is undoubtedly a fluent and compelling writer, I can pick plenty of holes in his argument. Just how 'friendly' are these nations with China? Do they really model themselves on this rather unique political and economic system? In most cases it is little more than an opportunistic alliance of communal interests, not a real affinity between values.

While it is true that relations between African nations and Beijing have improved, criticism of the latter's behaviour is also on the rise in several African countries. Besides, better relations do not constitute an embrace of the Beijing Consensus. Cultural differences remain a big obstacle. It is inconceivable that China's tightly controlled state capitalism might be introduced to Africa's often chaotic everyday reality. Including Saudi Arabia and Egypt on his list of China friends, Halper does not convince, as these countries are widely regarded as staunch American allies.

It is the same story in the Asian sphere of influence. Burma (Myanmar), which is also mentioned by Halper, has actually taken steps towards democracy and away from China. Today's biggest emerging countries, such as India, Brazil, Turkey and South Korea, all have a predilection for democracy. And while

Putin's Russia may have declared itself a big friend of China, it is in no way copying its political or economic system.

The Chinese leaders themselves are careful not to actively hawk the idea of a Beijing Consensus. Halper would probably say this is a cunning strategy, but I suspect they realise that it is too early for such boasting, given the country's many domestic problems. In 2009 a leading thinker inside the party, Li Junru, wrote in the official mouthpiece of the Central Party School, the *Study Times*, that talking about such a model is 'extremely dangerous' for the necessary reforms. Boasting about a 'Chinese Model' could easily lead to complacency. The leadership had better address issues such as corruption, pollution and the gap between rich and poor first. Besides, successful promotion requires soft power, and we have seen how slowly this is coming along. 'Its global soft-power appeal remains weak to nonexistent', American sinologist David Shambaugh concludes. He describes China as 'the partial power' in his book *China Goes Global*. 'China is not a magnet for others to emulate – culturally, socially, economically or politically. The problem for China in all four realms is that it is *sui generis*.'

It goes without saying that a country's image can change. After the testing Bush years, the US's popularity bounced back following Obama's election victory in 2008, only to decline again in his second term in office. And while Xi's charisma gives him the edge over Hu, China's soft power needs a lot more than that. The gap with countries with universal claims stretching back centuries, such as the United States, France and the United Kingdom, is immense.

It is understandable that China does not have a ready answer to this, all the more so since the country has been shaped by a mostly inward-looking, age-old civilisation. The country has only been pursuing soft power for less than a decade, and for now its initiatives are focused on disseminating the Chinese identity: the language, the culture and its take on current affairs. But this has a limited appeal to outsiders. You can study the identity, but not actually participate in it. An open system with values that are available to all has far more sex appeal. The US managed to attract generations of immigrants in this way. The Chinese Dream is restricted to the Chinese themselves.

Economic success is appealing, of course, which explains the growing numbers of foreign students and Chinese-language learners. But the downsides of this success make an actual move to the country far less attractive. The air pollution in Beijing and Shanghai is particularly off-putting. Moreover, there is no soft power to speak of until foreigners feel that they can and want to be a part of the culture. China, it is clear, is still struggling to generate it in any significant quantity. Internationally, the Beijing Consensus exists primarily in the minds of a few thinkers. It may well flourish in the long term, especially when China remains economically successful and the West continues its decline. This depends on the 'structural political and economic reforms' which were formulated in 2013 during the Third Plenum. So far, Xi has few concrete results to show for them.

# Chapter 22

# Chinese Disenchantment with a Powerful Europe

*The Vacuity of a 'Strategic Partnership'*

How much room is there for Europe in a Chinese politician's mind? There is no reason to have high expectations. The same is true the other way around: for the average European politician China remains a remote proposition. From Beijing's perspective, domestic concerns merit attention first, from the anti-corruption campaign and environmental problems to the endless Chinese game of favours for favours. The dragon is above all preoccupied with itself.

If a Chinese politician does look across the border, 'he focuses on the Asian region first, followed by the US and only then Europe', an experienced Western diplomat assesses the pecking order. The times when European countries were so remote their inhabitants could be nothing but barbarians are behind us, but the sense of distance is not gone. In fact, it has been reinforced by the disenchantment with Europe which Chinese leaders have experienced in the past decade.

At the start of the new millennium the Chinese had been optimistic. At that point in time, the Tiananmen Square uprising was far enough in the past, and most of the Western sanctions imposed in 1989 had been lifted by 1995, except for the arms embargo. And while the latter was (and is) certainly a sticking point, it did not prevent a flourishing trade relationship, especially after China joined the WTO. Around the turn of the century, Chinese policy makers cherished illusions about a 'powerful Europe'. They liked the look of it – for geopolitical reasons.

Following the collapse of the Soviet Union the US threatened to become overly dominant through its military, economic and political might. The French term *hyperpuissance,* which was used in those years to describe American supremacy, reflected not only the French, but also the Chinese fear of the American hyperpower.

China realised it was not in a position to counter this on its own and watched with interest as Europe enjoyed something of a boom. Not only was it doing well economically, but a big expansion with Eastern European countries was on the agenda and – the icing on the cake – the euro was launched. It had the potential to be a global alternative to the dollar.

In those years, the Chinese saw the European Union as 'a new pole capable of counteracting and weakening the US pole and thus serving their interests', according to French professor Jean-Pierre Cabestan in *La Politique internationale de la Chine* (China's International Policy). It was the right moment for a 'strategic partnership' with the EU. Launched in 2003, the exact content of this partnership, let alone its geopolitical meaning, remained unclear. Not a word was said about its relationship to the EU's real strategic partner, the US. But the term went down well at the European–Chinese summits which were hosted in turns by Brussels and Beijing.

On a political level, the Chinese hope that a stronger Europe could distance itself from the US's 'hyperpower' briefly appeared to come true in 2003. French President Chirac and German Chancellor Schröder jointly rejected US plans to invade Iraq. This move by the French–German axis, the engine of the EU, was welcomed by Beijing. It looked as if the 'multipolar world' in which the US could no longer call the shots unilaterally was on its way. Chirac paid lip service to this concept, to the further delight of Beijing.

But it was not long before the Iraq issue dealt a blow to the idea of Europe as a counterweight. A gulf emerged within the EU when the UK, as usual, opted for transatlantic loyalty. The gap in the French–German front widened when the ten Eastern European member states indicated that their loyalty also lay with the US. European discord reached its height when the French minister for foreign affairs issued a passionate plea against the Iraq invasion in the UN Security Council. But while the

Frenchman garnered applause, the Americans and the British sent their troops without UN approval.

## 'Into the marriage phase'

To the Chinese leadership this European division confirmed that a dreamed-of 'powerful Europe' was not on the cards. Further disillusion came in the spring of 2005, when a clear majority of both French and Dutch voters rejected a new European constitution. For the foreseeable future the EU would not take steps towards further integration, the Chinese leaders concluded rightly.

Moreover, Europe was proving itself a lot less assertive towards the US than Beijing had hoped for. All ten new Eastern arrivals opted to join NATO to guarantee their safety, which meant a choice for American security. The European leaders also failed to bring about China's main diplomatic targets: it was keen to obtain the status of market economy and to see the arms embargo lifted. President Chirac championed the case for the latter, in the hope of getting into China's good books and obtaining lucrative orders for his defence industry. He managed to get Schröder on his side, but in the end US opposition proved to be too strong. And so, with the arms embargo still in force, China has, besides producing its own, been buying mainly Russian weapons systems.

The other diplomatic bone of contention is China's status as a 'market economy'. With Europe dragging its feet on the issue, this too is a source of frustration for Chinese diplomats. The country will obtain the status automatically in 2016, fifteen years after joining the WTO, but China is keen to accelerate the process.

It would put the country in a better position to defend itself against Western nations complaining about the dumping of Chinese products. But failure to obtain the status also touched a more sensitive chord: it is seen as a lack of respect for its development model. China's frustration is evident from a remark made by a government advisor, who thinks it would be 'only polite' if the country was 'finally' recognised as a market economy, as China expert Jonathan Holslag cites him in his book *The Power of*

*Paradise*. In its defence, Europe points out that its own companies are not given enough access to the Chinese market. To Chinese ears this sounds suspiciously like a similar grievance expressed by the Americans – further evidence that Europe is marching to an American tune.

From 2007 onwards, irritations on either side mounted. 'From the honeymoon into the marriage phase' is how David Shambaugh characterises Chinese–European relations since that year in *China Goes Global*. The marriage phase, he implies, is not one of heightened pleasure. 'Both the atmosphere and the substance of the relationship turned sour during 2007–2010.' The Chinese were particularly unamused about the European reaction to the Tibet crisis in 2008. After the uprising was crushed, most international government leaders chose not to attend the Olympic Games in Beijing. Only the British Prime Minister Gordon Brown went, since the next Games would be held in London.

The atmosphere did not improve when the Dalai Lama was invited to visit Angela Merkel (2007), Nicolas Sarkozy (2008) and David Cameron (2012). They all defended their meetings with the 'important religious leader', but to the Chinese they were lending credibility to a 'wolf in a monk's habit' out to achieve Tibetan independence. The European government leaders were guilty of 'hurting the feelings of the Chinese people' and 'interfering with the internal affairs of China'. China retaliated by cancelling a European–Chinese summit in Lyon in 2008.

In 2009, the failed climate summit in Copenhagen did little to improve the atmosphere. A high-handed reproach was meted out to the Norwegian government when the Nobel Committee awarded the 2010 Nobel Peace Prize to the pro-democracy activist Liu Xiaobo. Four years later relations with Norway are still chilly, a demonstration of the unforgiving side of the Chinese leadership.

But the greatest irritations occurred in the realm seen as the most successful part of the relationship: the economy. The trade relations were developing well, but to the regret of the Chinese the Europeans began to complain more and more about their growing trade deficit and illegal dumping practices by Chinese producers. Southern European shoe and textile manufacturers took their complaints to the European Commission, which also proved responsive to the issue of the fake goods with which Chinese producers infringed Western intellectual property.

But the greatest challenge proved to be the euro crisis from 2009 onwards. The Chinese leaders had been able to respond positively and firmly to the earlier, Western-made credit crisis with a sizeable stimulus package for their own economy. This worked at the time, but when the euro crisis occurred their economic growth, the benchmark for their success and legitimacy, dropped to unseen levels: via 9.3 per cent in 2011 to 7.4 per cent in 2014. It would be unfair to put the entire blame on the EU, but disappointing demand from China's biggest customer is certainly an important part of the explanation.

A politically salient detail was that the drop in growth occurred mainly in 2012, just when Xi was about to take office, and economic stability had even greater priority than usual. Unfortunately, consultations in the backrooms of power in Beijing are rarely leaked, but I think we can safely assume that there was a great deal of ranting and raving about the 'strategic partner' after yet another euro crisis summit without clear results, as happened so often in 2011 and 2012. Publicly, the Chinese government kept it civil. 'Europe will have to get its own house in order' was the oft-repeated and wholly justified message. Prime Minister Wen and his successor-in-waiting Li Keqiang engaged in 'bond diplomacy' by expressing an interest to the leaders of weaker euro countries in buying up their government bonds.

To what extent this form of support actually materialised is officially unknown, as both China and European countries keep these transactions secret. But in a thorough article in *The Pacific Review*, Spanish economist Miguel Otero-Iglesias estimated in 2014 that China holds about 30 per cent of its foreign reserves or 1 trillion dollars in 'euro-dominated assets', of which government bonds are a very large part. For his own country he comes to the equally impressive amount of 12 per cent of Spanish government debt in Chinese hands, roughly 120 billion euros. 'The euro is too important for China to fail', he argues, not only because of the importance of the European market, but also because China has invested roughly a quarter of its foreign reserves in the euro since the European currency came into existence. The explanation is that Chinese leaders want to move away from the current dollar hegemony in the world's monetary system; they envisage a future with the dollar, the euro and of course the renminbi as core currencies.

At the same time Otero-Iglesias rightly states that the euro was 'too difficult to rescue' for China. The country's rulers would not have been able to explain to the average Chinese why they were buying up billions' worth of government bonds from the prosperous West. Moreover, in the course of the euro crisis Germany put pressure on China not to intervene too strongly in the sovereign debt markets as that would postpone structural reforms in weak economies in southern Europe. According to Otero-Iglesias this worked from the end of 2011 onwards, as China became more cautious. This caution can also be linked to a lack of political return on their European sovereign debt investment – the European leaders were not willing to grant China its much-wanted status of market economy, to the annoyance of Chinese leaders.

## A game of divide and rule

Once or twice it emerged what they really thought about the euro crisis. Jin Liqun, the chairman of the enormous sovereign wealth fund CIC, sailed close to the wind when he lost his patience at a meeting in London in 2012. He laid into the European welfare state and labour laws that were only keeping people from working hard, and the 'indolence' of Europeans who ought to 'stop languishing on the beach'. Writing in the *Financial Times*, he urged European politicians to look to the efficient way Asian leaders had solved their own crisis in the late 1990s. Instead Europe was just trying to alleviate the pain: 'Endless bargaining on terms and conditions for piecemeal bailouts has wasted a lot of time, each summit only reinforcing the belief that the eurozone is stuck in a cul-de-sac. This approach is anathema to a Chinese mindset: in *The Art of War*, Sun Tzu advocated setting fire to ships behind battling troops. Sometimes no way back is the best reason to fight for survival.'

His words ooze with self-confidence, bordering on arrogance. But to be fair, Jin had a point, especially when you pit China's successful handling of the credit crisis against the sorry sight of the EU in the sluggish euro crisis years. The political discord during the Iraq war was peanuts compared to the schisms with northern and southern Europe in opposite corners. The steps towards a banking union and the slight recovery of economic growth have taken the edge off things since 2013, but the differences have certainly not disappeared.

Beijing has drawn its conclusions. The EU, it turns out, is 'not a reliable partner in world affairs' and 'the EU remains disorganized in its foreign relations', as Shambaugh puts it succinctly. Therefore the Chinese government has turned to pragmatic negotiations with individual European countries, a strategy aimed at economic benefit. Technology, expertise and brands that could help China become a knowledge economy are of particular interest, and Chinese diplomats are quick to exploit discrepancies between European countries for a game of divide and rule. Those who behave, by not meeting the Dalai Lama for instance, are rewarded. Those who do meet him are punished, with other European countries ready to profit from such a 'slip-up'. 'The Chinese see the bilateral approach as a good and effective method to serve their interests', a Western diplomat notes.

Diplomatic rhetoric notwithstanding, Chinese leaders do not expect much of closer ties with Brussels. Xi was the first president of his country to visit European headquarters in 2014. He did so to plead for a comprehensive free trade and investment treaty, a project that had seen no progress in the previous seven years. The negotiations are tough, not least because China is not forthcoming in opening up its own market to European businesses.

Xi knows he needs Brussels for such a treaty – and with slowing economic growth at home he can do with the potential profits. At the same time his government has no qualms about making separate agreements with a group of Eastern European countries about investments within the so-called China–CEE initiative (consisting of sixteen countries, plus China). Of course the Chinese realise that Brussels is none too pleased, as the European Commission prefers to negotiate on its own. Justifiably so, as twenty-eight unanimous member states can provide a more effective counterweight to a superpower like China.

However, seduced by the ten billion euros Beijing is dangling before them, no fewer than eleven EU member states are participating in the China–CEE talks. The Chinese are playing yet another game of divide and rule, with the European countries involved happy to go along and the European Commission a reluctant observer.

Xi does not expect much beyond economic results. During his European tour he spent a lot of time talking about the 'New Silk Route', which includes a railway connecting the provinces in western China with Europe, as far as Germany. It should benefit mutual trade as well as the development of the turbulent province of Xinjiang.

But there is far less enthusiasm from Chinese quarters for talks on political issues with Europe. Via its highest diplomat, the High Representative for Foreign Affairs, the EU would like to enter into a dialogue with China about international issues such as Syria, Ukraine, Iran, etc. But the Chinese did not seem to take Lady Catherine Ashton, who held this post from 2009 until 2014, very seriously. Her successor, the inexperienced Italian Federica Mogherini, will have an equally hard time talking to Chinese top diplomats. There is no political kinship with the European nations, like that between Xi and the Russian president Vladimir Putin. Besides, in China's view Europe does not amount to much as a 'hard power', so it cannot be taken seriously in, for instance, talks about the rising tensions in the South and East China Seas.

Europe should want to get involved on this issue, since a disruption of the East Asian trade patterns would certainly have an impact on its economy. But mindful of Stalin's quip 'How many divisions does the Pope of Rome have?' the EU does not count for much to the Chinese. Their only opponent and partner in talks on this issue is the rival superpower in the region, the US. The ongoing political dialogue with the EU appears to be seen as perfunctory. And that's understandable – for more than one reason. How is China expected to take the European Union's High Representative for Foreign Affairs seriously if major European countries themselves don't?

# Chapter 23

# The Pitfalls of Imaginary Foes

When Nicolas Sarkozy was still only a candidate for the presidency of France in 2006, he consulted a dozen experts about his future policy on China. His conclusion was clear: he would have to make his first presidential visit to Beijing in the company of the British prime minister and the German chancellor. By making a joint fist, they could show that European discord had come to an end. But when Sarkozy made his first visit as president in 2007 he was accompanied by his mother and son. The anecdote sums up all that is wrong with the European response to the rise of China: despite realising that a joint strategy is the right approach, European governments persist in going it alone.

For years, China experts have been urging a united European front towards a country whose leaders think in terms of power and judge their interlocutors by those standards. As the economy of the country with its 1.3 billion people grows, the urgency of a joint approach increases. 'In the next twenty years or so, ultimately only the EU as an entity will be able to maintain a strong negotiating position with China', concluded Karine Lisbonne-de Vergeron already in 2007 in her study *Contemporary Chinese Views of Europe*. Experts in both the US and China fully agree that only an integrated Europe speaking with one voice has a chance to become a global player capable of speaking up to China.

Talk to a British, French or German diplomat and they will readily acknowledge that such a joint approach is the most sensible one in the long term. Germany, which has more reason than any other European nation to believe in the viability of an *Alleingang*, concurs. As a German diplomat told me: 'Our 82 million inhabitants would make us a medium-sized province in China.' He would love to see a united Europe, speaking with one voice: 'The Chinese would be surprised, somewhat alarmed even, because their policy of "divide and rule" would no longer work.' But then he goes on to outline all the complications.

## Being China's favourite European

Where did things go wrong, why was Sarkozy not on a plane with Merkel and Brown as he set off on his first trip to China? To answer this question, which is fundamental to Europe's role in the world, I will compare the attitudes of the main protagonists towards China.

Fear, ambition and distrust play their part in the attitude of all European governments. They fear that their national interest might be served less effectively if it were outsourced to a collective. Moreover, heads of government like to claim negotiation results, focused as they are on their electorate, but such a claim is hard to substantiate when results are obtained collectively. Thus a collective approach may frustrate them in their ambition to project themselves as statesmen.

Distrust also plays a role, because European countries have a tendency to capitalise on their colleagues' mistakes. France, Germany and Great Britain especially have a habit of not showing mutual solidarity. Or as the former Brussels correspondent of the *Financial Times*, Tony Barber, wrote: 'Each cannot resist the temptation to cuddle up to Beijing in the hope it will be adopted as "China's favourite European".'

The dilemma of receiving the Dalai Lama illustrates this. When Sarkozy welcomed Tibet's spiritual leader in 2008 on behalf of the EU, his country was promptly omitted from Wen Jiabao's 'confidence-building tour' around a number of European nations. Instead of showing solidarity with the excluded Sarkozy, Brown and Merkel unrolled the red carpet for the Chinese prime minister. This piece of theatre was repeated when David Cameron met the Dalai Lama in 2012. The Chinese reacted by freezing all ministerial contacts with the UK. It would be a year before the first signs of thaw. Meanwhile, Germany and France were doing everything they could to strengthen their ties with China.

In an effort to make up for lost ground, the British prime minister went to the other extreme during his next visit to Beijing in 2013, waxing lyrical about the success of Chinese growth and its implications for Great Britain. With a sales pitch including the Premier League, James Bond and the TV series *Downton Abbey*, Cameron praised his country as the best possible partner in the world. Other countries, in Europe and elsewhere, might have doubts about the rise of China, but not so Britain, he claimed: 'There is no country in the Western world more open to Chinese investment, more able to meet the demands of Chinese consumers or more willing to make the case for economic openness in the G8, the G20 and the European Union.' Listening to Cameron's words, one would never guess that his country was part of Europe. While in China he urged British children to stop learning French or German, but to learn Chinese instead. Europe was mentioned only in passing, when he promised the Chinese to place his 'full political weight' behind a comprehensive investment and trade agreement. In doing so, he waded straight into Brussels' territory, where officials were still discussing the conditions under which the EU might open talks. In his efforts to become China's 'favourite European' the British leader had spoken out of turn.

Even more remarkable was what Cameron failed to say. Not a single critical word passed his lips: human rights, Tibet, the Dalai Lama, environmental problems – none of it was raised and everything was amazing. He even avoided the Air Defense Identification Zone, which China had declared over the East China Sea, shortly before his visit. The Americans did get hot under the collar about this, as did the rest of Asia, but the British prime minister simply looked the other way. It earned him the accusation of 'egregious kowtowing', as one commentator put it succinctly.

The question is whether such obvious tactics have any effect. It is doubtful. His hosts must have seen a politician who, in their eyes, had made a faux pas and was desperately trying to get back into their good books. Their inclination would be to make him kowtow even more, as the writer of an editorial in the nationalist *Global Times* suggested: 'China won't fall for Cameron's "sincerity"', the headline ran. According to the author, 'the Cameron administration should acknowledge that the UK is not a big power in the eyes of the Chinese. It is just an old European country apt for travel and study.'

This cynical tone cannot be isolated from one of Cameron's earlier gaffes, when he made his first visit to China in 2010. He and his ministers refused to remove the poppies they wore in honour of the British war dead. Chinese officials had asked them not to wear them as they reminded the Chinese of what is unquestionably the blackest page in the history of British–Sino relations: the Opium Wars of the nineteenth century. It would have been only polite to consider their hosts' sensitivities, but Cameron and his team reacted haughtily. 'We informed them that they mean a great deal to us and we would be wearing them all the same', a British official explained. It may seem like a minor incident, but not to the Chinese, who are not in the habit of forgetting humiliation at the hands of Westerners quite so easily.

The lack of consistency in Cameron's attitude towards China, mixing assertiveness and submissiveness, is not unique for a British leader. His predecessor Tony Blair was similarly difficult to 'read' for the Chinese. Again, the Dalai Lama illustrates the point. Blair met him, then was scheduled to meet him again, but avoided the Tibetan leader because of 'diary pressures'. These came shortly after celebrating with Wen Jiabao the signing of around a billion dollars' worth of contracts between Chinese and British companies.

In contrast, their predecessor Margaret Thatcher was consistently critical towards China, albeit at a time when the country's economic clout was still negligible. It was with great reluctance that she handed over Hong Kong. And, interestingly enough, she warned the Chinese leadership back in 1996 that the internet ought to be open and free. Such a bold statement, bound to irritate the Chinese, is unlikely to be uttered by a British political leader nowadays.

Lacking consistency is a disadvantage in dealings with any country, but especially with China. Continuity and consistency are held in high regard by the Chinese leadership and are seen as a precondition for a stable relationship of trust. Those qualities carry more weight for Chinese, as they attach more value to personal relationships.

## German consistency

In that respect the British and the French could take a leaf out of the German book. If there is one country that has earned the title of 'favourite European' it is Germany. Not by swallowing every note of criticism, as Cameron and French President Hollande believe is necessary. During Xi's first visit to Europe it was Germany's President Joachim Gauck who dared to be critical. Quoting Confucius, he warned Xi that 'no state can exist without the trust of the people'.

Similar criticism could be heard from Chancellor Merkel. Standing next to her guest Xi, she stressed the importance of freedom of expression, which she described as 'of course a very important element to promote the creativity of a society'. While these are no earth-shattering remarks, they do show a preparedness to draw China's attention to the values the West stands for. In France, Belgium and the Netherlands, where Xi had been welcomed in the days preceding his German visit, this readiness was notably absent.

Ever since the door to the Chinese market opened in the late 1970s, Germany's approach to China has been characterised by a great degree of consistency. Aided by his fascination for the country, the then Chancellor Helmut Schmidt recognised the historic significance of that step and developed warm ties. His rival Franz Josef Strauß in Bavaria saw the situation no differently, nor did the later chancellor Helmut Kohl. Successive right- and left-leaning governments have gone down this route to this day – exactly the kind of continuity the Chinese like.

From a historical perspective, Germany has an advantage over France and the UK. While the Germans also acquired some Chinese territory during the 'century of humiliation', the real bad guys were the British and the French. Their Nazi past has been no hindrance to the Chinese. Mao saw World War II as a European war and to the Chinese it is no reason to change their view of Germany. The Germans owe their advantage to the reliability of their politicians as well as the quality of their products. They have garnered unreserved admiration from the Chinese and huge benefits for German industry. It would be hard to overestimate the importance of this.

Thanks to its economic success, Germany is generally referred to as the dominant political power within Europe these days. And while it managed to keep up with Germany until under Sarkozy's reign, France is now definitely trailing due to its much poorer economic performance. Those analysing Germany's economic success of recent years always mention China. It is largely thanks to Chinese demand that Europe's biggest economy has sailed through the crisis relatively unscathed from 2009 onwards. Growth on the Asian markets compensated for the drop in orders from the rest of Europe and the United States. The Chinese love of quality German cars such as those produced by Mercedes, Audi and BMW pushed profits to record highs. The backbone of German industry, its small and medium-sized enterprises, also benefited by selling their industrial machinery with the quality seal 'made in Germany'. Chinese entrepreneurs opted en masse for these machines to step up their own production. At the same time, German companies have started setting up Chinese branches. The days when those were established with an eye on export to the US and Europe are over. By moving close to the Chinese market, Germany honed its strategy.

However, this rosy picture does not tell the whole story. Whereas German–Chinese relations may be flourishing economically, the Germans are, paradoxically enough, quite negative about China. In 2012 only 29 per cent described China's image as 'favourable', which placed Germany right at the bottom of the countries surveyed by the Pew Research Center. This is a downward trend, because as recently as 2006 more than half of the population was favourably disposed towards China. Support dropped drastically from 2007 onwards, when both countries clashed openly over Merkel's meeting with the Dalai Lama. So while German politicians and business people may have been propagating the mantra 'China is an opportunity' over the past few decades, the German people are not impressed.

Why is that? For his book *Angst vor China*, the German journalist Frank Sieren explored his compatriots' motives. The authoritarian political system and human rights proved to be the main stumbling blocks. Dictatorship and human rights violations fill the Germans with disgust, for obvious historical reasons. Even the younger generations continue to experience the Nazi past as a heavy burden.

On top of that, China's reputation as a polluter does not please the Germans, who have a passion for the environment. With its industry heavily dependent on coal, China is known to be one of the world's greatest polluters and the biggest $CO_2$ emitter. The Chinese penchant for copying other people's products is another quality the Germans look down on.

Sieren offers a political and psychological interpretation as well. He believes both left- and right-leaning Germans have an axe to grind with China. The left is mainly offended by the environmental pollution and a rabid form of capitalism. The latter gives the population little or no social security and an 'unfair' competitive edge over the West. Germany's right has difficulty with a less-than-liberal state, which intervenes heavily in the economy, thereby undermining right-wing articles of faith such as privatisation and deregulation. According to Sieren, left and right not only share an aversion to China's non-democratic character, but also a fear: loss of control over 'the question of what is good or bad [...] for the world'.

This presumption of superiority is something I noticed during a debate in Berlin. The audience asked questions such as 'should we not sever all ties with such a reprehensible regime?' and 'could our democratic model serve as an example for China?' 'Absolutely not', the spry nonagenarian Helmut Schmidt snapped on stage in response to the latter query. 'Germany is Germany and China is China. The question betrays German arrogance. As Germans we are the last people to be teaching others a lesson in parliamentary democracy. The impertinence.'

With fine profits for German businesses and high-quality technology for China, the economic relationship may be in robust shape at the moment, but that is not to say that the future is rosy. People are worried about job losses if China catches up with German technology. In Schmidt's view this is a real danger, but if and when this comes to pass is a matter of conjecture. More concrete are the reservations German businesses have about the Chinese tendency to limit access to their market and to favour their domestic companies. China's 'national champions' receive subsidies from their government when they compete for orders in 'third' markets, so German businesses lose out on price. These are very real concerns, which call for European-level negotiations with China. Germany is too small to address this on its own.

Merkel's China policy is not completely above criticism. Her intervention in the Chinese solar panel case is a painful chapter for German diplomats. After the panels were dumped on the European market, the then European commissioner Karel De Gucht built a strong case against the Chinese manufacturers, backed by a German company that had brought the matter to court. But with an eye to some major deals for bigger German companies, Merkel chose China's side. The solar panel manufacturer was sacrificed and Brussels' negotiating position seriously undermined. So Merkel is certainly no stranger to political opportunism, although as a rule she manages to maintain a clever balance between pushing for economic benefits and retaining self-respect through emphasising Western values.

## 'Chinese tyranny' in Italy

Under China's increasing weight this balancing act is becoming more and more of a challenge to other European countries. With the possible exception of Merkel, no European leader is now likely to meet the Dalai Lama, the ultimate litmus test for a bilateral approach to China. Obama did so early in 2014, thereby defying the anger of the Chinese. But he could afford it, given the scale of his economy.

For individual European countries this is less of an option. They are increasingly inclined to 'leave human rights to Brussels', concludes Kerry Brown, the British professor of Chinese Politics at the University of Sydney. 'The attitude is one of "Let the European Commission take a hard line, so we don't damage our trade interests". But meanwhile the human rights problem is no less acute.'

This opportunism, using the EU as a welcome buffer, can be seen in both France and Italy. Unlike the Germans, the French are not engaged in a human rights dialogue with China and they are fine with that. It is something Brussels can take care of. The Italians have long since thrown in the towel. In his office in Milan Thomas Rosenthal, the young director of the Fondazione Italia Cina (a foundation dedicated to promoting business and cultural links between Italy and China), is honest about how his compatriots view the issue. 'The US can afford to keep welcoming the Dalai Lama and to criticise the Chinese currency. Germany is big and strong too and therefore in a position to speak freely about Western values. But we? Are we big and strong? We may be industrialised, but with a population of 60 million we are not that big. How outspoken on human rights can we be? We are talking about the superpower of the future here. We are small, while China is getting bigger and bigger. You need to strike a balance between your pragmatic interests and your values. In these circumstances the former is likely to outweigh the latter.'

The strategy of getting on their high horse and showing scant respect for China has badly misfired for Italian politicians in the past. The populist right of Berlusconi and his associates briefly tried to take advantage of the public's aversion to the rise of the Chinese. The Italians are just as critical of China as the Germans, according to Pew research, except that they do not take issue with environmental pollution and human rights. Their preoccupation is with jobs. Until China joined the WTO, many small Italian companies producing shoes, textiles and furniture were able to make a decent living. But their much cheaper Chinese counterparts left these family businesses gasping for breath as they witnessed the collapse of their domestic market and their exports to the rest of Europe. Allegations of 'dumping' were rife, both in Brussels and Rome. The subsequent import levies on the Chinese products were only a plaster on the entrepreneurs' wounds.

But there was not only suffering; the larger companies, led by luxury brands such as Armani, Gucci, Salvatore Ferragamo and

Ferrari, benefited hugely from the burgeoning Chinese demand for luxury. And, amusingly, Chinese consumers were keen for the manufacturers to continue production in their factories in Italy – nobody wants a Gucci handbag saying 'made in China'.

But these successes received far less attention in the Italian media than the suffering of the family-owned businesses. China also got a bad press because of what happened in the Tuscan town of Prato. A large colony of several tens of thousands of Chinese people descended on the textile town and moved into the factories that had been abandoned because they could no longer compete with China. Henceforth from Prato, the ever-increasing influx of Chinese workers could provide the clothing with the valuable 'made in Italy' label.

Initially, the local authorities saw this as the salvation of the town's textile tradition – and not without reason. They happily allowed it until the Chinese working conditions in the Italian factories came in for scrutiny in the media. The result: a textile entrepreneur was elected mayor in 2009 on the strength of a campaign against 'Chinese tyranny'. Once in power, he dispatched dogs, helicopters and police officers to the migrants, prompting the Chinese embassy in Rome to lodge a furious protest against these 'raids'.

Relations between China and Italy were, in a word, problematic. And Silvio Berlusconi would not have been his populist self if he had not tried to capitalise on this. The then prime minister, known for his fierce anti-communist sentiments, caused a row in 2006 when he urged a crowd of Forza Italia supporters to read *The Black Book of Communism*. It allegedly said that 'in the China of Mao, they [the communists] did not eat children, but had them boiled to fertilise the fields'. It was meant as a 'joke', which Berlusconi soon admitted was 'questionable', but the damage was done. His opponent Romano Prodi spoke of 'an insult to 1.3 billion people'. The Chinese authorities merely expressed 'displeasure', advising the Italian leader 'to use words and actions favourable to stable and friendly relations between China and Italy'.

Giulio Tremonti, multiple finance minister of his country and Berlusconi's fellow party member, offered an intellectual under-pinning to the discontent. In his book *La paura e la speranza* (Fear and Hope) he went on the offensive. 'The Chinese dragon will possess Europe', he predicted. He described Chinese immigrants, like those in Prato, as a 'fifth column' which had already embarked on the conquest. We were facing 'reverse colonisation', a 'new imperialism' even. Against this backdrop, he qualified the possible lifting of the arms embargo against China as 'suicide'.

Tremonti's hope consisted of a return to European values. Right now, 'Europe's identity is confused because it is based on a global culture based on indiscriminate equality and free import of merchandise and then people'. Again, this boiled down to 'suicide' for Europe. It would have to become a 'fortress', 'necessary to defend ourselves and to survive'. Protecting domestic industry is part of this strategy, through both import duties on non-European products and a powerful industrial policy.

But the Italian was forced to make a sharp U-turn in 2011. As finance minister under Berlusconi, he felt the immense pressure from the financial markets in response to his country's huge public debt. Tremonti was forced to receive the senior executive of Chinese sovereign wealth fund CIC with full honours. Investment in Italian government bonds would be more than welcome. Faced with a tough decision, Tremonti had come to the conclusion that fulminating against China would only harm his country.

## 'More Europe' as an answer to China?

Harping on about Western values to keep the enemy at bay only to be forced into a climb-down, like Tremonti; bowing down to China's economic might and leaving Western values unmentioned, like Cameron; point-scoring at other countries' expense with an eye to quick profits and leaving Brussels to its own devices if it happens to be more convenient – European politicians' answers to the questions raised by the rise of China are not very edifying. Is there an alternative to the concessions on principles, the occasional displays of arrogance and the kowtowing to China's economic power?

The best solution I can see for European politicians is a radical choice in favour of Europe, the compelling logic for which I outlined at the start of this chapter. If they chose Europe, they could be the proud representatives of the world's largest economy, the EU-28, instead of the anxious representatives of medium-sized national economies. Collectively, they could no longer be played off against each other by China and instead would present a much more powerful front on issues such as access to the Chinese market. Likewise, they could draw up plans for a common industrial policy. In Izraelewicz's view this is a crucial response now that China is abiding by only some of our postwar trade regulations. The state helps its domestic industry on an unprecedented scale, whereas in the West the distance between state and industry has actually increased. A more proactive industrial policy would help to offset this.

However, this road towards 'more Europe' requires politicians to jump over their own shadows. Policy coordination between Brussels and the member states, starting with the 'Big Three', will need to be stepped up. European government leaders such as Merkel, Hollande and Cameron, who like to use foreign policy to cut a good figure, should leave the initiative to Brussels, or at least work together more closely than they currently do, like Sarkozy had planned back in 2007. They must certainly avoid having so much distance between their positions that outsiders can take advantage, as China was able to do in the solar panel case. Established institutions such as Quai d'Orsay in France and the Foreign Office in London ought to subscribe to the longer-term perspective that the only foreign policy that stands a chance beside the superpowers of the US and China is a European policy. This calls for a powerful role for Brussels, with the President of the European Council and the High Representative for Foreign Affairs taking centre stage.

Unfortunately, there seems to be little interest in going down the route of 'more Europe'. The rise of euroscepticism, expressed by a substantial minority of Europeans in the European elections of 2014, is obviously not helping. As a result, politicians will be very reluctant to take any initiative. The weak economic recovery makes it unlikely as well. Germany, which in 2014 started to experience its own economic woes, is critically eyeing France under President Hollande. His unconvincing efforts to push through economic reforms nationally make French–German talks about a new common industrial policy extremely unlikely.

'More Europe' becomes even more complicated when the United Kingdom is added to the equation, as this country has traditionally been and is now increasingly opposed to the notion. With the announced in/out referendum on EU membership Prime Minister Cameron has effectively blocked any progress in this area. As for the referendum, it goes without saying that a potential exit will seriously weaken both the UK's and the EU's position in relation to China. Take trade agreements, for instance: in splendid isolation the UK would be the underdog in negotiations, while the EU would lose some of its strength too.

In the somewhat longer term there is the bleak prospect of massive job losses in the industries of rich northern Europe, following the example of small Italian manufacturers. This could happen when China becomes a truly serious competitor as a producer of high-tech products. Then it is likely we will start hearing voices echoing Tremonti all over Europe, labelling China as the enemy. From there it will be only a small step to protectionism. Besides counterproductive, that would also be short-sighted, as a drop in competitiveness is first and foremost a problem of one's own making.

Authoritative voices have argued that such threats must become reality before we can achieve 'more Europe'. This was the view of Érik Izraelewicz, who described China as 'the main argument in favour of a united Europe'. His 'personal hope' was that the country would fulfil the same role as the Soviet Union post-1945, when Europe opted for further integration out of fear for this external threat. But, he added, 'I fear we are not yet afraid enough of China'.

Belgian expert Jonathan Holslag is of a similar mind, describing Europe in its current state as looking 'like a sailing school, a bunch of Optimists with skippers paying more attention to each other's rear ends than to whatever is looming on the horizon'. By outlining the dark clouds on that horizon he hopes to highlight the need for a united Europe. Europe is set to become a 'playing field' for China and the US, he warns. These large tanker ships are bound to run down the tiny European vessels.

Is this kind of enemy thinking necessary to achieve closed ranks in Europe? There are plenty of historical examples to suggest that this is how it works. Then again, you might not want to go down that road with China. It would only fuel the country's already powerful nationalism. The great peril of enemy thinking is that it easily provokes a self-fulfilling reaction: create an enemy and you get one. It could play into the hands of those in Beijing who seek a more confrontational stance towards the West. One can imagine the consequences.

It is to be hoped that Europe will come to recognise the need for greater unity under its own steam. But current political and economic conditions are very unfavourable. The best we can hope for is that a second Cold War, this time with China, can be avoided. It would be a regression to a time of global division and of wrestling for a sphere of influence. Moreover, it would be to the detriment of all the shared issues the global community has yet to address, most prominently climate change.

# Chapter 24

# A Joint Approach to Global Problems?

Hopes for an international summit had seldom been this high. Around the world people had become aware of the danger of greenhouse gas emissions, which could lead to global warming and spell catastrophe for the whole of mankind. Now, in the final month of 2009, an approach to global warming would finally be agreed at the biggest climate conference ever held: the Copenhagen Summit. Limiting the global temperature increase to 2 degrees, a UN target agreed to in the 1990s, through binding engagements seemed within reach.

Images of the impending catastrophe, greatly exaggerated in Al Gore's documentary *An Inconvenient Truth*, had made a big impression, scientific consensus on the problem was virtually intact and the political climate appeared to be favourable to those blessed with an optimistic nature. The world's two biggest $CO_2$ emitters, the United States and China, seemed to be prepared to do business. Unlike his predecessor, President Obama had said he wanted to be a 'green' president, keen to start reducing his country's level of $CO_2$ emissions. From China the signals were positive as well, as there was an increasing awareness that without an urgent response the consequences would be dire. In Europe environmental awareness had a longer history and Al Gore's message was very well received by the public at large. With Copenhagen the European Union was hoping to take the global lead. And so the international environmental movement thought the conference could really deliver this time. Boasting no fewer than 27,000 participants, including 113 government leaders, it was nicknamed 'Hopenhagen'.

The conference was not just important for the issue itself, but could also be seen as a test case for an even broader question: is the global community capable of collectively solving a major problem? Can the disparities between the political systems and economic interests be overcome when mankind's future is under threat? These kinds of questions are relevant as the global population is expected to increase from 7 to 9 billion people by 2050. The resulting tensions, including a shortage of resources and food, call for global action.

Following the earlier Kyoto Protocol, there were demands for nothing short of a legally binding treaty to be signed in Copenhagen. But crucially, the two greatest $CO_2$ offenders would have to be prepared to accept such obligations.

The conference had been underway for nearly two weeks and was drawing to a close when US President Obama arrived in Copenhagen for a mere fifteen-hour stay. His secretary of state, Hillary Clinton, informed him of the latest developments, or rather the lack thereof. She described events up until that point as the 'worst meeting I've been to since eighth-grade student council'. The tensions between the Chinese and the US delegations had been running high, with mutual recriminations. American pressure to reach agreement on international verification of results did not go down well with the Chinese. They hit back with accusations over the US's modest efforts in the past.

From the word go, the Chinese chief negotiator, Su Wei, had it in for the Danish chair, Connie Hedegaard. In line with the European position she was aiming for legally binding commitments. Su tried to undermine her authority, first via aggressive interruptions and then through persistent silence. He also resisted all efforts to agree hard targets. The extremely remote target of a 50 per cent reduction in global emissions by 2050 was a bridge too far for him. He even rejected inclusion of the 80 per cent reduction that the Western industrialised nations had previously signed up for, although it was no more than a confirmation of a position adopted earlier and only bound the industrialised nations, not the emerging countries. The industrialising Chinese simply did not want to be confronted in any way with this figure of 80 per cent in the future.

Su Wei got what he wanted, to the despair of Angela Merkel, who raised her arms in exasperation. The German chancellor did not understand why she could not commit to her own objective. This was the atmosphere that greeted Obama upon his arrival. A snowstorm forecast for Washington meant he could only stay a short time, but agreement about a final declaration was nowhere in sight. And without such a text, failure would be complete.

## 'Saviour of the planet'

Where did it all go wrong? Anyone taking a closer look at the contrasting perspectives of the main protagonists would have been less surprised than the people who mistook Copenhagen for Hopenhagen. It was written in the stars that Europe would be playing a supporting rather than a pioneering role.

The Chinese negotiators' opposition to a legally binding treaty had nothing to do with climate change scepticism. One of the consequences of global warming is a decreasing supply of water from the Himalayas. This alone is reason enough for the leaders to take the issue seriously. China has a history of devastating water shortages and the Himalayas are an essential source. In fact, environmental experts see water shortages as the biggest threat to the country.

The fact that China has become the biggest investor worldwide in both solar and wind energy in recent years is another indication that the country's leaders are taking the problem seriously. Of course they realised that it does not do China's image any harm either. If China could use green technology and its large-scale application to promote itself as the 'saviour of the planet' it would compensate quite nicely for the troubling lack of soft power caused by human rights violations and other wrong-doings. With this second motive, the pursuit of political prestige in the international arena, China's approach to climate is not fundamentally different from that of European nations. They too like to show their moral leadership in this area.

But there are clear limits to the Chinese preparedness to do business with the West. As we saw with the human rights issue, the country will not have its sovereignty violated in any way. That principle is holy and the climate problem does not alter this, however grave and global it may be. So as soon as the prospect of international verification is raised, to determine whether a country honours its agreements, it is bound to meet with a Chinese veto. The leaders argue the UN should take them at their word.

At least as important as sovereignty is their premise that the economic development of China cannot be undermined, as long as some 10 per cent of the Chinese population lives in poverty. Prime Minister Li Keqiang may have declared a 'war on pollution', but he and his boss Xi are certainly not prepared to sacrifice economic growth to this war. It is a solution occasionally proposed by environmentalists, but something Western countries have never adopted either. This would be too much to ask, especially of China. The government was prepared to do something about its '$CO_2$ intensity', the emission per unit product. A few months prior to Copenhagen the country launched a concrete target: a reduction in intensity by an average of 40 to 45 per cent by 2020. But how many tonnes of $CO_2$ this would be in 2020 remained unclear, as they gave no absolute figure. As so often, they wielded the 'we are in a different development phase' argument. It came with an underpinning that was hard to refute: measured per capita, $CO_2$ emissions in Europe and the United States were still several times higher than in China. So they have no truck with Western environmental groups that claim the planet could not handle it if the Chinese were to start driving cars and eating meat on the same scale as Westerners. They pit their own 'survival emissions' against Western 'luxury emissions'. In their view it would be more appropriate to tackle the latter than to deny the former.

It will be even trickier for the West to impose demands on China if and when the European and American contributions to Chinese $CO_2$ emissions are acknowledged. Having moved industrial production to China, the West's pollution is now effectively taking place outside its own sphere. The 'made in China' consumer goods, which are being shipped to us by the millions of containers, are cheap not only because of the low wages, but also because the Chinese environmental costs have not been passed on. The Chinese leaders have a point when they say that it is easy enough for the West with its service economies, having subcontracted energy-intensive production with high levels of $CO_2$ emissions to China.

Finally, the Chinese believed that the US especially had done too little to reduce $CO_2$ emissions prior to Copenhagen. Again, this was a fair criticism: between 2000 and 2008 President Bush had blocked any progress by refusing to ratify the Kyoto Protocol at the Rio Summit. He argued that it did damage to US economic interests as there were no obligations imposed on emerging economies such as China. In the meantime Bush did not tackle the problem in his own country. So the Chinese had the right to speak their mind. Unfortunately it did not do the planet any good.

## A chair for Obama

To Europe, the subject had initially seemed ideal for a pioneering role. With Bush at the helm, the United States had been lagging behind – despite Al Gore's efforts. But in Europe's largest countries, most notably Germany, global warming was a particularly hot topic among the population. Since the climate summit was held under Danish chairmanship, Europe seemed to have every reason to hope for a key role.

In actual fact things took a wrong turn in the run-up to Copenhagen for a classic reason: internal divisions in Europe. During a meeting in Brussels the EU countries had managed to agree on the necessity of a legally binding treaty. But now that the economic crisis had hit, they failed to reach agreement on the financing of the necessary measures. Nor did they manage to increase their level of ambition from 20 to 30 per cent fewer emissions by 2020, thus compromising Europe's ability to demand extra efforts from the US and China. For lack of a unified position, Europe's 'Big Three' began to negotiate independently in Denmark.

This European lack of unity must have served Obama quite well. He had his own trouble on his home front, which made the pursuit of a legally binding treaty difficult. In 2010, Obama would have to drum up support in the US Senate for a national climate law with hard targets. Given the economic recession, this was always going to be a challenge, since the stimulus of growth would have to be a priority now, especially in the eyes of the Republicans. If Obama had returned from Copenhagen with an international 'Diktat' he would not have stood a chance. At the same time, he understood perfectly well that no final declaration at all in Copenhagen would be too much of a disgrace for a 'green president'. But after two weeks of futile talks, the summit was certainly heading towards that conclusion.

In his book *The Quest* the American energy expert Daniel Yergin describes how Obama, with only a few hours at his disposal, went in search of a compromise. 'At the end of a long corridor, Obama came upon a surprised security guard outside the conference room that was the office of the Chinese delegation. Despite the guard's panicked efforts Obama brushed right past him and burst into the room. Not only was Wen there but, to Obama's surprise, he found that so were the other members of what was now known as the BASIC Group – President Lula of Brazil, President Zuma of South Africa and Prime Minister Singh of India.' They were in conclave to arrive at a joint position and at least as surprised to see Obama. The US president was offered a chair next to Lula and opposite Wen.

Without immediately wanting to proclaim this party to constitute the new world order of the twenty-first century, I believe it is quite telling that both Europe and Japan were sidelined at this point. At previous UN conferences on this scale, that would have been unthinkable. In Copenhagen, however, Obama ended up doing business with the leaders of four emerging economies.

Premier Wen was in the company of his negotiator Su Wei. At a certain point, Yergin writes, the latter wanted to tear into an argument by the US president. But Wen silenced him. It created the necessary room for consensus and, after lots of back and forth, a text was drawn up at the last minute. Following the improvised debate Obama thrust the agreement into the hands of the European government leaders, telling them it was the best they could hope for.

## 'Fundamental deadlock'

The text contained neither legal obligations nor hard targets for 2020 and 2050. It said that the rise in temperature could not exceed 2 degrees. But it was an empty promise, since there were no $CO_2$ targets or dates. Both Wen and Obama said they were happy with this outcome. The Chinese leader kept a free hand, as did the American. For both superpowers, domestic considerations were the decisive factor for letting Copenhagen fail.

'I won't try to hide my disappointment', said the Portuguese chairman of the European Commission, José Manuel Barroso, afterwards. Behind the scenes, European leaders such as Merkel and Sarkozy were equally upset about the lack of binding obligations. Both China and the US were blamed. According to environmental organisations such as Friends of the Earth it had all gone wrong in Copenhagen because 'rich countries had bullied the developing nations'. Prime Minister Wen came under fire as well, because he had Su Wei speak to Obama when he should have done so himself. The civil servant Su had to keep conferring with his superiors, to the annoyance of the other leaders. China was so heavily criticised that a week later Xinhua news agency published an overview of all of Wen's diplomatic efforts. The Chinese hit back by highlighting the 'unrealistic and unfair demands' which Merkel and Brown were supposed to have imposed on China.

Obama described it diplomatically as a 'meaningful agreement'. He said they could not have achieved more because of a 'fundamental deadlock in perspectives' between him and the 'emerging economies'. The American president expressed sympathy with the unwillingness on the part of the Chinese and Indians to slow down the development of their disadvantaged populations. In his view the accord was better than no accord at all, since the latter might have fed 'frustration and cynicism'. Likewise, officials in China described it as 'meaningful and positive'. But Prime Minister Wen also expressed reservations. A better deal had not been forthcoming, in his view, because of 'distrust' between the nations.

Five years and a series of less prominent climate summits later, China and the US were able to come up with a joint climate initiative at the end of 2014. The Chinese, plagued by air pollution and therefore increasingly sensitive to the urgency of the topic, announced their carbon dioxide emissions would peak in 2030 – a rather vague, but still important statement, as any kind of ceiling used to be out of the question. In the same statement the US promised it would emit up to 28 per cent less in 2025 than it did in 2005 – a promise which was heavily criticised by the Republican majority in the US Congress. This initiative of Obama and Xi is meant to make a success of 'Paris 2015' and avoid a repetition of the Copenhagen disaster.

The lesson taught us by that episode in 2009 is clear: cooperation on global problems comes second to a country's self-interest, whether that country is China or the US. Both had their reasons for a meaningless final declaration. Consensus just about trumped the mutual distrust in American–Chinese relations. This is without doubt the most important bilateral relationship in the world. Its future will determine both China's place in the world and the relationship that is subordinate to it, that between China and Europe.

# Chapter 25

# China and the US

*G2 or Cold War 2.0?*

Squabbling between the United States and China, culminating in a feeble compromise that left the rest of the world none the wiser – that was the scene offered by the Danish climate conference of 2009. It seems fair to ask to what extent we should consider it a sign of things to come. What can we expect from future American–Chinese relations: is the world heading towards a 'Cold War 2.0', characterised by confrontation between the two most powerful countries in the world? If so, a period of bloc formation awaits us, with both superpowers fighting each other politically and economically to maximise their respective spheres of influence. Or will the US and China come to recognise that in view of their shared interests a 'G2' model of cooperation would be preferable, one that offers the prospect of a joint approach to global problems?

It is important to note that China presents the US with a unique challenge. For the first time in history the Americans have to position themselves in relation to an emerging world power which is not only based on a different political system and is currently in the process of building up its military power, but which is also economically strong. The latter makes China fundamentally different from the US's biggest rival to date, the Soviet Union. Many predict that at some point after 2020 the Chinese economy will outstrip that of the US. While this remains to be seen, it is clear that the Chinese have a lot more economic clout than the Russians ever had. The US's only other postwar rival, Japan in the 1980s, was an economic powerhouse too, but it posed no military or political threat.

As a result of this unique challenge, the Americans could well end up viewing China as an enemy. This is always a distinct possibility in the run-up to US elections, when politicians pander to the fear of job losses to China. The resulting sense of vulnerability is further reinforced when China's role in financing US government debt is highlighted. American public opinion is awash with speculation about the country's decline, in tandem with China's rise. In fact, the American public is now so familiar with this image that a majority believe the Chinese economy has already overtaken that of the US.

This tendency to think of China as bigger and therefore more threatening than it really is goes hand in hand with disappointment over its political development. The Chinese leaders are stubbornly refusing to meet the Americans' ideological expectations. The choice, in the late 1970s, in favour of a market economy should have been followed up with a different political system, in the eyes of many Americans anyway. Surely an expanding middle class ought to demand a say in how the country is run, just as the internet should lead to greater freedom?

Consecutive US governments have cherished the hope for more democracy and freedom. Americans appear to be more disappointed by the lack of progress than Europeans. This is probably a reflection of the former's more deeply rooted conviction that their ideology is superior and therefore worth emulating. While there is something to be said for this conviction, on the downside it tends to get in the way of a proper understanding of the Chinese perspective. I would like to give this perspective its deserved place when assessing whether the world is heading for a Cold War 2.0 or a G2 model.

Talk to Chinese people about their country's role in the world and it will not be long before someone airs the belief that the US are out to thwart China. Our economy is destined to become the number one in the world, I heard frequently, but Americans are doing everything to prevent this. They exploit Chinese workers, who have to do the hard work producing iPhones cheaply, while American shareholders net the profits. And the US is living beyond its means thanks to Chinese savings, so the complaints go.

Of course one can note plenty of admiration for American culture too. Lots of Chinese people are crazy about the clothing brands, high-tech equipment, pop music, television series and hamburgers. In these areas one can feel a sense of inferiority. Yet when it comes to politics, many middle-class Chinese seem to be convinced that the Americans harp on about human rights and democracy not so much out of genuine commitment, but to raise doubts and sow dissent about the Chinese political system. In their view the American goal appears to be a stagnating rather than a flourishing China. They feel strongly that the Americans are unscrupulously pursuing their own interests – although they admit, with a wry smile, that their country is no different. This state of mind is worth remembering when assessing whether a new Cold War is likely.

## China as a 'trapped giant'

A clash between the two superpowers over their spheres of influence in the Pacific is the most important test case in this respect. President Xi has made it abundantly clear in various speeches that he no longer wants to stand by the famous dictum of his predecessor Deng Xiaoping that China should wait its turn on the world stage and 'hide and bide'. In the Asian region Xi wants more control and hence more power, reflecting China's rise to superpower status. In the light of this aspiration it is a thorn in his side that control of the shipping lanes connecting his country with the oil and gas reserves in the Middle East is in the hands of the US navy. That is understandable; when the European nations and the US were emerging as world powers they too were keen to have such control. It would therefore be more conspicuous if China did not have this ambition.

What makes China's case special is that it has been such a superpower for a very long time – and that the awareness of this fact is very much part of the collective conscience. The country's return to the top, where it spent centuries until the early nineteenth century, is felt as a return to its rightful place – a sentiment that Westerners might view as arrogance. Underneath it all is another, less readily admitted feeling: a sense of getting even with the Western nations that inflicted the 'century of humiliation' on China through their 'hegemonic power politics'. The fact that China contributed to its own downfall in the nineteenth century does not get much of a look-in in the country's history books.

To settle accounts with a past in which China was weak and the plaything of foreign powers, Xi and his predecessors have made a significant commitment to strengthening the military. In recent decades, the annual defence budget has grown faster than its economy, which is no mean feat. These efforts have given the country the world's biggest military in terms of troops and the world's second largest defence budget (131 billion dollars in 2014). Nonetheless, it is still miles behind the US military (496 billion dollars in 2014), which defence experts estimate will remain superior for at least another ten years.

Still, the Americans believed this Chinese advance could not go unanswered. In 2011 Obama announced his famous 'pivot to East Asia', which involved the deployment of troops and resources to the area where China sought to step up its role. Obama purposely did not speak of aiming for containment – the strategy applied to the Soviet Union – as this could be construed as a hostile act. He argued that China ought to be pleased, since it would make the region more stable – and isn't stability its top priority?

The Chinese leaders were not convinced. Even before the pivot they felt that their country was being besieged by the US military. One does not need to be paranoid to believe this. With 35,000 troops in Japan and 28,000 in South Korea, the US has huge military bases on China's doorstep. Besides, after seventy years of military dominance in the Pacific the Americans have established a great many alliances in Asia, far more than China. To the Chinese leadership the 'pivot' made one thing clear: the US will not allow China to expand its sphere of influence.

Neutral defence experts agree with this view. Belgian professor Jonathan Holslag, an internationally recognised expert in the field of Chinese defence, describes China as a 'trapped giant' in his book of the same name. He believes the US is doing all it can to minimise China's maritime role. And that is a statement, not a reproach. Holslag is sympathetic to the ambitions of both superpowers, even though they seem incompatible. Analysing their collision course in the Pacific, he speaks of nothing less than an 'Iron Curtain of ships and sensors' which the Americans have positioned to contain China. Conversely, he points out that China is doing just as much to demarcate its territory. 'The Americans accuse the Chinese of engaging in "area denial" [attempt to deny others entry into an area, ed.], but what they are trying with the Chinese is "ocean denial".' It is a tense situation which has the potential to contribute to a new Cold War.

The territorial claims made by Xi have increased the tensions. Ever since he took office, he has been stressing the importance of what he describes as 'core national interests'. These include both the East and South China Seas, home to various island groups. A number of neighbouring countries also claim them, a fact that China blithely ignores: the country has been fishing in these regions, constructing oil rigs, building lighthouses and even creating entirely new islands. This all bolsters Xi's claim that the entire region belongs to China. The outcome has been an endless string of territorial incidents. Tensions with Japan, especially, have been running high over the Diaoyu/Senkaku Islands.

## Keep up the resistance or give in

An escalating conflict can have major repercussions for Asian trade flows to the West. Of course China and Japan have no rational interest in disrupting these flows, but the history between the two countries is charged and mutual distrust is deep – not least because of Chinese state propaganda still churning out films and television series emphasising the historical wickedness of the Japanese. Concealed behind this Chinese–Japanese dispute is the clash between China and the US. The key issue here is what the Americans will do when Japan faces war with China: what will their military guarantees, written down in a mutual defence treaty, be worth then?

The same question arises in relation to the Philippines, which has a similar agreement, and Vietnam, which looks more vulnerable without such a treaty. In 2014 it looked as if China was trying to find out through provocations. The US was provoked into responding to the construction of a Chinese oil rig not far off the Vietnamese coast. Beijing claimed it was installing the one-billion-dollar platform in its own territorial waters, but Hanoi begged to differ. During the anti-Chinese riots that followed, people were injured and killed. But despite Vietnamese and American protests China saw no reason to move the platform. The Americans did not think the issue was big enough to warrant escalation. Three months later China removed the platform after all.

Military experts are holding their breath over these kinds of incidents, as they can easily bring the two superpowers into direct confrontation. Isn't China isolating itself with this new assertiveness, which contrasts with Xi's rhetoric about his neighbourhood policy which features 'amity, sincerity, mutual benefit and inclusiveness'? It looks like it, because countries like Vietnam and the Philippines are increasingly turning to the Americans for protection. As the US is happy to offer it, China's tactics seem to be backfiring. But it cannot be ruled out that Xi is playing a smarter game. Former US Secretary of State Henry Kissinger, author of *On China*, points to China's staying power in these kinds of clashes. Arguing why a military confrontation would be unwise, he wrote in *Foreign Affairs* in 2012: 'In China, the United States would encounter an adversary skilled over the centuries in using prolonged conflict as a strategy and whose doctrine emphasizes the psychological exhaustion of the opponent.'

This observation is pertinent to the litany of incidents in the South and East China Seas. 'Xi is not playing this game with a timeframe of six months or a year in mind', the French China expert François Godement pointed out to me. Xi's aim is to bolster Chinese power by putting permanent pressure on other countries. These then face a choice: keep up the resistance or give in. China hopes they will eventually relinquish their opposition. This may well happen if China's military and economic might continues to grow and the US finds it increasingly difficult, due to budget constraints, to play the role of the world's police officer.

The economic sphere may well provide another source of heightened confrontation in the future. When it comes to investments, Chinese takeovers in the US are eyed with suspicion. Conversely, American businessmen complain about the Chinese market being increasingly difficult to penetrate. Both countries subscribe to the importance of free trade, but here too their strategic manoeuvring is becoming all too apparent: whereas the US favours a new free trade zone without China called TPP (Trans-Pacific Partnership, with eleven other countries), China wants the twenty-one members of APEC (Asia Pacific Economic Cooperation) to form a free trade zone, thus including the US.

An economic area rife with Cold War sentiments is industrial espionage, which, as we have seen, has become a permanent source of tension between the two countries. China excels in this field of expertise. Other countries engage in this too, but not on the same scale and not with a coordinating role for the military. That said, US espionage activities came to the fore as a result of the Snowden affair. This caused the US to lose the moral high ground in this debate in 2013, something that suited the Chinese leaders very well. My worry is that industrial espionage will continue to add a Cold War dimension to the bilateral relationship. A levy on all Chinese exports to the US and allowing American companies to 'hack back', as the Huntsman report proposed in 2013, would pave the way for both a trade war and a cyber-war.

## Kissinger's fear of confrontation

Political hawks, most of whom can be found in the conservative camp in the US, think such a belligerent approach is the best way to handle China. Harking back to the successful defeat of the previous opponent, the Soviet Union, they would like to directly confront China. Among this assertive faction is former UN ambassador John Bolton. Writing in the *Wall Street Journal*, he urged the US in 2013 to shed its naïvety and no longer believe in the 'peaceful rise' the Chinese leaders are propagating: 'The rosy "peaceful rise" theory ignores countless other possibilities, particularly its polar opposite.'

These Republicans believe Obama is not taking a hard enough line now that a coalition between China and Russia is emerging, with presidents Putin and Xi agreeing on most issues. Together they have thwarted the US by blocking Security Council resolutions on, for instance, intervention in Syria. Against this 'alignment of the world's two leading anti-Western powers', as a conservative commentator put it, Obama ought to form a bloc of democracies with the aim of containing China.

These Republican hawks find an opponent in Henry Kissinger, the founding father of American rapprochement with China. Instead of bloc formation, he pleads for a 'Pacific Community', a political alliance in which both superpowers participate. He cautions against 'a new version of historic patterns of international rivalry' and recommends 'a genuine effort at cooperation'. China and the US 'owe it to themselves, and the world, to make an effort' to transcend their rivalry.

This statement is not inspired by idealism in his old age. True to his vision of global politics, Kissinger's conclusion stems from an analysis of the balance of power. The US will never manage to do to China what it did to the Soviet Union, bringing about the disintegration of the country. The reasons are many, but above all economic in nature. China's economy is so much stronger than the Soviet Union's ever was that there is simply no comparison. And given the many links between the two countries, breaking them down would hit the Americans themselves quite hard. 'A prolonged confrontation between China and the United States would alter the world economy with unsettling consequences for all', Kissinger argues.

This interdependency is best illustrated with reference to US government bonds, of which China is the biggest buyer. The US has been able to partly finance its public debt of 18 trillion dollars through China's investment of roughly 1,300 billion dollars. This huge investment has created a mutual dependence. Given these dollar reserves, China would not benefit from an American decline, while export to the US, its second export market after the European Union, would also be hit.

The 'dollar trap' that China has fallen into with its investment in US government bonds actually contributes to global financial stability, according to American Nobel Economics laureate Joseph Stiglitz in his book *Making Globalization Work*. Whereas financial markets are guided by 'periods of irrational pessimism or optimism', the Chinese authorities are a beacon of calm. Given this 'mutual hostage situation', conflicts between the US and China 'seldom move beyond rhetoric', he believes. The facts bear this out. While tensions may be running high at times, the Chinese sovereign wealth funds hold their considerable investments in US bonds.

The links between China and American 'Big Business' further bolster this interdependency. Wal-Mart alone buys so much from Chinese suppliers that if the retailer were a nation it would be China's sixth-biggest export market. The political ramifications are huge: multinationals such as Wal-Mart and Apple profit enormously from a low renminbi and gain no benefit whatsoever from their government's pressure to push the rate up. This is mainly meant to help American companies hit by Chinese competition on their domestic market. The major multinationals that have their products made in China want none of this, let alone a Cold War. In *On China* Kissinger describes the price to be paid quite succinctly: 'A cold war between the two countries would arrest progress for a generation on both sides of the Atlantic.'

To my mind Kissinger is less persuasive when he cites China's domestic problems as a reason why Xi would not pursue military adventures. He believes the president will be too preoccupied with internal issues to even consider it in this decade. This appears to be a case of wishful thinking, because these problems could actually make a military adventure all the more attractive. Military aggression as a distraction from national concerns – it would not be the first time in world history. Russia's interference in Ukraine is the most recent example.

Such a conflict between China and one of its neighbours might push the US, with its many military guarantees in the region, towards direct confrontation. While inflicting catastrophic damage on both parties, it would fail to resolve anything in the long run, as Kissinger remarks: 'By the time any such hypothetical conflagration drew to a close, all participants would be left exhausted and debilitated. They would then be obliged to face anew the very task that confronts them today: the construction of an international order in which both countries are significant components.'

## China's refusal of the G2 concept

So what to make of the 'G2' model, the pursuit of shared responsibility for joint global problems? Above I outlined the threat of a Cold War between China and the US. I believe the risks are all too obvious and it is self-evident that both countries should do everything in their power to avoid it. Striving for the opposite – a 'G2' – might help. But how realistic is it in the light of the above? And what are the experiences with it to date?

When he came into office in 2008, Obama was a strong proponent of the G2 model. He welcomed 'China's efforts to play a greater role on the world stage' and expressed a willingness to make room for the new superpower. The American–Chinese relationship would be the 'landmark bilateral relationship of the twenty-first century', which is why he favoured coordinated action. His political opponents condemned his position as soft on China, but Obama ignored them, trying to manoeuvre China towards the US standpoint on a range of issues, from global warming and nuclear weapons in Iran to the uprising in Syria. To this end he invested in nine meetings with his counterpart Hu Jintao. But to the frustration of the US government, success eluded him.

Prime Minister Wen Jiabao actually admitted that he did not believe in the 'G2' concept. 'Some have floated the idea that America and China are going to rule the world together. It is a false and unreasonable idea', he told Western journalists. During Obama's first term in office, the 'G2 notion' gradually receded into the background. There was a brief revival in the summer of 2013, at least in the media, when Obama and the new Chinese president met for a two-day summit 'with their shirtsleeves rolled up' at the Sunnylands estate in California. But this has not led to a rapprochement. Xi is emerging as an outspoken nationalist, who sees more of an ally in Putin than in Obama. A critical stance towards the US, together with his Russian counterpart, serves Chinese interests best in his view. He appears to have as little affinity with the 'G2' concept as his predecessors.

Why does China refuse to see American advances as a chance to gain international recognition? The aforementioned suspicion rears its head again: Xi is unwilling to accept all kinds of international obligations foisted onto him. He would rather serve directly what he perceives to be key Chinese interests than function as the 'responsible stakeholder' the US wants him to be. He has therefore come up with his own Asian Infrastructure Investment Bank (AIIB), an alternative to the Asian Development Bank, which is dominated by Japan and the US, and the World Bank. I will discuss this initiative later in this chapter.

But there is a deeper underlying cause for Chinese reluctance to participate fully on the international stage as well. Such a prominent role requires ample self-confidence. Now Xi might be good at radiating this, but that does not tell the whole story. I tend to agree with Érik Izraelewicz's observation in *L'Arrogance chinoise* that the arrogance the Chinese are so frequently accused of flaunting also conceals fear and insecurity over their position in the world and their economic and political system.

## A sense of vulnerability

This insecurity cannot be dismissed as an attempt to pull the wool over foreigners' eyes. Andrew Nathan, an American China expert and professor at Columbia University, provides the most persuasive underpinning for this. He interviewed Chinese policy makers and academics about their self-image and their perception of the US. 'China is uncertain about its territory, its control over it is contested and that is a major difference with western countries', he identifies one source of insecurity in *Foreign Affairs* in 2012. In his fascinating article 'How China sees America', he points out that Beijing is forced to deploy vast resources to retain power over two-fifths of its territory, including the western province of Xinjiang and greater Tibet. Uyghurs, Tibetans and Mongolians are dissatisfied with Beijing and sometimes actively oppose central government – often with support from abroad. The efforts to suppress this opposition put permanent pressure on the state apparatus. For Western countries, on the other hand, this kind of primary uncertainty about their territory belongs to a distant past.

Just beyond China's borders the sense of vulnerability increases, as does the hostility. Hong Kong may have been officially part of China since 1997, but it boasts a political system with democratic elements and a substantial part of the population has protested fiercely against attempts at imposing limits to democracy by Beijing. In the autumn of 2014 a pro-democracy movement which attracted worldwide attention protested for months against the 'vetting' of political candidates, as proposed by Beijing. In vain, as the central government refused to compromise. It did little for its popularity, both in Hong Kong and worldwide.

The relationship with Taiwan, at a distance of only 180 kilometres, is equally complex. The island wants to chart its own, independent course, with the US as its protector in the background. But China's economic importance is increasing. For local politicians in the 'renegade province', as Taiwan is seen by Beijing, it requires a difficult balancing act. If they play along with China, which is tying the island economically to the mainland and expecting this to lead to a single, united country in the long term, they risk punishment by voters. As in the case of Hong Kong, an important section of the population fears that Beijing's growing grip on the island will culminate in total Chinese domination.

China is not popular among its big Asian neighbours either. Here too the suspicion that epitomises the country's relationship with the US dominates. In the past seventy years China has been at war with five neighbouring countries (India, Japan, Russia, South Korea and Vietnam). That said, relations are not all bad. Ties with Putin's Russia, especially, have been strengthened. But there are doubts among China experts about the depth of the alliance. It has done nothing, for example, to remove Russian fears that a scarcely populated Siberia might de facto be taken over by immigrants from an overflowing northern China. Conversely, the Chinese leaders view Russia's modest economic achievements with contempt. What really counts for them is their relationship to the US.

Other neighbouring countries offer serious competition to China: arch-enemy Japan is a much more advanced knowledge economy – with only 127 million inhabitants its economy is around 40 per cent the size of China. South Korea is smaller, but far more prosperous than China in terms of GDP per household. India is a young colossus with its own problems – as well as potential with an almost equally large, but younger population. And tiny Vietnam, with which China has been at loggerheads for thousands of years, attracts a great many foreign and, intriguingly, Chinese investors these days, because its wages are lower.

The list of China's true friends is short, featuring four former Soviet republics (Kazakhstan, Uzbekistan, Kyrgyzstan and Turkmenistan) and weak states such as North Korea and Pakistan. The latter, incidentally, also comes under the US's sphere of influence. Just how hard it is to make new allies is demonstrated by the case of Burma (Myanmar). Having enjoyed years of Chinese assistance, the country is now trying to extricate itself from China's clutches and is seeking rapprochement with the West.

Looking at more remote regions such as Australia, Africa, the Middle East and Latin America, we find evidence that China's increasing economic clout is also meeting with renewed resistance. In some countries local politicians are scoring with anti-Chinese rhetoric, taking aim at China for unscrupulously pursuing its own interests. As their interests in those regions grow, Chinese leaders feel more rather than less vulnerable, being unable to defend them militarily. This further increases their sense of insecurity.

But to the Chinese policy makers Nathan spoke to, the main source of vulnerability is an internal one: the political system. They have a sense that it is 'in a transitional phase'. Nathan draws a comparison with Japan. The government's economic performance there has been mediocre for decades, but it never seems to prompt a fundamental debate about the multi-party system. In China, on the other hand, such fundamental doubts keep popping up in internal debates, even though the country's economic performance has been outstanding for decades. At the prospect of threats, be they deflation, environmental problems, property bubbles or rising labour costs, the conversation quickly turns to the political system as such.

Nathan tried to instil those he spoke to with a different perspective on the US by highlighting the American contribution to China's development. 'The United States has done more than any other power to contribute to China's modernization. It has drawn China into the global economy; given the Chinese access to markets, capital, and technology; trained Chinese experts in science, technology, and international law; prevented the full remilitarization of Japan; maintained the peace on the Korean Peninsula; and helped avoid a war over Taiwan.' But he was unable to remove the distrust, as the experts' prevailing view of the future remains: 'As China rises, the United States will resist.' Fascinating, too, is their prediction about the future balance of power. In sharp contrast to Western analyses about a decline in American power, they believe the US will continue to be 'the global hegemon for several decades'.

## More Chinese influence leads to more suspicion

What does all this mean for the most 'important bilateral relationship in the world'? I agree with Chinese policy makers that the West tends to perceive China to be a bigger threat than it really is. In comparative analyses, the scale of its domestic problems and its international isolation are rarely fully appreciated. The growth figures and the size of the population have a blinding effect. This is reinforced by the dynamism of the place with its expanding skylines and extreme manifestations of wealth. But that shiny exterior blinds us to the other, equally real China with its long list of problems. The solutions will have to come from a political system that may seem stable from a distance, but which is surrounded by doubt. The result is a strong conservatism, a 'don't rock the boat' mentality, especially among the many bureaucrats and the enormous state-owned enterprises. Whether President Xi manages to break this deep-rooted desire for the status quo with his anti-corruption campaign remains to be seen.

China's international position is likely to improve, as Xi has embarked on a clever strategy of offering other Asian countries help with their infrastructural problems. Roads, bridges, ports and railroads are needed to accommodate the economic growth in Asia and to this end China, with its huge building experience, has created and funded the Beijing-based and aforementioned AIIB. With 50 billion dollars as starting capital, likely to be doubled, various European countries, including the 'Big Three,' chose in 2015 to participate in this new multilateral but China-dominated bank, much to the frustration of the US. The American diplomacy failed to convince its European allies of the danger that the AIIB would strengthen China's position in Asia. The Europeans preferred to take their economic chances, thus underlining the weight and influence of China's economic power.

But this influence will also lead to more suspicion about China's political agenda, as we have seen in Hong Kong and Taiwan. With its current political system China may be the ally of non-democratic countries, like Kazakhstan and Uzbekistan, but it is hard to see a true alliance with any of its democratic neighbours. In this respect the gap with the US is still considerable and perhaps more fundamental than the equally considerable gap in military power.

The size of the Chinese economy may exceed that of the US at some point in the next decade, provided a serious economic downturn can be avoided. But measured in terms of prosperity there will still be a world of difference. In China the same pie will have to be divided among roughly four times as many people. Whether China will be able to overtake the US also depends on the latter's performance in the years to come. It is up to the US to get its own house in order by addressing the twin deficits of government debt and budget deficit and by reducing unemployment. Frustrations over this should not be vented on China.

Efforts at cooperation are obviously preferable to the path of confrontation. Steps towards the containment of China are in my view counterproductive and will only play into the hands of the hardliners in Beijing, thereby increasing the chances of a Cold War 2.0 with adverse consequences for both parties. Striving for the other extreme, a G2, is too ambitious in the light of the disparate strategies and Obama's experiences in this area. When American and Chinese interests converge there may be room for collaboration. This is particularly true for the economic sphere, where there is a common interest in stable markets and open trade.

A positive and encouraging event in American–Chinese relations was the APEC Summit in Beijing in 2014, when both countries were able to agree on a variety of issues. A joint climate initiative drew most attention. Although some scepticism about its content and effectiveness is justified, the fact that both countries were able to come to some kind of understanding on limiting $CO_2$ emissions is positive. During the same summit deals on much smaller issues (such as extending visas and eliminating tariffs on two hundred information technology goods) were concluded, to the surprise of many sceptical observers of the US–Chinese relationship.

To my mind these positive developments indicate that Xi and Obama understand the wisdom of Kissinger's observation that a Cold War between their countries would be detrimental to both. But this observation does not mean they are able to deepen their cooperation. So far Obama has resisted Xi's call for a 'new model of major country relations', a debate which would put the Asian strategic interests of both countries on the table. Avoiding this debate and holding on to the status quo is seen as more in the US's interest by the current government. However, Xi is probably right when he indicates that 'the growing trend towards a multipolar world will not change', a reference to the Chinese view that America's post-Cold War role as the sole superpower is drawing to a close. According to the Australian China expert Hugh White in his book *The China Choice*, the US has little choice but to share power with China in Asia, at some point in the future. I tend to agree with him.

Avoidance of hostility may well be the best the US and China can achieve in the years ahead. All efforts at cooperation will primarily serve that purpose. In this respect the improved relations between the two countries' armies are encouraging; contact has been established at the highest level and information has been exchanged. Whether the minimum target of avoiding hostility will be achieved depends on the extent to which both parties manage to curb their assertiveness and suspicion. The decisive factor will be the psychological condition that underpins mutual contacts.

The insecurity and vulnerability felt by the Americans in

relation to China is mirrored by at least as much insecurity and vulnerability on the part of the Chinese – seasoned and covered with feelings of superiority on both sides. Given the many differences, mutual recognition of these handicaps could go some way towards facilitating the process of cooperation in all areas where this is possible. Understanding and respect are the basic ingredients.

It is vital to understand that China's ample suspicions about the West's intentions meet their match in the West's suspicions about China's intentions. In my experience Westerners find it just as hard to suppress those feelings when they judge both Chinese people and events. Even those who are determined not to lapse into enemy thinking are often guilty of it and end up oscillating between suspicion and trust.

There is no harm in nurturing some suspicion towards the other, if only to avoid the pitfall of naïvety. In view of the tensions and conflicts we will be facing in the next few years, that suspicion will stand us in good stead. The creation of trust, however, is a very different matter. It requires the necessary readiness to listen to the other. In light of the many obstacles we share with the Chinese, that will be no easy feat.

# Chapter 26

# Suspicion and Trust

The call for trust is one of the rituals performed at meetings between Chinese and Western politicians. When President Xi explains what he means by a 'new type of major power relations' with the US, 'strategic trust' is a key notion. When he underlines the importance of 'building a bridge between Europe and China', he is also referring to trust. On his visit to France in 2014, Xi quoted Napoleon, who had warned: 'When China wakes, she will shake the world.' His country is awake now, he said, but it is 'peaceful, pleasant and civilised'. His predecessors followed the same vein: Wen Jiabao's tour of Europe in 2009 was called the Trip of Confidence. 'We are bringing trust to Europe' and 'have no fear, trust us' were lines he kept repeating.

This persistent emphasis on trust merely points up its opposite. Those who trust one another do not need to emphasise it so much. It is no surprise that suspicion continues to prevail at the start of the twenty-first century: the global balance of power is changing so rapidly that we can barely get our heads around it. The West's self-image, shaped by two centuries of world domination, is based on its superiority. One expression of this is our inability to truly accept that other countries do not want to adopt our political system. The Chinese have their own sense of superiority, based on their millennia-old culture in which foreigners were seen as 'barbarians'. Under the influence of the 'century of humiliation' this sentiment became muddled up with a feeling of inferiority. Now, following their economic successes, Chinese self-confidence is on the rise again, but, as we saw earlier, this also conceals fear and insecurity. More often than not the outside world confuses the resulting attitude with arrogance.

The rise of other parts of the world, most notably China, has only just begun, and the West's realisation that its power is waning has been slow to follow suit. On the economic front, both the US and Europe have seen their image dented by the protracted, self-inflicted crisis, which has had repercussions for the global economy since 2008. Politically, the West has felt increasingly powerless, especially towards the many trouble spots in the Middle East. Since the failed interventions in Iraq and Afghanistan there has been a growing awareness that the US can no longer fulfil its ambition of being the world's policeman. Other centres of power, particularly China, are coming to the fore.

## 'A dragon chasing its own tail'

When it comes to what seems to be this century's greatest development, the shift of power to Asia, Western politicians are as much in the dark as ordinary citizens. It does not really infringe on their day-to-day practice, distracted as they are by smaller events closer to home. As a result, there is little room for considering the consequences of changing East–West dynamics. It is no different on the Chinese side, where domestic issues equally take up the bulk of politicians' time, due to both the size of the country and its growing pains.

Chinese society is extraordinarily dynamic, but also riven with tension. An added complication is that its problems have to be tackled by a political system which, as outlined earlier, is part of the problem. 'China is a dragon chasing its own tail', an expert once described the country to me. That phrase keeps haunting me as I try to get to grips with China. Governing a fifth of the world's population – to Western politicians the enormity of this challenge is practically impossible to comprehend; to their Chinese counterparts it puts the importance of international affairs into perspective. Domestic affairs dominate their thinking and their international awareness begins with their neighbours in Asia and the United States, with Europe coming into the picture only later.

Yet for all their preoccupation with their own spheres, Chinese and Western politicians need to work together in order to avoid confrontation, as our worlds become increasingly connected. The dominant process in the world economy sees the US and Europe buying their products in China, which in turn gets the necessary resources from Africa and Latin America. When things go wrong with Western demand, as they have been since the credit crisis of 2008, the entire chain is affected. Of course globalisation is more complex than that. The web of people, goods and capital spreads in many directions. But consultation between the main players, China and the West, is necessary to manage the sometimes converging, sometimes conflicting interests. The issues at hand exceed the economic realm, as they include countering global warming, terrorism and the spread of nuclear weapons. To secure cooperation in these areas we do not only need converging interests, but in my view also a minimum of trust. What are the chances of achieving it?

There seems to be little cause for optimism, either economically or politically, on either side. Western countries are still grappling with poor to mediocre economic growth, high public debt and high unemployment. The necessary cuts in public spending tend to jeopardise consumer confidence and are unfavourable to growth. Europe seems to be the weakest link in the world economy, after years of crisis which has sorely tested the trust between European member states, especially between the north and the south. Although the most acute phase seems to be over, distrust lingers. Suspicious northerners wonder whether the south, especially Greece, is serious about its austerity measures and reforms, while suspicious southerners assume that the north is full of cold bookkeepers without empathy for their social suffering.

This crisis of confidence raises an important question in relation to China. If the distrust between fairly like-minded cultures within Europe can be so acute, how do we develop a relationship of trust with a country that is both culturally and politically far more remote? What's more, a country which is perceived to be a threat, because it cherishes the ambition of becoming a rival knowledge economy and is prepared to use every means available, including espionage, to achieve it?

At least part of the answer is that Western politicians should avoid fanning the flames of this fear. Chinese competition ought to be an incentive for Western innovation, not for scaremongering. Opt for the latter and you end up with protectionist measures. They always provoke retaliation, most certainly when China is involved. Such a confrontation is ill-advised, since protectionism or even sanctions on the world's second-largest economy would hit the West much harder than, for instance, the sanctions on Russia in response to the Ukraine crisis – the Chinese economy being more than five times bigger than Russia's.

## China's trust deficit

On the Chinese side the overall economic and political constellation is unfavourable for trust as well. Since 1978 the CCP has derived its legitimacy primarily from economic growth. In the past thirty years hundreds of millions of people have been lifted out of poverty, which is a formidable achievement. No other country has made as big a contribution to the global fight against poverty as China. But the country's growth has now dropped to a structurally lower level, where it is predicted to remain for the rest of the decade. At around 7 per cent it is still at an enviously high level to Westerners, but considering that it takes 6 per cent growth to absorb migration from the countryside it is clear that the margins are getting smaller for the leadership.

For Xi, who should stay on as party leader until 2022, the year 2021 is the speck on the horizon. It will be the centenary of the CCP, which he hopes to celebrate with surpassing the US as the biggest economy in the world. By 2049, on the first centenary of the People's Republic, China should also have overtaken the US as the world's biggest military power. As far as Xi is concerned, the country will get there via his 'Chinese Dream', which is propagated with the help of enormous billboards in the cities: 'My Dream, China's Dream', the slogan goes.

However, the people's dreams are not focused on 2021, but on today and tomorrow. In their everyday reality, the population is experiencing the downsides of the tremendous growth of the past decades. It starts with the polluted air they breathe. In many big cities, the level of particulates greatly exceeds the safety standards set by the World Health Organisation. The human costs are considerable: the estimates vary, but at least 350,000 people died prematurely in 2014 as a result of outdoor air pollution alone – land and water pollution add to the toll. The economic repercussions are considerable as well: from higher health costs and lower food production to rising emigration of rich Chinese and foreign expats and tourists staying away.

Another downside is the greatly increased gap between rich and poor, with China's Gini ratio having surpassed that of the US. This indicator of rising social tensions must be seen in the context of the problem of corruption, which can affect citizens in a range of areas: from the quality of buildings (their home or their children's school) to food safety and health care. Xi's fight against corruption, announced in 2012, has therefore been welcomed by ordinary Chinese, but the campaign could also trigger more frustration over the gap between rich and poor when people do not see tangible results in their daily lives. Those will be very hard to obtain. For now, the government has also failed to provide a reliable social safety net for the unemployed and the elderly – a serious shortcoming in a country with an ageing population, where the tradition of children looking after their parents has been undermined by the one-child policy. All in all, this has led to what Jonathan Fenby, in his book *Tiger Head, Snake Tails*, describes as a 'trust deficit' between the leaders and the people.

Historically, the Emperor could be ousted after losing the trust of his people. Whether it will come to this with the CCP is of course impossible to say. In 2007 the government stopped publishing figures on 'mass incidents' – those with a hundred or more protesters. In that year the number came to 80,000. Fenby quotes an academic from Tsinghua University who claimed there were around 180,000 in 2010. This is obviously a huge figure, more than 500 a day, but it should be noted that these are local actions. The majority concern farmers protesting against expropriation of land, wage conflicts and local environmental pollution. The demands are frequently met, but the organisers tend to be placed under surveillance or in prison afterwards. These kinds of disturbances do not represent a threat to Beijing. The secret services prevent the protests from moving beyond a local level and if necessary the army can be deployed to restore order. Add to this the fact that the country's financial reserves give the leaders leeway to buy off social problems, and one could be led to believe that they can continue to rule comfortably in the years ahead.

In reality this is not the case, as the many social tensions in the country indicate. Xi has thought it wise to increase the level of scrutiny of people. The repression of civil society has been stepped up under his rule. Under his predecessor civil activists, lawyers and religious communities were relatively free to do as they pleased as long as they did not cross a 'red line', such as propagating democracy. Under Xi they even get into trouble without doing so. And on the internet the hunt for free-thinking bloggers and disobedient tweets is intensifying. Likewise, academics affiliated with think tanks and universities must tread carefully. The influential research institute, the Chinese Academy of Social Sciences (CASS), has been upbraided by the party for showing insufficient loyalty. The institute is also suspected of being 'infiltrated by foreign forces'. Just how far-reaching these repressive measures will be is, as of this writing, hard to tell.

This tougher approach to dissident thinkers is part of Xi's view on the party; in the next few years nothing less than its survival is at stake, he has repeatedly warned. The anti-corruption campaign is meant to purge the CCP from within, while the repression of civil society is supposed to crush attacks from the outside. My expectation is that the CCP will stay in power this decade. But with it the characteristic 'trust deficit' between the leadership and the people will remain in place.

## 'Superficial friends'

A similar deficit characterises China's relationship with foreign countries. Xi's ambition to turn China into a superpower requires the cultivation of more trustworthy allies than the handful of states that currently merit this description. To do so he has adopted a clever strategy of offering Asian countries help with their infrastructural problems. This is likely to improve China's international position, but will also arouse suspicion of its political motives, as we have seen in the cases of Hong Kong and Taiwan. I agree with Yan Xuetong, a renowned Chinese expert in the field of foreign policy, who emphasises that in order to gain true allies China will have to acquire something it currently lacks: a model that inspires people abroad. Once it possesses that, China can use its soft power to get other countries on its side. Economic clout alone is not enough, as it only offers the prospect of what Yan describes as 'superficial friends', not a relationship of trust.

How could China arrive at a more inspiring model and overcome the internal distrust? A first step would be the above-mentioned social safety net, providing for both unemployment and old age. In its 'China 2030' report the World Bank advised establishing this for both social and economic reasons. It would provide the population with the confidence to curb what is seen by international standards as excessive thrift, which is currently slowing down the rise in their standard of living. Higher living standards could spell the beginning of the restoration of trust. But there is a big stumbling block in the shape of the vested interests: the big banks and state-owned enterprises still stand to gain too much from people's savings accounts and local governments tend to profit as well. It remains to be seen whether Xi's anti-corruption campaign is capable of breaking this broad-based opposition.

When it comes to forging a relationship of trust not only with its own people, but also with the West, it seems to me that the economic sphere, consisting of mutual trade and investments relations, can serve as China's healthy bedrock. The US was China's biggest importer in 2014 with 466 billion dollars' (428 billion euros) worth of goods and 124 billion dollars' (114 billion euros) worth of export in 2014. Despite six consecutive years of crisis Europe still imported 302 billion euros from China in the same year and achieved even higher export levels than the US: 167 billion euros. Those abstract figures conceal many thousands of individual contacts.

In spite of the political and economic wrangling on a global scale, this microcosm of daily interaction flourishes unabated. To my mind it presents the main reason for some optimism about the Chinese–Western relationship. This micro level encompasses a lot more than the stereotype of Western and Chinese entrepreneurs sounding each other out over dinners where the Maotai or whisky flows freely. In the past ten years business people have been joined by tens of thousands of scholars and students. Now that every respectable Western university must boast at least one partnership with a Chinese institution, the number of contacts has multiplied. Doctoral posts in both Europe and the US are frequently awarded to Chinese scientists, while the numbers of Chinese bachelor's and master's students in the West has also increased dramatically, especially in natural sciences. Likewise, more and more Western students are showing an interest in learning Chinese and studying in China.

This has had largely positive results. China has really come into focus and is now being studied far more intensively by Westerners than only a few decades ago. It used to be the almost exclusive domain of sinologists, but now engineers, economists, lawyers, sociologists and even psychiatrists have started engaging with the country on a large scale. This will not only boost its ongoing development, but also help to shape China's image. As the British ex-diplomat George Walden puts it: 'After centuries of projecting fears and dreams, we are finally developing a realistic picture of China.'

These contacts are making their effect felt in another way. Both the Chinese and Westerners can benefit from the cross-fertilisation of ideas and knowledge. This process is illustrated by an anecdote I heard in Germany about leading Chinese scientists. Together with German colleagues, they were on a review committee for the allocation of research grants. Initially the Chinese were reticent about voicing criticism, worried as they were about loss of face. But after a few years they grew used to a more open form of communication. Now, ten years on, they take the lead in the critical evaluation of colleagues, whether Western or Chinese. In contrast, having developed more empathy for the Chinese sensitivity to loss of face, the German scientists are now more cautious, one of the scientists involved told me. It is a fine example of the cultural melting pot. Having said that, the Chinese willingness to learn from the West seems to me greater than the other way around.

## Learning from China

This brings me to one of the questions I most enjoyed asking Westerners: Can we learn from China? The cultivation of a relationship of trust goes hand in hand with respect and appreciation of the other's ways. The willingness to learn is a good test case. The silence that often followed my question said a lot about the sense of superiority that plagues us still. Many did not get much further than the obligatory 'hard work'. But what struck me was that the younger generation appeared to be more open to learning. A young member of Germany's parliament, for instance, cited Chinese people's knowledge of Europe as an example. We can learn a lot from their systematic research into European best practices, she explained.

I also remember a young Dutch architect's enthusiasm for his Chinese clients. They understood much better than their European counterparts that an architect needs a degree of freedom. Western clients, he implied, tend to want to 'board up' their projects in advance. Various interviewees also lauded the Chinese readiness to admit women into the higher levels of management, something that only happens piecemeal in many Western countries. These are the first tentative signs of a change in perception, away from the prevailing picture of Western knowledge being transferred to China. This might pave the way for more equal relations, which is beneficial for mutual respect.

But will this microcosm of cultural exchanges and cross-fertilisation remain intact, or should we anticipate a decline as a result of political or economic setbacks on the world stage? The Chinese leaders feel ambivalent about this. Their country's development benefits from Western expertise and technology, they know, but at the same time they are worried about the uncontrollability of this process. Their concern was reflected in the message outgoing President Hu gave to fellow party members during his final year in office. 'The international culture of the West [is] strong, whereas we are weak. Hostile forces abroad are trying to westernise and divide the country', he lamented in 2012, echoing an earlier complaint by Deng Xiaoping. Counter-measures were needed, according to Hu.

But there is little Chinese leaders can do about the consumption of Western products. This is just as prevalent among the upper echelons of the party, who all drive Audis, as it is among young urbanites. The latter are as fanatical about their iPhones and iPads as their Western peers. The translation of American, British, French and German novels into Chinese has also got underway, offering young people the opportunity to familiarise themselves with a non-Chinese way of thinking. Conversely, Chinese films, novels and artworks show us the world through Chinese eyes.

Contrary to Hu's fears, this reciprocal influence will not spell the end of Chinese culture, but it does challenge the notion of the unique, 'eternal' China, adhered to by the authorities and some Western experts. I personally share the vision of another movement, which counts the German writer and government advisor Tilman Spengler and the Hungarian anthropologist Pál Nyíri among its ranks, who describe the country as first and foremost a consumerist society. The rise of individualism has led to a debate on the loss of social values, which suggests another similarity with Western societies.

Such similarities tend to be largely ignored. What separates us is simply more eye-catching, but I also believe the lack of attention to the similarities is a paradoxical effect of globalisation. It makes us cling to our national identities: the bigger our world becomes, the greater our need for smaller scales. On this point, too, China and the West are on the same wavelength.

One consequence of this focus on identity is that 'we have a strong tendency to make them stranger than they really are', to quote Spengler. The attention to their singularity obscures our common ground. In addition to social trends such as consumerism and individualism, I am thinking of shared basic needs: from clean air and safe food to a stable private life and finding pleasure in a gadget or a good book. But we also share a more profound longing. Like Westerners, the Chinese do not want a tyrannical state to interfere in their daily lives. Freedom from tyranny is, in my view, a basic human right. Although it is not yet within the Chinese people's reach, as the conflicts over the expropriation of land indicate, that is not to say they do not want it.

What they have acquired in recent decades is a different kind of freedom: the freedom to do business. And they have embraced it. Those seeking an explanation for the country's economic success are bound to arrive at the energy and dynamism that this form of freedom has unleashed – and not at the state, intervening heavy-handedly in the economy. Western success has the same entrepreneurial basis, so in that respect we are similar too. As the Italian missionary Matteo Ricci concluded at the start of the seventeenth century: 'They are human beings, just like us.'

The complex web of contacts in the physical world, which the Chinese authorities are ambivalent about, is bolstered in the virtual world. Quite a number of Chinese internet users know how to circumvent the Great Firewall and further increase the authorities' lack of control. These exchanges have a political dimension too, as Robert Guest observes in his book *Borderless Economics*: 'The more contact China has with the rest of the world, the more Chinese people will be exposed to that alternative [the democratic constitutional state].' I expect the internet to lead to a further intensification of relations between China and the West. Despite all the efforts put into increased control, the exchange of information between professionals on both sides is bound to grow.

## A balanced approach to China

The Chinese authorities are not the only potential threat to the process of cross-fertilisation and cultural exchange. It can just as easily come from Europe. Antagonism towards China can complicate matters in politics and in public opinion. Moral indignation about 'Chinese conditions' can prove counterproductive. This was the case in 2011, when the German media turned against *Die Kunst der Aufklärung*, an art exhibition about the German Enlightenment, held in Beijing. Co-organised by the two countries, it was the biggest exhibition Germany had ever mounted abroad and the biggest China had ever welcomed. It showed in a neutral way how Germany had arrived at its enlightenment ideals, which are at the root of Europe's contemporary values. The exhibition took place near Tiananmen Square and the day after the opening the artist Ai Weiwei was arrested. Latching onto this, the German press heaped scorn on the exhibition. How could one collaborate with such a reprehensible regime at such a sensitive location, the critics wondered. In the Netherlands the media were similarly indignant when a delegation of Dutch authors visited China, when their country was the guest of honour at the Beijing International Book Fair. They were also accused of lending credence to the regime.

These responses reflect a sloppy way of thinking. The intrinsic value of these kinds of exchanges, as outlined above, is far too easily overlooked. Besides, they betray a lack of understanding of the effect such a negative attitude might have in China. It is grist to the mill of the hardliners who do not like these kinds of exchanges in the first place. And it is a slap in the face to the reformers who organise such events in the hope of contributing to the further opening of their country – by importing Western ideas instead of cars or handbags. Globally, such a negative Western attitude adds to China's international isolation, while on the home front the hawks are likely to beat the doves. We will derive far greater benefit from the opposite – i.e. China's integration with the rest of the world.

I fear that the temptations of 'enemy' thinking will only increase in the coming years, particularly under the influence of the growing strategic rivalry between the US and China. President Xi might be tempted to use nationalism as a replacement for faltering economic success to legitimise the power of his CCP. In Europe, politicians may equally try to tap into fear for domestic political gain. You do not even need to be a populist for that. A committed European such as the late Érik Izraelewicz hoped for European unity by projecting China as a common enemy, arguing that the erstwhile fear of the Soviet Union did speed up European integration.

In my view we should not go down this route. Fear of communism may have helped Western Europe bridge historic chasms. But should China be our next *Angstgegner* or bogeyman? A balanced approach to China would be better. We should remain critical of aspects of China and confident of our own values, but not suspicious of the country as such. Mindful of the fact that China has come a long way, we should give the country credit for its economic achievements in recent decades, which have helped lift hundreds of millions out of poverty. We should also acknowledge the immense challenges the Chinese leaders face in governing a fifth of the world's population. Finally, it is important to put the country's dominance into perspective. There is no doubt that China will become more powerful, but it also has a great many domestic problems to contend with and few allies internationally. China will certainly not eclipse the rest of the world. The most likely scenario seems to me a multipolar world, in which China plays an increasingly important role; its engagement with the international community should generally be welcomed, criticised when necessary and above all not feared. This balanced approach should enable the daily undercurrent of contact between peoples to continue to prosper.

Unlike the news about the broader political and economic developments, these contacts cannot be captured in catchy headlines. But in contrast to the former, the latter do provide cause for optimism. There is a parallel here with the debate about the so-called multicultural society. That too revolved around people from vastly different cultures, regarding each other with a mixture of suspicion and trust. After identifying all kinds of wrongdoings and engaging in heated debates in the media, more and more politicians felt compelled to describe it as a failure. But meanwhile daily life went on and now there is no denying the existence of a multicultural society. However imperfect, the foundations are in place, and we are continuing to build on them. Not through the media, but through everyday life. Not overnight, but over the course of generations. Not as a straightforward success story, but through trial and error.

I foresee a similar scenario for China and the West. The contacts will continue to broaden and deepen – not spectacularly, but steadily. And given this increasing interdependence, the effect of any scaremongering will be felt in our wallets. When both the authorities and public opinion manage to avoid this, the human exchanges at micro level can do their work. Slowly, but surely. In the long run they might create the foundations for a relationship of trust.

# Acknowledgements

Help in writing this book has come from many quarters. I'm indebted to my newspaper *de Volkskrant* for the time they granted me. While travelling through Europe and China I spoke to many people who offered me new insights. I found particular inspiration in my conversations with the British ex-diplomat George Walden, the late French editor-in-chief of *Le Monde* Érik Izraelewicz, the Chinese-German author Luo Lingyuan and the German sinologist and writer Tilman Spengler.

In the Netherlands I enjoyed the support of two eminent China experts, Henk Schulte Nordholt and Stefan Landsberger. From Oxford, Rogier Creemers brought his expertise and enthusiasm to bear on steering me past all kinds of pitfalls.

Friendly and detailed editorial support came from Emile Brugman, who made me feel as though we had been working together for years. My good friend Pieter van den Blink and his great feel for language deserves a special mention; his enthusiasm throughout the project was heart-warming. And finally, Laura Vroomen produced what I feel is a fine translation with admirable speed. If, despite their input, any flaws have crept into the text, the responsibility lies entirely with me.

My thanks also go to my beloved parents, my late father Pieter Obbema and my mother Mieke Obbema-Smeets, who gave me the necessary means to make this book possible. By far my biggest thanks go to my great love, Carine Holties. Without her I would not be the person I am now. The value of her mental support and the energy she mustered to allow me to lose myself in the writing process cannot be expressed in words.

Fokke Obbema
Amsterdam, January 2015

# Bibliography

Brautigam, Deborah, *The Dragon's Gift: The Real Story of China in Africa,* Oxford University Press, Oxford, 2009

Brown, Kerry, *Hu Jintao: China's Silent Ruler,* World Scientific, London, 2012

Cabestan, Jean-Pierre, *La politique internationale de la Chine: entre intégration et volonté de puissance,* Presses de la Fondation nationale des sciences politiques, 2010

Cardenal, Juan Pablo and Araújo, Heriberto, *La silenciosa conquista China*, Critica, Barcelona, 2011

Chu, Ben, *Chinese Whispers*, Weidenfeld & Nicolson, London, 2013

Cohen, Philippe and Richard, Luc, *La Chine sera-t-elle notre cauchemar?*, Mille et Une Nuits, Paris, 2005

——— *Le Vampire du milieu*, Mille et Une Nuits, Paris, 2010

Domenach, Jean-Luc, *La Chine m'inquiète*, Perrin, Paris, 2008

Fallows, James, *China Airborne*, Pantheon Books, New York, 2012

Fenby, Jonathan, *Tiger Head, Snake Tails: China Today, How it Got There and Where it is Heading*, Simon & Schuster, London, 2012

Friedman, Thomas, *The World is Flat: A Brief History of the Globalized World in the Twenty-first Century,* Farrar, Straus and Giroux, New York, 2005

Guest, Robert, *Borderless Economics*, Palgrave Macmillan, New York, 2011

Halper, Stefan, *The Beijing Consensus,* Basic Books, New York, 2010

Holslag, Jonathan, *De kracht van het paradijs: Hoe Europa kan overleven in de Aziatische eeuw*, De Bezige Bij, Antwerpen, 2014

Izraelewicz, Érik, *Quand la Chine change le monde*, Grasset, Paris, 2005

—————— *L'Arrogance chinoise*, Grasset, Paris, 2011

Jacques, Martin, *When China Rules the World: The Rise of the Middle Kingdom and the End of the Western World,* Allen Lane, London, 2009

Kissinger, Henry, *On China*, Allen Lane, New York, 2011

Kynge, James, *China Shakes the World: The Rise of a Hungry Nation,* Weidenfeld & Nicolson, London, 2006

Lee, Felix, *Die Gewinner der Krise: Was der Westen von China lernen kann*, Rotbuch, Berlin, 2011

Lemos, Gerard, *The End of the Chinese Dream: Why Chinese People Fear the Future*, Yale, New Haven and London, 2012

Leonard, Mark, *What Does China Think?,* Fourth Estate, London, 2008

Mahbubani, Kishore, *The New Asian Hemisphere: The Irresistible Shift of Global Power to the East*, Public Affairs, New York, 2008.

Li Zhang, *News Media and EU–China Relations,* Palgrave Macmillan, New York, 2011

Lisbonne-de Vergeron, Karine, *Contemporary Chinese Views of Europe,* Chatham House, London, 2007.

McGregor, Richard, *The Party: The Secret World of China's Communist Rulers,* Penguin Books, London, 2010

Putten, Jan van der, *Verbijsterend China: Wereldmacht van een andere soort,* Nieuw Amsterdam Uitgevers, Amsterdam, 2011

Sandschneider, Eberhard, *Der Erfolgreiche Abstieg Europas: Heute Macht abgeben um Morgen zu gewinnen*, Hanser Verlag, Munich, 2011

Schmidt, Helmut, *Nachbar China, im Gespräch mit Frank Sieren*, Ullstein, Berlin, 2007

Schulte Nordholt, Henk, *De Chinacode ontcijferd*, Byblos, Amsterdam, 2006

Shambaugh, David, *China Goes Global*, Oxford University Press, Oxford, 2013

Sieren, Frank, *Angst vor China: Wie die neue Weltmacht unsere Krise nutzt*, Econ, Berlin, 2011

Sorman, Guy, *L'Année du Coq: Chinois et rebelles*, Fayard, Paris, 2006

Subramanian, Arvind, *Eclipse: Living in the Shadow of China's*

*Economic Dominance,* Peterson Institute for International Economics, Washington, 2011

Stiglitz, Joseph, *Making Globalization Work,* Norton, New York, 2006

Walden, George, *China: A Wolf in the World,* Gibson Square, London, 2008

Walter, Carl and Howie, Fraser, *Red Capitalism: The Fragile Financial Foundation of China's Extraordinary Rise,* Wiley, Singapore, 2011

Yan Xuetong, *Ancient Chinese Thought, Modern Chinese Power,* Princeton University Press, Princeton, 2011

Yergin, Daniel, *The Quest, Energy, Security and the Remaking of the Modern World,* Allen Lane, London, 2011

Yu Keping, *Democracy is a Good Thing,* Brookings Institute, Washington, 2009

# Index